Faith and Unbelief

Uncertainty and Atheism

Herwig Arts, S.J.

A Liturgical Press Book

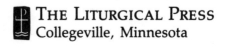
THE LITURGICAL PRESS
Collegeville, Minnesota

Cover design by Greg Becker

Faith and Unbelief: Uncertainty and Atheism was published originally in Belgium under the title *Het ongeloof gewogen* © De Nederlandsche Boekhandel / Uitgeverij Pelckmans, Kapellen, Belgium, 1982.

1	2	3	4	5	6	7	8	9

Library of Congress Cataloging-in-Publication Data

Arts, Herwig.
    Faith and unbelief : uncertainty and atheism / Herwig Arts.
        p.   cm.
    "A Michael Glazier book."
    Includes bibliographical references.
    ISBN 0-8146-2010-8
    1. Faith. 2. Apologetics—20th century. 3. Atheism. 4. Language and languages—Religious aspects. 5. Religions. I. Title.
    BV4637.A68   1992
    239—dc20   92-22894
                                                                CIP

For
Helen Rolfson and Rita Van de Wiele

Contents

Introduction

In his book *L'Amour et l'Occident*, Denis de Rougemont demonstrates the radical difference between the way East and West experience human love. In the author's view the relationship between man and woman as known to the Western world, characterized as it is by permanent conflict between passionate erotic love on the one hand and conjugal fidelity on the other, is a phenomenon completely unknown to Indian or Chinese literature. What the East understands as love does not correspond at all to the Western concept of eros. It remains an open question as to whether there is a similar divergence of views between East and West when it covers the relationship between human beings and God or to matters of religious belief.

In the case of human love relationships, whatever differences there may be in the cultural expressions of love, everyone—with the possible exception of people suffering from deep frustration or psychological disabilities—experiences love in some shape or form or at least aspires to it. Love is thus a generalized human phenomenon. The same can no longer be said of the relationship between human beings and God. There are lots of intelligent, good-living people around today who have no religious faith whatever, yet who feel perfectly happy, well-adjusted and sane. Faith can no longer be assured to be an integral component of the average person's view on life, even if for centuries it had been so. Atheism is a creed of relatively recent vintage, and one which is typically Western. Outside of the West and its sphere of influence the phenomenon of atheism is virtually unknown. The Jewish Marxist philosopher Ernst Bloch claimed that: "Only a Christian can become a good atheist."[1] The reason why his claim holds true, lies, he asserts, in the fact that Christ was the first

1. E. Bloch, *Atheismus im Christentum*, Frankfurt, 1968, 15.

to liberate human beings from every form of "theocratic superstition," then put them in centre stage before, finally, challenging them to rise in "active rebellion against all forms of intellectual slavery or ideological imperialism" and against all outmoded superstitious fairy tales. Was it not the Christian martyrs, asks Bloch, who were the first to receive the accolade "atheoi" at the emperor Nero's court?

Bloch wonders whether Christianity is not as much the religion of "human dignity" as of the "incarnation" ("Menschwertung und Menschwerdung"). He would thus see Christianity as a humanism which is radical and consistent, even if institutionalized Christianity has alas degenerated into just one more new form of religion. In the opinion of Bloch, himself naturally a fervent atheist, it reverted to slavery to a mythological tyrant deity.

Bloch was not the only Jewish thinker who attempted to explain why there were no traces of atheism outside the Western Judeo-Christian sphere of influence, and why neither Lucretius, nor Buddha nor Confucius had ever been considered "atheoi." In the view of G. Steiner, atheism came about because the God of Sinai and the God of the early Church was too abstract, too monotheistic, too transcendent and too difficult to conceptualize. From this interpretation it follows that for Steiner "the entire Old Testament is one long story of mutiny against that God and of spasmodic relapses into idolatry of the old deities (golden calves etc.) which could be fashioned by hand and be represented and conceptualized by the human mind." He believed that Christianity itself very soon developed into a "polymorphous trinity" and emerged with a surplus of saintly figures and a diversity of Madonnas which made a more immediate appeal to the popular mind. "The christian churches, with a few possible exceptions, have always been the bastard products of monotheistic ideals on the one hand and polytheistic practices on the other. Therein has lain their flexibility and synthetic power."[2] In other words this uncompromising Jewish monotheism at an earlier stage rejected the more primitive and antiquated forms of religion. In the longer term such a religious ideal transpired as too exalted and too transcendent for the conceptual powers of the ordinary person. It was Steiner's assertion that a pure spiritual, invisible and intangible God held no appeal for anyone. Steiner believed that the radical transcendence of

2. G. Steiner, *In Bluebeard's Castle: Some Notes towards the Redefinition of Culture*, New Haven, 1971, 39.

the Jewish God, i.e., his infinite indifference to all that is human, material and conceivable, was at the root of Western atheism. Then there is the impossibly radical character of Christian morality, summarized in the Sermon of the Mount. In the light of what happened, for example, to the Jews in the concentration camps, the celebrated French proverb came to Steiner's mind: "Qui trop embrasse, mal étreint."

Whatever one's view of the accuracy of Bloch's and Steiner's analysis, it is an incontrovertible fact that throughout the West, traditional belief in God is going through a severe crisis. Both these Jewish philosophers manage to demonstrate *why* it was impossible for atheism to come into being outside the Judaeo-Christian sphere of influence. *How* it was that this atheism was born in the West admits of a more nuanced explanation than that advanced by either of these Jewish authors. Atheism does not flow directly from either Judaism or Christianity. If that were the case why would it have taken seventeen centuries before the first symptoms of disease at the heart of Christianity manifested themselves? The link between Christianity and atheism was provided by the modern sciences and industrialization which—as Teilhard de Chardin so astutely observed—by no mere accident came into being in the West (and not the East). According to Teilhard it was the "Judeo-Christian yeast" which produced the positive sciences. The high degree of specialized scientific activity in many cases produced in its turn positivism and an agnostic worldview. Modern industrialization transformed the conditions of human labour, modern scientific methods transformed ways of thinking: both resulted in division and specialization. Just as an increasingly radical division of labour often led to the self-alienation of many workers, so too an increasingly radical scientific specialization led to the "Fach-idiotie" of many one-dimensional intellectuals. As a result of increasingly detailed knowledge of the different trees, these latter have often lost complete sight of the woods. What is more serious is that they have become suspicious of and allergic to universal insights or world views. In the degree that specialization sub-divides, a global vision of the whole of reality becomes dimmer. One does not discover God under the microscope of empirical investigation. Since the emergence of atheism in the Parisian salons and British laboratories of the eighteenth century, no one in his right mind could any longer hold that belief in God is a centralized human phenomenon. This fact becomes more obvious with each passing year.

In the wake of Voltaire's anticlerical liberation cry "Ecrasons l'infâme!" more and more enlightened spirits have rallied in a struggle involving the weaning away and deliverance of man from all forms of superstition, mythical tales and irrational illusions. One has to readily admit that their "work of deliverance" has achieved considerable success. It remains an open question whether the people thus "enlightened" are happier and more well-adjusted, or are more fully-rounded human beings. Is it not rather the case that there is considerable evidence to show that a growing number of people today (particularly numerous young people, whom one can hardly accuse of excessive religious imagination) turn their backs on the "system" of society and on the modern way of life? The young atheist Karl Marx wrote that "the abolition of religion as illusionary happiness for the people is the first step towards authentic happiness." One is sorely tempted to ask all those who have been trying for more than two centuries to wean man away from his "imaginary God": whatever has happened to that increase in happiness?

Since the Enlightenment, atheism has been on the increase in both the West and all other milieux which have been subject to Western influence. This atheism promised to liberate humanity at long last from every unacceptable superstition which for so long stood in the way of its freedom and happiness.

The logical question that then arises is: do today's human beings feel themselves to be truly freer and happier than their 1750 counterparts? If the answer is yes, would it necessarily empirically prove that religion is genuinely repressive and that atheism is liberating? Even the most superficial examination of contemporary society, however, calls into question this beaming happiness. The growing need for "psychiatric therapy" would seem to signify a bad omen for the cure for all self-alienation, guilt and anxiety so often promised.

The relationship between humanity and God has broken down almost entirely in the Western world. It has largely disappeared or slipped into the realm of the unconscious. No serious person can deny the existence of this religious crisis. It is an open question whether interpersonal relations, too, have not suffered as a result. Had it been the case that as belief in God faded, interpersonal relations underwent a dramatic improvement, then such a development would have been a bad sign for such belief. Has human experience of human love actually improved or become healthier? Is it not rather the case that loneliness, insecurity and anxiety have increased in the psychiatric wards of the atheist establishment? Faith is not something confined to the area of religious experience alone. The fact that an individual does or does not believe has far-reaching consequences for every other area of his life.

Would it not be true to say that the Western industrial revolution had its impact not only on the relationship with God but on *all* human relationships? Furthermore is it not the case that it resulted not only in the "recession of God" or atheism but also in growing self-alienation? Right across the board it would seem that human relations have run aground and a desperate scramble has begun in the area of psychology as well as that of religion for some way of setting them afloat again. "What most fundamentally characterizes modern society is the loss of the human relationship" claims the economist J. Baudrillard. "Patented psychologists and sociologists are paid hefty fees for injections of a modicum of solidarity, contact and communication in relationships between human beings which have become opaque."[3]

Are we not witnessing the application of new techniques with a view to breathing fresh life into both relations between human beings and their individual relationship with the divine? On the one hand we find marriage encounter, sensitivity training, group dynamics, conversation therapy, nonverbal communication, psychodrama, etc., and on the other we have techniques of transcendental meditation, yoga, courses for initiation in Zen Buddhism: both are examples of attempts to overcome inhibitions which have penetrated the heart of interpersonal relations and religious experience. They are also examples of what the futurologist A. Toffler has called the great future eagerly awaited by the "experience makers" and the "experiential industries."[4] They are examples which, one way or other, demonstrate that serious communication problems have arisen not only between human beings and God but also (and in perhaps more dramatic fashion) between human beings themselves. For the believer this generalized psychological crisis comes as no surprise. The man who slashes the artery of faith can have a good guess at the consequences. If the young person of today is content and actually grateful for the godless society which his leaders are dishing up to him, then this would represent an undeniable plus for atheism. The energy, the brutality even, with which young people reject this "enlightened" dish, seems to set

3. J. Baudrillard, *La Société de Consommation*, Paris, 1970, 255–256.
4. Cf. A. Toffler, *Future Shock*, London, 1970, 202ff.

few people thinking. While the enlightened spirits tremble about ingratitude, young people turn increasingly Eastwards to still their spiritual hunger and try to discover their authentic religious "orientation."

This book sets out to try and shed light on what is specific to the Christian faith by comparing it not only with other forms of religion but principally by confronting it with the atheistic vision of Western invention. Faith is possible for persons of the West only in a context of mounting unbelief. There are few believers who have not been infected or inspired (depending on one's viewpoint) by the prevailing climate. It is indeed to contemporary atheism's credit that everyone's faith is now "troubled" by serious questions which no one can deny. These questions, which have been raised by the various sciences, form the agenda of this study and it is our purpose to treat them as objectively as possible.

The atheist has obliged believers to meditate more profoundly on the "why" and the "how" of their faith. The believer ought to be eternally thankful to the atheist. As a result of being challenged, faith is no longer a set of conventional beliefs that can be taken for granted. For this reason it is henceforth essential to discuss this faith in the light of the often far from banal objections raised in scientific critique as well as our improved knowledge of non-Christian religions.

The intellectual climate of tacit atheism in which contemporary human beings generally live, makes discussion of God at any level a delicate and difficult enterprise, and for a number of reasons.

Just as it is quite impossible to provide an adequate explanation of a love poem to those who themselves have never experienced love, so too is it a hopeless task to discuss an experience of God with people who have never been touched by religion. As a general rule people are most easily moved by books or films where they can spontaneously identify with the principal character, i.e., a character into whose shoes they can easily put themselves. The problem where religious language is concerned is that modern human beings find it extremely difficult to identify with it. It is a language which sounds odd, far-fetched or simply unreal to the ears of an increasing number of people. Moreover, it is quite impossible to speak "objectively" about one's relationship with God. God is simply not an "object" which can be put under the cold microscope of critical analysis. In all major religions God is actually experienced as a Person. There is no one on earth who can speak "purely objectively" about someone he or she loves and with whom he or she knows themselves to have an intimate relationship. Objective language simply does not fit when it comes to describing someone experienced as a "Thou."

In any case it remains an open question as to whether "objectvity," the favorite buzzword of critical spirits, is actually able to furnish searching information about a person, regardless of whether that person is human or divine. Doesn't a mother who worships the ground her child walks on (and is consequently "subjective") generally know that child a good deal better than the unprejudiced psychologist who forms his opinion on the basis of objective tests and cool, detached observations? Hölderlin points out that one will never track down God by looking on from a distance. One must rather enter into God's mysterious reality: "Outsiders are never touched by God" ("Göttliches trifft Unteilnehmenden nicht"). How do I know, some will ask, whether or not my experience of God has been coloured by subjective and illusory influences? In other words, do I not project onto God characteristics which exist exclusively in the realm of my own personal fantasy? This, it cannot be denied, is a constant danger. No two people know God in quite the same way, just as no two daughters have exactly the same image of their mother. The medieval monk William of St. Thierry made the same point as follows: "Each person forms his own image of God. To the extent to which someone prays to God, he also forms an image of God." Which is not to suggest of course that each and every view of God (Buddhist or Christian, Jansenist or Ignatian) is equally valid or equally orthodox. A mother is now and then misunderstood even by her own children. No human being ever sees "through" God. For that very reason everyone's image of God has to be enriched, revised or reviewed up to the very end of their lives. Just as one only partly knows one's friend and never acquires exhaustive knowledge of him, so too God reveals himself only partially and then more in the context of prayer than in that of cool, detached scientific observation. In other words, there exists no other path to religious knowledge or the insight of faith than that of personal and "subjective" contact. Even if I am greatly helped in this regard by the witness of a figure such as St. Paul or St. Teresa of Avila, in the last analysis the witness they bear, too, rests on personal experience.

Were atheism a purely intellectual problem, then it would possibly be enough to counter it with philosophical concepts or "proofs." Yet what is at issue is a problem which concerns the total person. It is a problem which, in addition to its spiritual dimension, also has affective, moral or psychological aspects. Nonetheless, myriad ecclesiastical writers must have been repeatedly of the view that any doubt in regard to God's existence could be reduced to a strictly intellectual or philosophical matter which could be countered with a blast of apologetics. Discussions concerning the existence of God were thus virtually always held in the groves of academe, based on the conviction that serious objections to belief in God could only be philosophical in character.

In reality, though, from the late Renaissance onward, religion has been called into question and has come under attack from the various non-philosophical disciplines. The natural sciences were the first to raise objections to the totalitarian-theological world view which prevailed in the Middle Ages. They objected, in other words, to a Weltanschauung which was based completely on the Bible, as if the Scriptures contained not only religious information but also cosmological and anthropological data. This information was above and beyond any human doubt or questioning.

In the nineteenth century, biology raised its objections to the static biblical view of the world, and the other nascent human sciences were now on its heels: psychology, sociology and anthropology. Medieval theology had indeed constructed a grandiose Weltanschauung in which world view and faith-content nicely complemented each other. It was a system in which physics, anthropology and theology made up an almost "totalitarian" unity. The schism between profane and religious sciences had not yet been completed. Nature was not yet secularized nor robbed of its divine mantle. The natural and the supernatural were still interwoven. It is interesting in this regard to note that the leading Christian thinkers and mystics accepted and used the cosmic and scientific data of their own day, without taking any stand on its veracity or scientific authenticity or even interesting themselves greatly in the matter. They used profane stones to build a religious house, and not a scientific laboratory, i.e., they spoke about God in the human language of their own time without losing sleep over the scientific precision of that language. It was never their intention to analyse or criticize that language. The Church's magisterium and the official theology of the "system-builders" were the only ones who believed that this language fell into their specific area of competence. It is to their credit that such men as Galileo and Darwin demonstrated that the Bible was not a scientific or biological manual, but rather a religious message, even if it took the Church centuries to perceive and admit this fact. The path traced by sun, moon or stars is not the central theme of revelation; rather, the path on which God encounters human beings. The essential contents and unique richness of the Bible were cast in a sharper light thanks to the criticisms levelled by the various disciplines, even if they were at first experienced as painful.

Bit by bit physics, biology and the human sciences from the time of Copernicus, Galileo and Darwin up to Durkheim, Marx and Freud demonstrated that significant components of the impressively harmonious Weltanschauung of the Middle Ages were incorrect and untenable. Medieval cosmology and anthropology were especially shaky. There had been a general conviction that the Bible guaranteed their accuracy. People quite simply did not see that the Bible was concerned with other, and indeed far more weighty matters. God had not revealed any scientific insights to human beings: human beings had in any case been gifted with a creative and heuristic intelligence. What God revealed to human beings was a new insight into the mysterious love-relationship between God and humankind.

When in the seventeenth century Galileo hazarded a new perspective on physics, curiously enough it was not the Christian physicists but rather the theologians and philosophers who dismissed his insights as patently false. The same scenario repeated itself when biologists such as Charles Darwin and Thomas Huxley proclaimed as nonsense the static, nonevolutionary doctrine of creation. It was the Anglican bishop Wilberford who, in the company of a series of theological and philosophical advisers entered into the fray against Darwin. The Christian world had to wait for the arrival of Teilhard de Chardin, scientific genius and religious thinker combined, to see clearly how enriching the theory of biological evolution was for theological thought. God not only created the entire universe, the whole of reality, but he created it in a state of permanent development and growth. The fact that matter actually evolves is ironically perhaps the most impressive feature of the divine creative activity. It matters little that a modern astrophysicist like C.F. Van Weizsäcker should speak about the "Galileo myth" and that a Nobel prize-winning physicist like W. Heisenberg should remark apropos of Galileo's propositions, condemned by the Inquisition, that they are partly "wrong," very relative and therefore also "irrelevant." What really matters is that Galileo and Darwin, once conceived as such formidable adversaries by the Church, actually had a beneficial effect in producing a purer

and more adequate theology which must remain in continual dialogue with science without trying to absorb, annex or gag it. Here,
too, our Lord's words are to the point: "The truth will set you free"
(John 8:32), even if the scientific fraternity possesses no monopoly on
that truth.

After biology it was history's turn to aim its fire at "the biblical
stories" and subject them to the rules of historical criticism. The Catholic magisterium initially felt itself cornered once again and kept its
exegetes as far away as possible from this new "danger," failing to
see here, too, how fruitful a dialogue between the scientific discipline
of history and biblical theology could be. The Protestant reaction to
the new challenge seemed much more positive. The evangelical
"Leben-Jesu-Forschung" was to open up the way to the methods of
"Formgeschichte" and "Redaktionsgeschichte" which in the meantime
have become universally accepted in Christian intellectual circles.

The questions posed by the historians made it abundantly clear
that the gospels were not historical reports of precise events or authentic sayings. One came to the realization that a gospel was more truly
a theological reflection on actual events and on the Lord's original
words. The question about the historicity of Christ's resurrection, for
example, has been answered with a very nuanced affirmative. That
question led people to see that the stories about the empty tomb and
about the encounters between the disciples and their apparently risen
Lord, were also rich in kerygmatic content. Those stories suggest a
message which is much more than a procès-verbal of a historical
fact. Tolstoy's *War and Peace*, too, is more than the historical report of
Napoleon's military adventure and disaster in Russia, even if Tolstoy
never could have got across his pacifist message separate from the
real facts. What is unique in Tolstoy is that on the basis of unforgettable events he was able to depict, in extremely concrete terms, the eternal link between humans and war, as well as between love and hate.
The technique of historical criticism has enabled us to understand
more clearly the literary genre of the gospels and of all the books of
the Bible. As a result we have been able to appreciate more the richness of these texts. The gospel is neither a mythical story nor a
bland, uninspired factual report.

Originally many Christians were afraid that historical criticism
would lead to a systematic peeling off of the heart of biblical truth,
layer by layer, like an onion, and that ultimately there would be nothing left. This overanxious, suspicious, reductionist argument was mis-

placed as the impressive strides made by Protestant and Catholic exe-
gesis have amply demonstrated. Without the pioneering work of D.
Strauss and W. Bauer, the achievements E. Käsemann, H. Schlier, G.
von Rad and C.H. Dodd would have been impossible. These latter
scholars were clear examples of both scientific-critical rigor and
kerygmatic-religious wisdom. Rather than subject everything to universal doubt, one has been able to see a lot of things more clearly
and uncover a hitherto hidden wealth of riches.

In our days it is sociology and psychology which have been sharpest in their critique of religion and have most frequently cast it in a
relative light. Since the time of Marx, Durkheim and Freud, various
doubts about the truth of religious convictions have been expressed
in sociological or psychological terms. Is the emergence or disappearance of religious opinions not the result of a given individual's sociological context, i.e., of his milieu? Is religion but an illusion which
can be explained away by psychology? Can one not simply reduce
faith to certain retarded or infantile psychic processes? Those are
questions which would seem, consciously or unconsciously, to under-
mine the once rock-solid religious convictions of many.

The menacing shades of unbelief masquerading in philosophical
vestments borrowed from philosophy are no longer floating about.
Thanks to Feuerbach, atheism and agnosticism were understood and
explained in terms of sociology and psychology. Isn't J. Delumeau ar-
ticulating the heartfelt fears of many of the faithful with the question
posed in the title of his study *Le Christianisme va-t-il mourir? (Is
Christianity Going to Die?)*. In his preface the author asks where all
those fervent Christians, who used to fill our churches to capacity
and filed in processions through our streets, have disappeared to?

"Drawing on scientifically established figures, statisticians inform
us today that religion appears to be on the way out . . . God's future
seems to be a thing of the past. The religion of ceremonial, power
and control of conscience is undeniably in its death throes."[5] There
are many Christians who feel as if they are "the last of the
Mohicans." Regardless of whether the answer provided by this Christian sociologist is particularly encouraging, it cannot take away from
the fact that many contemporary believers have been profoundly af-
fected by the atheistic blast of incredulous sociology. Religious faith is
not just a matter of which T. Veblen called a "cultural layer" or a

5. J. Delumeau, *Le Christianisme va-t-il mourir?* Paris, 1977.

"cultural arrears." Have the religious institutions not simply been left behind by technical and scientific developments? Are they not merely out-of-date "survivals" (Darwin) or the last hangover from a pre-scientific era? Will the slightest grain of "sociological imagination" (W. Mills) not necessarily lead people to see that a lot of what believers accepted as obvious has now become no longer tenable?

Does what people thought, did and practiced in faith in former days not admit of a "sociological explanation"? To put it bluntly: does not a soundly based sociology necessarily raise a whole series of religious questions, particularly when psychology points in the same direction? Have not many people become "unaware of God" (V. Frankl)? Has he not rather become a "Fremdkörper" (foreign body) who no longer fits in the life of modern human beings? Isn't humankind at last well on the way to complete emancipation from what H. E. Richter called "his God complex"? Wasn't the religion of the past simply the result of "human fantasy" so long as humans had no accurate perspective on reality (E. Bloch)?

Regardless of one's own private opinion on the matter, it is undeniable that modern sociology and psychology have put to religion a series of shrewd and pointed questions. The believer who refused or deemed it superfluous to give these questions serious consideration could easily be accused of lacking guts or intellectual honesty. This is not simply because the Christian by definition ought to be a "protestant" or "public witness" of the truth which inspires his own life and which he believes to be of universal application, but also because history demonstrates that every serious scientific critique has in the long run greatly enriched religious faith. The whole development of dogma, for example, emerged from an honest, indeed, sometimes pretty aggressive confrontation with a variety of heretics and people whose opinion was at variance with the official line. In the same way, too, a more faithful and profound insight into the Christian message is only to be expected if the Church engages in serious dialogue with the best brains of our scientific community. Their questions and suggestions are certainly deserving of mature reflection and a serious reply.

The purpose of this book is certainly not to build an apologetic rampart round the limited ground still left to faith, but rather to focus the critical intellect, shaped by modern science, unblinded and free of fear, onto the possibility of faith in the contemporary world. Not so much to save what can still be saved, but to establish as fact what up to now was merely supposed. The believer is not asked to take an irrational jump in blind faith into a sea of religious sensibilities, but rather to use to capacity the rational powers God has given him/her. The searching journey that humankind makes towards God requires that he muster all the talents with which as a human being he is endowed. The greatest of these talents is the mind.

There are two reasons why a Christian has an obligation to explore the questions and objections raised by those who think differently (i.e. those who do *think*, even if they form different opinions, and not just those who are bitterly anticlerical of fanatically atheist). To begin with, it is actually quite enriching to become familiar with the ideas of a genius like Marx or Freud. It is not necessary to swallow totally their theories in order to benefit from the wealth of ideas contained in their new way of viewing things. St. Thomas Aquinas did not shy from addressing the questions raised by Greek-Arabic philosophy and logic concerning a wide area of Christian thought. On the contrary he familiarized himself with these "foreign" ways of thinking, not to make them innocuous or neutralize them but rather to integrate what was best in them into his new scholastic philosophy. It was only then that he attempted to provide an "answer" to what was unacceptable in various elements of the pagan view of things.

When at a later stage the intellectuals of the Renaissance, thanks to emigrants from the Byzantine world, discovered the unsuspected riches of the Greek heritage, it was the Jesuits, following in Erasmus' footsteps, who attempted to integrate these riches into a revamped secondary education (humaniora), i.e., an education largely based on pagan texts and works of art which were not Christian in inspiration. Terence's rule of thumb was their guide: "Homo sum, humani nil a me alienum puto" (I am a man and nothing human is alien to me). It was thanks to a highly regrettable misunderstanding that the Christians labelled the unbelievers with names which would far more fittingly apply to themselves. By using the terms "free-thinkers" and "humanists" to describe "non-Christians" we run the risk of forgetting that it is the task of each and every Christian to think and search "freely," without fear or favour. It is furthermore the duty of Christians to hold all human values in high regard and to defend them, and fight any defeatism unworthy of human beings.

When the biological insights of Darwin and his colleagues and the spectacular discoveries made in various branches of the positive sciences in the nineteenth century raised serious questions about the

Christian world view (which does not mean the Christian faith) it was necessary to wait for a figure like Teilhard de Chardin to come to grips with this challenge without being scared by it. Then it was not a question of refuting or rejecting the discoveries of these sciences, but rather as a Christian to come to a more adequate world view. Teilhard did not launch a rescue program for Christianity. He attempted rather to stimulate a more considered and mature use of language when it came to talk of God and his creation. It was never the aim of Christianity to absolve humans from thinking or to free them from thinking. Christ actually set thought free from a certain number of taboos and superstitions. Pagan cultures had a rich baggage of mythical tales but no profane history, magical practices and incantations but little true medicine, astrological prophecies but rarely scientific astronomy.

There is a second reason why Christian thought should face up to the questions and objections of dissenters. To borrow Tillich's words, all discussion of God has to be "correlative," i.e., should be an attempt to answer the real problems of real people. The Christian message is a genuine answer and no airy-fairy luxury. "The answers provided by Revelation are meaningful only in so far as they are in *correlation* with the questions which concern the whole of our human existence, i.e. existential questions." For that very reason it is essential that the theologian take as his point of departure real, living *a priori*, problems and objections, precisely in order to show that the Christian message "truly does provide an answer to these questions."[6] In other words it is imperative for the theologian to remain in dialogue with the representatives of the human sciences of his own day and give undivided attention to his problems and objections. If he fails to do that then he will soon be talking an esoteric jargon, intelligible only to the initiated and relevant only to those trained in theology. Theological reflection will flourish only where real people are asking real questions and not in the cloistered havens of dogmatic certainties. The great questions of our day are no longer byzantine quibbles in the ethereal realm of deductive theology. It is the modern sciences which preoccupy believer and non-believer alike. There is, however, a hidden danger in this justified demand that we use "contemporary" and "correlative" language when talking about God. The euphoria of the Sixties, when people swore by all that was "modern"

6. P. Tillich, *Systematic Theology*, I, London, 1951, 69–70.

and were quite indiscriminate in the way they saw all "modernization" as progress, is a thing of the past. The enthusiastic raptures
with which the achievements of our own day are greeted have died
down. The mounting Green Party lobby is even asking whether our
"modern approach" has not actually led to disastrous destruction of
our natural environment. Psychologists see in the "modern mentality"
the cause of growing self-alienation. Moreover not all those in political office believe any longer that economic progress is necessarily a
boon for humanity. Even the most modern of our theologians realize
that the charismatic revival and the renaissance of Eastern religions
are no longer just "cashing in" on their worldly way of speaking
about God. It is gradually being realized across the board that much
that is contemporary and modern is disappointing and one-
dimensional. Thus while the theologians of the secular city—often
mustering the most bizarre conceptual armoury—attempted to
"adapt" the Christian tradition to the modern way of viewing things
(even at the expense of throwing overboard or passing over in complete silence whatever did not massage modern sensibilities), the concept "modern" has lost a lot of its lustre.

> The death of God theology was the grotesque climax of this theologi-
> cal disembowelment. At the same time the church functionaries, in-
> creasingly panicky about the faith of their organizations, tended to
> jump on whatever cultural or political bandwagon was proclaimed by
> the so-called opinion leaders as the latest revelation of the Zeitgeist.
> As was to be expected, all these efforts "to make the church more rele-
> vant to modern society" had the effect of aggravating rather than alle-
> viating the religious recession.[7]

To put it more simply, precisely at the moment when one particular
school of theology had just about completed a grandiose theological
edifice in "contemporary language," the concept of "modern society"
is becoming less attractive to more and more people. It is no longer
so evident that today's one-dimensional man is any more sophisticated than that of his forefathers. So, for example, it would no
longer be claimed that a modern garage-owner is more broad-minded
and humane in his judgement on questions of life and death than a
nineteenth-century shepherd or craftsman. There can be no doubt
that a major leap forward has been made in technology. Yet an in-

7. Berger, *Facing up to Modernity,* New York, 1977, 197.

creasing number of people are coming to realize what the cost is in spiritual terms.

To address the issue of God in appropriate language is not the same as to slip into using popular jargon like: "somehow I thought a little bit of alternative faith comes across as O.K. if it responds to our modern sensibilities." Today more than ever before religious reflexion supposes what Berger has called the need "to transcend modernity." One has to see beyond one's contemporary nose. One must try and see beyond the present (often rather sorry) state of affairs. It is imperative to introduce nuances into certain forms of modern thought which are alarmingly one-sided. This implies, of course, a familiarity with modern thought as well as the myriad questions which that thought has not answered nor even addressed. It is essential in the first instance to recognize the symptoms of the one-dimensional person, so as then to be able to detect the origins of this syndrome because only then is it possible for the Christian message to contribute to the debate. It is no mere optional extra. It confers salvation. It may very well be that it is the only door which opens a way out of the present impasse.

This study begins thus with a critical look at religion with the assistance of the X-rays of modern sociology. The initial question it will address is whether religion is anything more than a phenomenon admitting of a sociological explanation. Is faith something more than the top layer of socio-economic structures? More than the consequence of a not tenably successful collective internalization? Then there is the question as to whether religion, the age-old stabilizing factor in society and source of cultural inspiration, still fulfills these functions in contemporary society. Is religion not completely out-of-date precisely because it is no longer functional on the one hand and on the other has lost all credibility? These are questions posed by sociology which provide the point of departure for the present study.

A further chapter will examine religion in the light of a critique levelled by psychology. Is religion anything more than the psychological projection of a humankind which is still naive? Is being a believer something more than being a member of a religious institution which is completely passé? Do the religious convictions of modern humans not necessarily run into a barrage of insuperable psychological objections? Can religion stand up to the critique advanced by psychology? It would appear from all these questions that modern humanity is indeed so "handicapped" that it suffers from worrisome narrowing of its experience and awareness. The language, thought-systems and the whole cultural ambiance in which humans think and speak are so one-sided that it finds itself unavoidably trapped between what W. Blake called "single vision and Newton's sleep." On the one hand humans seem particularly fascinated by the objective reality of empirical things; on the other hand they seem to be in a deep sleep or under total anaesthetic whenever they are confronted with whatever transcends the positive sciences. To put it more plainly: they are empirically alert but doped when it comes to metaphysics. Particular attention will be devoted in this study to the most potent anaesthetic possessed by modern atheism: contemporary language. Only then will it be possible to discuss the age-old problem of the diverse religions which so often contradict one another. If there is one universal deity, why, many ask, does he not reveal himself more clearly so that at least the scandal of religious conflicts and polemic can be avoided? After comparing the different forms of religious belief and somehow classifying them, a key question arises: what actually is "faith"? Furthermore, what is Christian faith and what is it not? It may well be the case that the "kairos" of contemporary believers resides in the fact that, stimulated by the critical remarks and the pertinent questions posed by "dissenters," they themselves arrive at a clearer idea of what it actually means to "seek God, in the hope that they might feel after him and find him" (Acts 17:27).

CHAPTER ONE

Faith: A Matter of Mere Sociology of Knowledge?

Modern sociology has launched an attack on religion from two angles. Sociologists of knowledge like to claim that a person's religious
convictions are nothing more than the result of his milieu, i.e., of the
social context in which that person grew up and by which such a person was indoctrinated. Change a person's milieu and his or her "personal convictions" will very soon change too, especially if that person
is still relatively young and therefore malleable. The Spanish migrant
worker was a believer and active churchgoer so long as he lived in
his native village in Castile. As soon as he moves to Paris or Stock-
holm one can be virtually certain that his new environment will reduce to zero his religious practice and his faith will not be far
behind. After a short time he will start behaving like an unbeliever; a
little later he will feel like an unbeliever and describe himself as
such. Sociologists of knowledge point out that his social milieu initially changes a person's behaviour and shortly afterwards their
world of experience. Generally the first thing to change is a person's
outward behaviour, and then later their inner feelings and theoretical
opinions alter.

Functionalists, on the other hand, point out that in every age religion has been necessary to maintain social cohesion. Religion had a
"function" in every society. It provided a series of collective propositions, ideas and moral norms which saw to it that within the group
order and social solidarity were guaranteed. Any breaches of the
rules were considered a "sin" and were consequently reduced to a
minimum, at least as long as the members still preserved this sense
of sin. On the one hand, religion gave some sense to existence, and
particularly conferred meaning on work, suffering and death. On the
other hand, this same religion prescribed laws and duties which were

mandatory for all. What was allowed and what was not, what was obligatory and what was not was all decreed by the gods and sanctioned by the priests. In our day that function is gradually being taken over by more rationalist authorities.

Religion just does not "perform" any more. Its role seems to be played out. Religion has simply lost its credibility in the eyes of modern human beings. When it comes to deciding what is good for them and what is not, they are more likely to consult a psychologist than a priest. What acts as the cement of social cohesion are no longer "collective religious propositions" but rather cold, scientifically established insights and laws.

Even if not all sociologists of knowledge and functionalists are unbelievers, it cannot be denied that their discoveries raise serious questions which challenge traditional faith. This first chapter will investigate the degree to which sociology of knowledge poses a major challenge to a personal faith in God. A subsequent chapter will examine the objections which functionalists, following in E. Durkheim's footsteps, made to traditional religion which was for so long taken for granted.

1. The Concept "Sociology of Knowledge"

The sociology of knowledge emphasizes the intimate link which always exists between a person's social milieu (a bourgeois milieu, a working class area, a monastery, a university campus, etc.) and their so-called personal convictions. The opinions a person holds are determined by the social group (or groups) to which he or she happens accidentally to belong. A social group creates an environment in which ideas and values are acquired and become part and parcel of a person's approach to life. Not only the contents of a person's thought but the very way in which they think is sociologically determined. One has only to think in this context of technical, artistic, sensual, business or scientific interests. The problem that arises, of course, is that any given individual belongs to any number of different groups: his family, colleagues, generation, language group, church, political party, sport's club etc. In the eyes of the Marxist, class is decisive; for Freud it is the family environment; for the teenager it is the "modern mentality" of his peers; and for the nationalist it is the blood in their veins, their native language and their native hearth. This does not mean to suggest that a person is always aware of the external forces which have most strongly influenced him or her. Students can be of the opinion that they became a Marxist through their own personal choice of reading while in fact they absorbed the left-wing ideas which were then the fashion at the Catholic university chaplaincy. Furthermore, the number of groups of which a person is a member is far greater in a big modern city than in a Papuan fishing village. The average Papuan belongs to one of fifty families of fishermen, and that is about it. The modern city dweller's mind is reeling with contradictory views and opinions, and sooner or later they have to make their choice. The traditional village-dweller of long ago, on the other hand, lived by a stock of self-evident received ideas and knew perfect ideological rest. It just seemed as if there was no such thing as intellectual problems. All that one could and ought to know and believe was obvious. As society became more complex, it became correspondingly difficult to get a "clear view" of things and people began to have more and more doubts.

The sociology of knowledge can consequently be defined as: the study of the way an individual's mind works in so far as this is limited to the social and cultural factors which, consciously or unconciously, have had an influence on him or her. "Being linked to" is of course not at all the same as "being determined by." To put it another way, the link between a person's social milieu and their way of thinking (a link no sane person could deny) is not necessarily a "causal" link. A social milieu can influence a person's ideas without actually being their irreversible cause. The latter only happens in the case of those who follow the herd or the ideological fellow-traveller. One cannot simply "reduce" ideas to nothing more than the result of social influences. Rembrandt is not just a product of Amsterdam's Calvinist bourgeoisie, a class which was anyway rather cool in the way it received his avant-garde artistic creations. Whoever reduces ideas to the mere by-products of social determinism has but two choices. "A person either sinks into a negative cynicism or he reacts to this tendency by hurling himself into the arms of one or other pseudo-religion or ideology. In both cases the end result is the same: a fanatical contempt for all that is humane and a hefty dose of violence and negativism."[1] This is a prophecy which has sadly come true in the case of many who repudiated all forms of thinking for themselves.

1. Cf. W. Stark, *Die Wissenssoziologie: Ein Beitrag zum tieferen Verständnis des Geisteslebens*, Stuttgart, 1966, 149.

Karl Mannheim, considered by many the father of the sociology of knowledge, prefers to speak of the "existential link" between every thought and a social milieu without which no original thought can be explained. It is impossible to fully understand and appreciate Rembrandt without some understanding of the puritanical Calvinist atmosphere which he breathed, and the baroque age in which he lived. In the same way one cannot really understand the gospels without some notion of the Pharisaical-Jewish environment in which Jesus lived and against which he often vigorously protested.

It was Mannheim's view that the principal thesis of the sociology of knowledge is that there are ways of thinking which cannot adequately be understood as long as their origin remains obscure.[2] (One ought not to lose sight of the fact that the almost imperceptible source of the Mississippi in Minnesota is no adequate explanation of the strength of this mighty river at its estuary in New Orleans.) In other words if one really wants to understand a thinker properly one must always look into his or her historical, existential and social background. A sociology of knowledge, properly understood, is thus a hermeneutic or a method of interpretation. It sets out to understand the sense of claims or assertions human beings may make, and not a scientific, critical exposition of "explanatory causes" or of automatic determinism. There are still quite a number of serious open-minded sociologists who believe they can explain someone's faith by pointing the finger at their "sheltered environment" or at an old-fashioned way of thinking typical of certain rear-guard ideological reactionaries.

Before attempting to answer objections of this kind it is important to have a look at the positive, illuminating insights a great sociologist like Max Scheler has into the phenomenon of religious faith. In *Die Wissensformen und die Gesellschaft* he points out that every form of thought, observation, acquaintance, knowledge etc. has a "sociological character." It is not so much the contents of our knowledge which is socially determined, but rather our selection of certain objects of our knowledge. It is not so much *what* I feel, think and enjoy while standing in contemplation before a Rubens painting which is the consequence of my education but rather *the fact that* I come to look at the picture at all. The fact that I am more easily attracted to a classical art gallery rather than a busy shopping hall, a friendly pub or a

2. K. Mannheim, *Ideology and Utopia*, New York, 1969, 2.

porno-cinema is the result of a certain form of education which attempted to make me sensitive to or interested in certain types of objects, while the very same education dismissed other objects as being trivial or unworthy of attention.

It is not so much my personal awareness of God which is the result of my environment, but rather the fact that someone taught me to be open to religious reality. In Scheler's opinion our "forms of knowledge" are strongly influenced by social factors. The question therefore is, for what sort of knowledge have I developed a sensitivity? For empirical observation, sports scores, classical literature, mysticism or economic forecasts? It is not so much what I think about Dostoevsky which is the result of my milieu, conservative or liberal, but rather the fact that I apparently am more inclined to turn to a classical Russian author than to the latest potboiler. The effect which reading Dostoyevsky may have on me or which of his works is my favourite cannot be completely explained by social pressure or cognitive conditioning.

Long before the term "Wissens-soziologie" was ever invented and launched by thinkers like K. Mannheim and M. Scheler, other German philosophers such as K. Marx and M. Weber had emphasized the intimate link between ideas on the one hand and socio-economic circumstances on the other. One could even speak of two contradictory schools in the sociology of knowledge: "materialists" and "idealists."

2. "Materialist" Sociology of Knowledge

The "materialists" find in Karl Marx their most articulate spokesman. New convictions are, in their eyes, always the result of a new socio-economic environment. If a Mayan Indian from Mexico goes on to study at Harvard he is bound to lose whatever residual belief he has in a "Sun-God" within a very short time. Such a belief is quite simply not tenable in the context of an international university. For the "idealists" the contrary is the case: for them new socio-economic circumstances (e.g. Western capitalism) are the *consequence* of a set of widespread ideas (e.g. puritan Calvinism with its strong work ethic and tradition of sobriety). For both schools convictions are "relative" in the sense that they are always directly related to specific social environments.

Marx believed that religion was the result (and thus not the cause) of a particular economic infrastructure, e.g., of feudalism or capitalism. Religion is purely a structure of ideas or an ideology which buttresses an existing class system and keeps it stable. Thus, for example, the Indian caste system seems to have been an efficient religious instrument in that it prevented an intermingling of the races on the Indian continent during the waves of Indo-European and Aryan migration. The caste system, rooted in religious belief, fitted nicely into the context of a conservative class society governed by Brahmins. At a later period, the emperor Constantine saw in strict Christian monotheism an ideology which more successfully legitimized his imperial monarchy than did confusing polytheism. Hence Constantine's "conversion" to Christianity.

It was Marx's view that the "material means of production" determined the intellectual climate. "It is not a man's consciousness which determines his existence, rather it is his social existence which determines his consciousness."[3] In other words, it is not what I personally feel and think which determines my social behaviour, rather the social environment in which I live will restructure my brain. "In direct contrast with German philosophy (i.e. Hegelian idealism), which always descends to the earth from the celestial realms, we climb up from the earth to heaven. In other words, we do not take as our point of departure what people claim, imagine, or think; nor do we start with man as he is described, presented or assessed in order to get to the creature of flesh and blood. We start with the real, active human being and, on the basis of his day-to-day life, demonstrate what ideological traces or echoes are the result of this life-process."[4]

"Upon the different forms of property, upon the social conditions of existence, rises an entire superstructure of distinct and peculiarly formed sentiments, illusions, modes of thought and views of life. The entire class creates and forms them out of its material foundations and out of the corresponding social relations. The single individual, derives them through tradition and upbringing."[5] The ideas in circulation at a particular period, i.e., the mentality or spirit of the age, are nothing more than a reflection of the socio-economic relationships of the day. Were one to change the dynamic of these relationships, one would immediately create a new climate of opinion and a

3. K. Marx, *Zur Kritik der politischen Ökonomie*, K. Marx und Fr. Engels, Werke XIII, Berlin, 1972, 9.

4. K. Marx, *Die Deutsche Ideologie*, K. Marx und Fr. Engels, Werke III, Berlin, 1969, 26.

5. K. Marx, *Der achtzehnte Brumaire des Louis Bonaparte*, in: N. Abercrombie, *Class, Structure and Knowledge*, Oxford, 1980 n. 13.

new set of sensibilities. Industrialize a traditional rural society, and its faith will collapse like autumn leaves falling from the tree of tradition. Send a "right-thinking" seminarian to a world-famous university and his religious, intellectual and moral consciousness will undergo a pretty rapid transformation.

Do different social classes have different convictions and religious beliefs? Despite the class structures of the feudal system, were not the Middle Ages rather remarkable in the homogeneity of their religious opinions? Marx was no stranger to such questions and objections. His answer was disarmingly simple: "The ideas of the ruling class are in every age the prevailing ideas."[6] The rich and powerful force the conceptual system and mentality—from which they reap most advantage—onto all other classes in society. In this way the people get a "mistaken" or "false" consciousness and end up being alienated from their true selves. For that very reason it is essential for the ordinary person or member of the proletariat to take over the controls themselves, even using dictatorial methods initially. The powerful force not only their system of production on everyone else but also set the trend in the distribution of knowledge. The social class which possesses the material means of production has at the same time control over the apparatus of "mental" production. It was Marx's view that the very same people who launch material products on the market also manage to sell off their spiritual values as part of the same package. The modern enlightened revolutionary will have to emphatically reject that alienating package which, for ages past, bears the unmistakable stamp of Christianity. The new knowledge will have to be "realistic" (i.e., materialistic) in character. It will have to defend the interests of the new generation and no longer of the established order. This clarion call is music to the ears of the intellectually unarmed, the emotionally disenchanted and the "new man," who have nothing to lose precisely because they have never possessed anything in the first place.

Marx was pretty withering in his criticism of metaphysics and spiritual values in general. He was particularly sharp in his attack on religion. Religion rocks human beings to sleep. It is an opium or a spiritual tranquilizer which manages to close its disciples' eyes to material reality. His jibe that "religion is the opium of the people" is known to one and all. He saw religion as the cheapest epistemologi-

6. K. Marx, *Die Deutsche Ideologie*, K. Marx und Fr. Engels, Werke III, Berlin, 1969, 47.

cal anaesthetic that the lords doled out to their servants to keep them quiet and "high" despite all their pain and toil. One must remember that in nineteenth-century England Marx saw with his own eyes how many textile factory workers resorted to opium exported from the colonies in order to forget their misery. The use of drugs is not something which just started in the twentieth century. The only thing that is different is that there is a sociological shift in the class of person who takes flight into the "paradis artificiels" (Baudelaire) in comparison with the past. It is no longer the worker living in material poverty but rather the middle-class teenager starved of spiritual nourishment. There is more than enough food available in our consumer society. Spiritual food has become pretty scarce however, and this is an intolerable situation for anyone who is intellectually alert.

It was Marx's belief that religion effected on the cognitive level what alcohol and opium effect on the physical level. One can forget the pressures of hopelessness and despair and sink into a short-lived "transcendental intoxication." "Religion is the sigh of the oppressed creature, the heart of a heartless world and the soul of soulless situations."[7] In other words the weary person finds in their religion a little comfort and privacy in this valley of tears, and above all that their patient resignation to suffering here below will be rewarded in the world to come. Religion is thus a compensation for those in positions of servitude. For their lords, on the other hand, religion represents a reassuring "way of life." According to Marx both parties need to be "informed" and have the scales removed from their eyes.

One of the reasons why Marxism has managed to mesmerize the simplest Latin-American labourer as well as the most enlightened Western intellectual is that the truth of some of its basic, self-evident premises seem so palpably obvious. These premises are what the Swiss psychologist J. Piaget termed "thought schemes." Thought schemes are cognitive structures or intellectual tentacles by which one gets a "grip" on reality and enable one to feel one understands that reality. A thought scheme is a mechanism of interpretation. It is a sort of intellectual pincers by which one extracts from reality or from history as much as fits into the pincers, while one forgets about whatever necessarily escapes its grip. It was Piaget's view that a growing child understood just as much as fitted into his thought scheme at any given age. The child will divide his world into "good"

7. K. Marx, *Frühschrifte*, Landshut, Ed., 1953, 208.

and "naughty" things and people. Later on the child will see that such a black and white structure is much too simplistic (nobody is entirely good nor is anybody completely naughty). Intellectual growth basically involves a refinement and increasing complexity of a person's thought schemes. Only a fanatic or a complete reactionary slots all of reality into out-of-date thought structures. The true philosopher is continually searching for better cognitive structures which will enable him to understand and interpret reality as much as possible. It seems a little odd that those who were most successful in bringing thought structures onto the intellectual market seem to be A. Comte, K. Marx and S. Freud, or perhaps a combination of the three. The strength of their thought schemes lies in the fact that not only do they seem to explain a lot but also that they do this with disarming lucidity and in terms which anyone can understand. Their thought schemes have become common property to such an extent that one can join Dilthey in speaking of a "spirit of the age."

Since the time of Comte many people (even those who have never read him nor are even familiar with his name) are inclined to see faith in terms of his three-stage thought pattern according to which, in a particular culture as well as in an individual person, we can discern three stages of development. After a period of religious or mythological belief (the "theological" stage) a person's critical faculties sharpen and they begin to philosophize more for themselves (the "metaphysical" stage) to end up as a mature, adult humanist: the final stage is that of "positive science." This scheme "explains" both the young adolescent's difficulties as well as the later apostasy of the teenager. By extension it also explains the religious naivete of primitive peoples as well as the unbelief of the informed psychologist in contemporary society.

A similar simplicity and clarity of thought makes Freud equally attractive, especially when he sees the roots of neurotic complexes in family structures and repressed sexuality. (We all know that family background and sex are the scapegoat and hobby-horse respectively of modern human beings).

The great advantage with Marx, whose philosophy, it cannot be denied, was extremely nuanced and complex (how many of his disciples have ever gone to the bother of reading him?), is that he offers his disciples a solution which is disarming in its simplicity and appears to be an intellectual "passe-partout." His scheme admits of two types of person: the exploiter and the exploited. This categorization can apply to an incredibly wide range or realities: bourgeoisie and proletariat, whites and coloured, academic mandarins and revolutionary students, male chauvinists and liberated women, conservative parents and the new generation, the Church hierarchy and a gagged laity, supermarkets and the local grocer, the silent majority and the "emergent class," etc. It remains a big question as to whether such schemes do not lead to gross simplifications which were perhaps not consciously the intention of their inspired and brilliant "Urheber."

Problems of faith are far more rarely the fruit of an intense perusal of the works of Marx or Freud than of a "spirit of the age" which is inseminated or contaminated by a popularization of their ideas. It is precisely this spirit of the age and the spectacular drift from faith to unbelief which is part and parcel of it that will be examined in this study. There is no attempt to furnish an exhaustive interpretation or even summary of Marx or Freud. Our concern is with their spiritual step-children: today's unbelievers.

Marx himself was far too intelligent and intellectually honest not to realize that the scheme "socio-economic structures as the determinant of ideological superstructures" was not in need of certain qualification. Marx, and to a greater extent his sensible friend Engels, saw clearly that reality was a good deal more complex. In other words he was no "pure" materialist. Ideas too (e.g., his own) appeared to have the power to influence and even change socio-economic conditions. "The materialist doctrine concerning the changing of conditions and education" wrote Marx in his *Jugendschriften,* "forgets that those circumstances must first be changed *by people* and that the educator has first to be educated himself."[8] The socio-economic infrastructure and the mechanism of indoctrination must be changed and refined by revolutionaries who cannot just be the result of existing structures against which they had just protested.

Is it reasonable to claim, for example, that Luther was "the product" of a sterile late medieval Church or that Jesus was a "spin-off" from the Israel of the Pharisees? Wasn't Socrates put to death by his own milieu because his religious convictions were viewed by that same milieu as subversive and pernicious? Religious founders such as Ignatius Loyola and social reformers such as Las Casas cannot be explained away as merely the result of a set of socio-economic circumstances. They in fact react *against* these "circumstances." Moreover,

8. K. Marx, *Dritte These über Feuerbach,* Werke III, Berlin 1969, 5.

the fact that religion can be an opium for the people and can anaes-
thetize the masses demonstrates at the very least that ideas can have
a major impact on socio-economic structures. This explains Marx's
positive hatred of religious ideas. In his eyes they were much more
than a mere "paper tiger." Furthermore, the Russian obsession with
controlling and censoring Western and "capitalist" information and
their neurosis about "dissident" literature demonstrated clearly the
enormous power they ascribed to the spread of ideas. Their concern
for ideological orthodoxy is best explained by R. Laing: "All those
people who seek to control the behaviour of large numbers of other
people work on the experiences of those other people. Once people
can be induced to experience a situation in a similar way, they can be
expected to behave in similar ways. Induce people all to want the
same things, feel the same threat, then their behaviour is already
captive—you have acquired your consumers or your cannon-fodder.
Induce a common perception of Negroes as subhuman, or the Whites
as vicious and effete, and behaviour can be concerted accordingly."[9]

In his earlier writings (1844) Marx readily admitted the existing interplay between economic substructure and ideological superstructure. Later Marxism was to lose sight of this dialogue. Ideas were to
be viewed as a mechanical consequence or an epiphenomenon of
"real" material circumstances. For Lenin, thought was nothing more
than a "reflection" or automatic mirroring of economic reality. Within
the Marxist camp it was necessary to wait for the study *Geschichte
und Klassenbewustsein* (1923) from the pen of the Hungarian communist Georg Lukàcs to rediscover the mutual influence of social context
and ideas.

Frederick Engels was fully aware that religious convictions could
indeed act as a spur to political action. In 1890 and 1893 he admitted that he and his friend Karl Marx had on two particular points
ventured an inadequate opinion. To begin with they had "over-
emphasized the economic factor and under-estimated the dialectical
interaction between ideas and infrastructure." Furthermore, Engels
continued, they had never clearly explained exactly how ideas
emerged and subsequently developed within a given society.

Engels' common sense led him gradually to put water in the wine
of Marx's extreme materialism by claiming that the economic situation and the class struggle were at the basis of everything, but that

9. R. Laing, *The Politics of Experience*, London, 1967, 80–81.

"certain elements of the superstructure . . . such as political, juridical, philosophical and religious theories can have an influence upon the course of historical processes, and can even in certain cases become decisive . . . there is in fact an interaction of all these elements."[10] In other words, the economic structure is actually nothing more than the framework within which certain ideas can develop and become socially relevant and effective. Economic circumstances are the "conditio sine qua non," but not the explanatory cause of certain intellectual convictions. "Primum vivere, deinde philosophari" is an adage of which even the monks of the Middle Ages were convinced.

One way or the other, even after Marx and Engels have balanced one another out, the only beliefs which can survive are those which seem to be in the interests of one or other social class. The two materialists will, however, grudgingly admit that social frameworks themselves do not produce ideas. They can make them possible or promote them. The initially radical materialism of the sociology of knowledge is thus diluted (even if the penny has not yet dropped for many popular Marxists).

No one will deny that faith is not something up in the clouds but rooted rather in a concrete historical situation, riddled with social, national and ideological conflicts. That situation can evolve or even change radically. Nevertheless it is quite striking how through all the ages biblically-inspired Christian faith has remained basically the same. Moreover, any cultural historian cannot but agree with the observation of the Jewish philosopher of religion, Heschel: "To us it seems obvious that the great ideas were born in spite of social pressure, in spite of circumstances. Moses had to wage a battle not only against Pharaoh but also against his own people. Upon the masses which clamored for a golden calf the prohibition to make a graven image had to be imposed. The essence of religion lies beyond the grasp of sociology."[11]

3. "Idealistic" Sociology of Knowledge

We find a completely different vision of sociology of knowledge in the works of Max Weber. This German Protestant set out to demonstrate that ideas and religious convictions were not so much the re-

10. Letters of F. Engels to J. Bloch (21-9-1890) and to J. Mehring (14-7-1893) in *Marx and Engels, Selected Correspondence*, Moscow, 1955.
11. A. Heschel, *Man is not Alone, A Philosophy of Religion*, New York, 1951, 230.

sult as actually the cause of a whole series of historical developments. He is often considered an "idealist" on account of the seminal influence he attributes to religious ideas (an idealist in the German philosophical sense of that word, i.e., primacy of the spirit over matter). His most celebrated work is *The Protestant Ethic and the Spirit of Capitalism (1920)*. In this study Weber argues that it was no accident that the rise of Protestantism in Switzerland, northern Germany, Sweden, Great Britain and the Netherlands went hand-in-hand with the rise of capitalism in the same countries. Weber compares the world of ideas which characterized puritain Calvinism (and which were later transferred to North America, resulting there, too, in industrial development and the growth of capitalist wealth) with the religions of ancient China, India and the Middle East which wielded no socio-economic power whatsoever.

Weber demonstrates that economic rationalism or "sober matter-of-factness" was caused by certain religious values emanating from the tradition of Puritan Protestantism—e.g. sobriety, the work ethic, a strictly regimented life, prohibition of alcohol, rigorous Sabbath day observance, a severe code of sexual ethics, etc. Furthermore, in the Calvinist doctrine of predestination worldly success was an extremely important sign of God's blessing and grace. Catholics, too, practiced asceticism but it was generally confined to monasteries or convents and "did not really touch the spontaneous and lively character of daily life in the world. . . . The Calvinists brought asceticism onto the streets, they slammed the convent doors firmly shut behind them, imported their strict and methodic time-table into daily life, and made of it a generally accepted lifestyle."[12]

Protestant countries became the wealthy countries, in contrast with countries like Ireland, Spain, Poland, Italy or Latin America. It was Weber's view that the Protestant elite ruled the roost for centuries precisely because of their puritan ideas. It was those very same Protestant countries which at a later period would witness the most violent reaction against every form of prudish inhibition. In this regard one has only to think of the hippy phenomenon which imported its anti-work, anti-war, and anti-inhibition morality with the greatest success into societies where work, competition, military power, discipline, and a non-permissive ethic were held in high regard.

12. M. Weber, *Die protestantische Ethik und der Geist des Kapitalismus, in Gesammelte Aufsätze zur Religionssoziologie*, I, Tübingen, 1947, 163.

And yet Weber was no "naïve idealist." Within the context of certain socio-economic and geographic conditions which formed the prerequisite, Protestantism supplied a number of ideas deeply coloured by religion which would then become the cause and motivation of a new economic style and order. The power of Weber's argument lies in the fact that, in contrast with Marx and so many other sociologists, he had assiduously studied the major religions and knew them intimately.

Twenty years later Weber's vision was to be confirmed from a totally different quarter. Teilhard de Chardin, who spent much of his life in China, came to precisely the same conclusions as Weber in his study *Le Phénomène humain*. Teilhard wondered why man's evolution stagnated for so many centuries in non-Christian cultures such as those of the Mayan Indians, the Chinese, the Indians or the Polynesians, while during the same period the West experienced a tremendous élan. The progress is so impressive that the West is copied and even envied by the developing countries. In addition to geographical and physical factors, Teilhard saw the cause of the discrepancy between the West and other countries as lying in the difference between their respective religious convictions and ideals. China never really bothered to elaborate a "pure" physics. Astronomy, for example, never developed beyond para-religious astrology. India lost itself in metaphysics which viewed matter as in principle less worthy. "Through an exaggerated passivity and detachment they became incapable of constructing a world. . . . The (empirical) phenomena were conceived of as an illusion or "maya." How could such doctrines stimulate and give direction to human development? . . . . By contrast, in the West first Greece, then Rome, and finally and principally that mysterious judaeo-christian yeast gave Europe its spiritual form and structure."[13]

How do we explain the West's strength? By two essential combinations which the Eastern religions neglected or simply did not see, according to Teilhard. In the West the spirit is anything but blind to material reality, and contemplation and action were never viewed as mutually exclusive. Spirit and matter go hand in hand, and St. Benedict's *Ora et labora* is just as typically Christian as St. Ignatius' *Contemplativus in actione*. The West's strength lies in its dynamic vision of life. In this context one has only to think of socio-economic

13. P. Teilhard de Chardin, *Le Phénomène humain*, Paris, 1955, 232–234.

expansion or mass communications, the school infrastructure, opinions surrounding marriage, legal custom and tradition, the structures
of democratic or socialist stages, etc. In all domains there is a constant search for change, improvement, growth, or even revolution. In
"an ancient China which had completely ground to a halt" (Teilhard),
the revolutionary movement and economic development only got underway once there had been a massive influx of Western ideas. This
occurred when Marxism swept the boards and took over the role of
static Confucianism and Taoism. It is unthinkable that the Marxist
phenomenon—a conglomerate of Jewish and Christian ideas—should
have emerged within an Islamic or Hindu cultural setting. It is no accident that Marx was the son of a Jew who had converted to Protestantism. One could even go so far as to consider him a typical
"heretic," who made a lucky strike (or "hairesis") and branched out
from the tradition of Judaeo-Christian faith. For him, respect and justice for the oppressed "poor of Yahweh" is of such primordial importance that, with a view to achieving this noble aim, he is willing to
unburden himself of a whole series of other Christian values and
throw them completely overboard.

Marxism is, as it were, a secular eschatology. It is a prophetic doctrine which preaches a future paradise—even if it is to be established
on this earth—for which the convinced communist rather than the
Christian believer works with all the fire and fury of an ardent missionary. It was Weber's view that both capitalism and Marxism are
not so much the result of a bourgeois-romantic "belle époque" but
rather an amalgam of heretical Judeo-Christian ideas.

CHAPTER TWO

The Limits of the Sociology of Knowledge or the Relativity of Relativism

What specific problems and objections does Christianity face in the light of the sociology of knowledge? To what extent is it now more difficult or even impossible to still believe after the X-rays of the sociology of knowledge have cast their withering light on our ideas and faith?

To begin with, a whole series of old "certainties" and self-evident truths, now called into question and at best viewed as dubious, are slowly disappearing into the mist. It is indeed true that every society rests on a number of "evident propositions" which are accepted by everyone and considered completely normal. They make life easier and smoother. They free human beings of the constant pressure to look up everything for themselves and then make their own choices and decisions. Today so many of these self-evident propositions are questioned and challenged. "Why must we do that? Why can't we do this? How on earth can you prove that this is really true?" Young people in particular no longer see the sense or justification of certain beliefs and customs. For the first time in history, perhaps, there are many who find themselves aliens in the society in which they live. Such a thing would be unthinkable in a primitive or traditional society, whatever its nature. A young Papuan boy from a fishing village finds it quite normal that one day he too will become a fisherman, that his parents will find him a nice girl as a bride and pay for her, that he will participate to the full in all the rites of initiation of his tribe, etc. It is only eventual contact with a Westerner whose lifestyle and mentality is so totally different that might set him thinking about whether it would perhaps be to his benefit were he to go to school, leave his native village and look for work elsewhere, dress

16

differently henceforth and gradually turn his back on his traditional gods. Contact with Westerners represents a "culture shock" for him. By virtue of their lifestyle and the way they talk, they call the whole Papuan milieu ino question. Age-old customs and laws lose that self-evident quality, and now become relative and problematic. The young Papuan will have to choose for himself and go his own way, even at the risk of the deep disapproval of his fellows.

Every modern youngster is exposed to similar "culture shocks" whenever he or she travels, reads a book, or looks at television. They quickly become aware that in other parts of the world people live and think in a completely different way. They live in a pluralistic society which by virtue of its very pluralism has become anonymous, where different convictions and lifestyles can be found within one single apartment block, or even within one and the same family (or at least try to live and let live). Everything suddenly appears to be relative. Given that religion in particular is concerned with the Absolute (i.e. fixed values, unalterable natural law and God's eternal commandments), it is usually the first casualty of this questioning relativism. How can one still talk about eternal truths at a time when everything is in a state of flux and a handful of old certainties seem to be vanishing behind a rising wave of questions and problems?

Modern humans ask the why and the wherefore of the existing institutionalized rules and regulations which have been rammed down their throats since they were children (religious Sabbath day observance, monogamous marriage, pre- or extra-marital sexual abstinence, clerical celibacy, etc.). The question as to the whys and the wherefores is far more than mere intellectual curiosity. It is an existential questioning. The perplexed questioner is, in the essence of his being, already a doubter who is no longer content with the social milieu into which he happened to be born. "The person who asks what the sense of something is betrays the feeling that he may have gone astray (i.e. has been wrongly brought up) or has discovered in himself a need for different and better structures than those which at present exist."[1]

It cannot be denied but that society exerts a major influence on the thought and action of the individual. A traditional society afforded security and did not trouble their peace of mind. Shocked and as it were rudely awakened by contacts with other cultures, modern soci-

1. A. Gehlen, *Urmensch und Spätkultur*, Bonn, 1956, 69.

ety has a radically different effect. It makes people anxious and insecure, and furthermore hypersensitive, allergic even, to values, customs and ideas which were once considered "established."

Individuals are increasingly obliged to pass judgement for themselves, to look for solutions and to find answers on their own. They
have to make their own way through the growing minefield of complex issues with which they are confronted at an early age. They live
constantly in an atmosphere of "decision stress," i.e., of options and
decisions where they themselves must make the choice. One can, of
course, welcome the fact that at long last the individual is at the controls in his or her own life. It could well have been a disaster that
this step forward had to occur at the very moment when they sallied
forth from their safe and cozy nest only to end up in the bewildering
confusion of an increasingly complex world.

Perhaps what is most typical of the modern self-consciousness is
the ability, and the corresponding duty to choose for oneself, while
in earlier societies everything was cut and dried, laid down from
above and endowed with an unquestioned inner necessity.
Kierkegaard detected the roots of modern "Angst" in this duty to
choose for oneself. The obligation to choose creates a fear of freedom
and an anxiety about its exercise.

There are two ways of escaping from this obligation to make one's
own choices, both of them attractive: a fanatical and virtually blind
decision for a fixed ideology which offers "security" (at the present
time this is usually a left-wing Marxist ideology or a neoromantic "retour à la nature" under the Greenpeace banner), or a cynical universal doubt so as to escape the hurtful accusation that one is still "so
naive." In either case one ends up with a "precarious vision of life"
and develops a mentality which makes one ill at ease and alien in
the world in which one lives.

The sociologists of knowledge have even more disturbing facts in
store. Just at the moment when persons feel obliged to adopt a more
personal approach, to choose their own ideas and opinions and to
work out their own vision of life, the sociology of knowledge comes
along and tells them that their so-called "personal standpoint" is in
large measure determined by the social milieu in which they live. In
other words, not only are the cultural habits of the milieu in which I
happen to live "relative," but so too are my most deeply personal experiences, decisions and convictions. "Perhaps the greatest shock
comes when one suddenly locates oneself . . . within a certain place

in society. . . . One's very private life and convictions are seen to be crucially connected with this social location."[2]

Even my own retrospective view of my own past and life-history is apparently relative. Someone who runs along to a Freudian psychiatrist is doing nothing more, according to P. Berger, "than buying a new autobiography." The "alternative" psychiatrist will also draw to his patient's attention a number of episodes and details from his past life which he had totally forgotten. The psychiatrist will go on to show the patient how important certain principles were to which in their naivete they were deeply attached but from which they must now try "to emancipate themselves." The specialist will encourage them to subject themselves to a mild and benign form of healing and therapeutic "brain-washing" by means of a "scientific reevaluation" of their most intimately personal experiences and memories. What is our life-history more than the history of our experiences with society (i.e., our family, school, church, youth movement, clubs, etc.)? Society is a map and our biography is but a route on its surface. Our life is thus, in P. Berger's view, a trip through society.[2a] The big question is who is to be our guide on this perilous journey? There is a big chance that one will follow a different path and accumulate different experiences if one follows in the footsteps of a Freudian psychiatrist rather than those of a Marxist activist or, for example, a Catholic priest.

The sociologists of knowledge assure us thus that everyone will try to see reality from their own individual standpoint, but that this "standpoint" is in the meantime profoundly influenced by "others," i.e., by their milieu. The result of all of this is naturally a general widespread feeling of uncertainty, changeability and relativity of each and every conviction and belief. For the traditional Arab, Islam is self-evidently true and any other set of religious beliefs is unthinkable if not absurd. For the modern Christian this is no longer the case. They no longer view their religion as obvious and beyond all possible doubt. Thanks to his ecumenical spirit and open mind they can easily appreciate and identify with Weltanschauungen other than their own. This tendency so prevalent in the West, thanks partly at least to the sociology of knowledge—to feel unsure about one's own position and to be only too happy to revise or change it—Berger terms "alteration." One could even consider it intellectual humility: a tender

2. P. Berger, *The Precarious Vision, A Sociologist Looks at Social Fictions and Christian Faith*, New York, 1961, 15.
2a. T. and B. Berger, *Sociology*, New York, 1972, 18.

plant which in an odd way only sprouts in the shifting sands of sun-drenched pluralism. It is no accident that the term "alternative life vision" has become a fashionable buzzword. To put it more simply and brutally, modern humans belong to what H. Schelsky as early as 1975 called: "Die Skeptische Generation."

One of the fundamental reasons for this very widespread philosophical scepticism or religious agnosticism is the fact that the sociology of knowledge has made human beings aware (or at least claims that it has) of the reasons why they hold a particular belief or none at all. The flip answer of many youngsters today is "I believed probably only because my parents or teachers drummed it into me." This type of reasoning weakens and undermines a childhood faith. This growing tendency among the young to feel "unsure" about positions they had taken at an earlier stage (often so-called "indoctrination") and the growing ease with which they are willing to revise them seriously, call them into question or change them, lies at the heart of what Berger stigmatized as "alternating thinking." People constantly get a kick out of being "dissident." I am fascinated by everything but nothing manages totally to convince me; I am willing to try or experiment with any number of ideas, yet I will not allow myself to be definitively bound by any firm choice or option. Life goes by in an atmosphere of intellectual browsing and spiritual dilletantism. One overlooks the fact that faith or belief (either in God or in a permanent spouse) is impossible for those who constantly avoid a definitive decision. Impossible thus for all those who on principle continue to hesitate and are always on the lookout for "alternatives." It would almost seem as if procrastination, doubt, and the cultivation of uncertainties have become the status symbol of an "open mind."

Those who do take the risk of faith still have a shadow of doubt in the inner depths of their heart. All visions are termed relative and of equal value. This seems to be about the only affirmation of which the modern doubter is sure. Speaking of the current "cult of tolerance" J. Baudrillard noted: "The fact that today former enemies are so quick to talk to one another and that radically opposed ideologies manage to launch a dialogue, in no way signifies progress in the field of human relations or mutual understanding. . . . It simply means that ideologies and convictions too have become consumer products which people barter and vary when the mood takes them."[3]

3. J. Baudrillard, *La Société de Consommation.* Paris, 1970, 277.

A conviction, much like a piece of antique furniture or a snazzy sports car, becomes a status symbol. In this case it is a status symbol which indicates "a modern mentality." Baudrillard calls it "un signe différentiel," Bourdieu terms it "une marque de distinction"; "open-minded" persons change Weltanschauung like they would change their brand of cigarettes, i.e., not terribly often, yet when they do so it is not as if they feel they have turned their back on something of enormous importance or a matter of life or death. It is somewhat surprising that the most virulent opponents of a liberalized economy are usually the most furious proponents of ideological liberalism, at least in theory.

What answers can a believer come up with in the face of this barrage of objections from the sociology of knowledge? To put it another way: what religious affirmations are still possible in such a climate of dizzying relativism?

To start with, the sociological tenet that a person's religious convictions are quite simply the result of the milieu in which he or she just happened to be born becomes a two-edged sword. The idea, if it is true, could also be made to apply to atheism: the fact that many people now consider themselves as unbelievers is just the result of the general atmosphere of agnosticism and religious doubt in which everyone these days "is born and brought up." Unbelief could thus be merely the result of the "spiritual pollution" (Roszak) and of the "intellectual contamination" which modern humans are obliged to breathe. If one were to claim that in the middle ages people were obviously believers because at that time faith belonged to the "bon ton," then by the same token one can equally legitimately claim that their modern counterparts feel themselves to be agnostic for precisely the same reason: because the tendency to doubt and cast everything in a relative light is part and parcel of the atmosphere in which "progressive" people live, they want at least to live up to their reputation. What is rather peculiar is that the sociologists of knowledge usually relativize every form of thought, with the notable exception of their own insights. They see everything as relative, except for their own relativity. Relativity is the only absolute.

On the other hand it is often said that conversions are purely the result of social pressure, i.e., of a change in the ideological climate. It is perfectly possible that someone becomes an unbeliever simply because the new social environment (e.g., a big city or university) does not allow faith to influence the way they think or live. The opposite reaction is also possible. One-sided materialism and the spiritual vacuum of the world can put someone off so much that he or she turns to religion. Moreover, the facts would suggest that this second reaction is increasingly frequent. The reason why a trickle has not turned into a flood is explained by means of the sociology of knowledge: a social climate in which unbelief rules the roost is alarmingly widespread. Van de Pol was right when, after the most recent council, he spoke of "the end of conventional Christianity." The end of conventional unbelief is still a long way off, alas.

One could make a second criticism of those who would seek to relativize religion. It is obvious that every personal conviction will have a social dimension, i.e., has emerged and developed within a social context. This does not mean, however, that the group is the origin of an idea or its inspiration. A seed cannot be fertilized in barren soil, the deep brown earth does not itself create grains of wheat. They must come from elsewhere.

As Bergson correctly pointed out, there are two sources of religion. First, there is the static structure or the sociological circumstances in which an individual lives. Secondly, there is the dynamic inspiration provided by one or other religious figure with whom a person may come into contact. I can have been born and reared in a strict Calvinist environment but have come into contact with a figure such as Roger Schutz in Taizé.

Church order is always the result of fixed norms and structures (no religion thrives on anarchy). The propagation of a spirituality is usually the work of a very singular personality. It is generally the "religious virtuosos," to borrow a phrase from Weber, who create the atmosphere in which the spirit could breathe more freely and spread its wings. The primary source of religion is thus the social substructure. Without the Jewish people, prepared for centuries by their prophets, Jesus Christ would not have been possible nor even imaginable. And yet Jesus was to turn the existing structures on their head and give them a new purpose. The conformist or the one who follows the herd never advances beyond the automatic habits of that milieu. "Individuals differ in their capacity to transcend the situation into which the accident of birth has thrown them: There are a thousand dull conformists for every Socrates."[4] And yet that is precisely

---

4. P. Berger, *The Heretical Imperative; Contemporary Possibilities of Religious Affirmations.* New York, 1979, 8.

what makes the present time so fascinating, i.e., that which was formerly a person's fate now becomes an opportunity and a chance for an individual to achieve personal fulfillment.

When Marx claims that it is always "the ideas of the ruling class which become the ruling ideas," it is important to remember that Marx's division of classes into bourgeoisie and proletariat is rather out-of-date. The so-called "middle-class" (to which more and more people now belong) is actually split into two new classes which are diametrically opposed. On one side stand the producers, managers, and distributors of material goods. To this class belong industrialists, technicians, traders and the "liberal professions." On the other side we find the manufacturers and distributors of ideas. These people are active in the areas of education, communication media and the social services. Like their colleagues from the material department, they too have gone into the business of mass production and propaganda. Their business is the "forming of opinion." In contrast with the first group, which wants to limit state intervention as much as possible, the second group demands even greater state involvement, i.e., a more socially-oriented body of laws on which they themselves are actually financially dependent. Left and right is no longer dependent on different salary scales but rather on the role an individual plays in society. Both classes have their own symbols and flags. The "silent majority" is in favour of work, law and order, family life, industrial development, technical progress, military security, but against feminism, abortion, the romantic Green Party, etc. The "new priestly caste" takes a completely different stand on all these issues. Schelsky calls them the "priestly caste" because these people—in contrast with the "silent members" of the majority—are so keen to explain, inform, protest, meet, supply information and massage "the soul of the child." That second group is indisputably the "governing class" on the present idea-market. The products which they offer in the display cases of the mass media are more redolent of unbelief than of faith. The mass media have this much in common with the priests of old, according to Schelsky: they are both out to proselytize. (Where the genuine priest is concerned, Schelsky speaks of what his older colleague Benda called "La trahison des clercs": they deserted to the crying minority.)[5] It is quite remarkable how modern people have been

5. H. Schelsky, *Die Arbeit tun die Anderen*, München, 1975, and P. Berger, *The Class Struggle in American Religion, The Christian Century,* 1981, 194–199.

spurred to think more critically (by all these developments), but then in such a way that their attention is often focused on archaic forms of power, such as those exercised by the Church and family. They are seldom aware of the far stronger pressure exerted by the "new priestly caste."

In his study *The Lonely Crowd*, D. Riesman stresses how young people are no longer successfully "indoctrinated" by venerable traditions, nor by parents or any authority from above, but rather by their own contemporaries, i.e., by their peer group. They do not consult their parents about how long they should grow their hair. They just imitate those they see around them. The music they like is not the same as what their parents enjoy; they like the pop music their peers all over the world listen to. The social pressure "from above" has slackened; the pressure "from the side" has become markedly greater. Nineteenth century humans knew that they were bound by their environment and accepted the fact. Their counterpart a century later is shaped by a far more efficient environment which remains imperceptible. In that respect they run just as great a risk of becoming an ideological mass product as their colleague from "la belle époque." The reason is simple: the influence of the present-day "hidden persuaders" (Vance Packard) has become stronger and more effective. Just because one no longer feels the intellectual injection does not mean that the dose in the syringe has in any way been reduced. While one holds one's right arm in a firm protective grip, the injection is painlessly doing its work on the left arm. Just as the medieval shoemaker was less well able to persuade the consumer to purchase his handwork than is the modern manufacturer of detergent, so too the indoctrination-potentialities of the nineteenth-century catechist were modest indeed compared with the power of a contemporary bestselling novelist or TV journalist.

One of Christianity's most brilliant enemies was without doubt Nietzsche. His influence may have gone into somewhat of a decline as a result of certain associations with later Nazism. And yet everything points to a succesful "comeback" for this celebrated adversary of Marx. It is striking how both Marx and Nietzsche were violently anti-Christian, but then for diametrically opposite reasons.

For Marx, Christianity was a "tranquilizer" which was invented by the rich and intended for the poor on whom it was hoped it would have an immobilizing effect. For Nietzsche, on the other hand, Christianity was the invention of the small, enslaved "Unmensch"

with fateful consequences for the talented "Übermensch." In Marx'
eyes, Christianity was a religion created by and for the wealthy
bourgeoisie. In Nietzsche's eyes it was an ideology for slobs and
good-for-nothings.

Christians flunk the challenge of life. They are scared to "live
dangerously." They prefer to take refuge in such "cowardly virtues"
as humility, prudence and obedience. In other words, in the virtues
of a good slave. Christianity prevents its adherents ever becoming
"grown-ups." In Nietzsche's opinion it is an unnatural reaction
against Darwin's "survival of the fittest." If only it were true that
the fittest drew up the laws! In the same way that tiny microbes can
actually kill a lion or fungi and parasites can fell a mighty oak,
Christianity represents an attempt to make the slavish and the
petty-minded seem as if they are powerful. Because of his terror of
sin, the Christian avoids "living." So, asking to keep people firmly in
their place, anxiety and guilt feelings are pumped into them. The
result is that people are "just as afraid to live and to love as to die."
(R. Laing)

Although in their eyes religion, seen in a historical perspective, has
been repeatedly misused to rock the little people of this earth to
sleep and to put bright, intelligent people down, it is evident that
neither Marx nor Nietzsche ever fully understood the true nature of
Christianity. It was precisely in order to frustrate the establishment of
the capitalist jungle, in which the law of the survival of the fittest
would prevail just as it does in the natural world, that the leading
figures in the history of Christianity have always taken up the cause
of the little people, the sinners burdened by a heavy weight of guilt,
in order to set them free and emancipate them. However great may
have been the deviations from this noble aim, this is the heart of
Christianity and not what Feuerbach, spiritual guide and mentor of
both Marx and Nietzsche, saw as "Das Wesen des Christentums."

Does this all mean that personal religious convictions are the exclusive preserve of a few privileged individuals or a strong elite capable of setting themselves against the sociological current? And that
the rest just scamper along, joining the herd? Must one be gifted
with the brilliance of a Socrates to escape social determinism? No
way! In a pluralistic society such as ours, where nothing is taken for
granted any more, everyone has to choose for themselves. This does
not, however, mean that everyone has to blaze a completely new
trail. Such a task falls to truly exceptional figures such as Buddha, St.

Bernard or Las Casas. There are many different paths through the cognitive labyrinth of modern society. There is a huge range of possible choices and lifestyles. Before investigating how one makes the best choice and one on which one treads new ideological paths or changes one's Weltanschauung, it is worth nothing that there are three sorts of people who cannot choose or are not willing to do so. These are people who stick to their guns no matter what. A normal child accepts and takes for granted the views of his or her parents and first teachers. We can overlook for the moment the enormous psychological handicap which several children suffer at an early age, namely in an environment in which mother and father, or parents and teachers differ among themselves and even contradict one another. These are later always the first victims of agnosticism.

It makes no sense to ask a child whether or not it wants to be baptized. A child is but an infant and cannot make such a decision. Were one to conclude from this that it might be better to wait before conferring Baptism, then by the same token it might be better to wait before educating the child in English or letting them have piano lessons. It might later transpire that the child would prefer to be brought up in French and play the violin rather than the piano. Parents usually try to give to their children the best of what they themselves possess: their native language, their customs, their religion, etc. At a later stage children will have to decide on the path they wish to follow or rectify the one they are on. In order to change direction, one has first, at least, to be on a path. And if one is to choose French rather than English, then one must at least be able to talk.

Both faith and unbelief are "states of the soul" (Bergson). In contrast with organic things like hair and fingernails, the spiritual dimension of humanity does not grow "on its own." A child has to be brought to "insight" through education. There are still many people who have grown up in a pre-pluralistic spiritually homogeneous framework. Every deviation from their education seems to them to be not only treachery, but even silly. What "dissidents" believe one way or other is of little interest to them. The air which young lungs breathe in is not yet infected with strange ideas. Such people—even though their number is dropping rapidly—have no need of a choice or of "conversion." To them everything seems simple: for one person it is faith, for another it is unbelief. Hans Küng has pointed out that at the present time not only are an increasing number of believers beginning to doubt their faith, but also more and more unbelievers are beginning to wonder whether it is so certain that "nothing exists" outside of the empirical universe. Besides children, there is another class of people who never experience anxiety when faced with a choice. These are those few who live in an intellectual reservation in which they manage to escape from the dizzy confusion generated by mutually competitive views of life.

There is, then, a third class of people who try to duck every new choice, i.e., the sceptics. Their attitude is simply: "I won't make any statement because whatever I say is relative and dubious." Naturally what they fail to see is that their utterance is itself a very categorical pronouncement which is anything but relative or tentative. Scepticism is their dogma. Very often this scepticism is again the result of a particular sociology of knowledge. Maybe the oldest aphorism of all is Pascal's famous jibe: "What is considered true on this side of the Pyrenees, is considered untrue on the other side." The conclusion which many apparently immediately draw from this is that when French and Spaniards do not think on precisely the same lines, this fact in itself proves that both are wrong. It is as if the fact that a Zulu medicine man holds a different opinion about the cause of an eclipse of the sun than an English scholar in itself proves the opinions of the Englishman are just as suspect and mythological as those of the African fetishists.

None of this makes it very clear what personal position or view of things is absolutely necessary for modern humanity, i.e., why it is advisable to have one's own set of beliefs, rather than to keep everyone else company hemming and hawing over everything. In order to understand why this is necessary one must first be aware of the transitory spiritual vacuum in which a person lives when his "Sitz im Leben" is a shifting pluralism. One must also realize that floundering about in a sea of uncertainty is not only hard on the nerves but also leads to cynicism. This is not to suggest that "it is better for a person to choose something; it doesn't matter what" but rather that persons simply must search for their own way forward in the spiritual forest. Moreover, they know that others before them have found ways through this particular forest which led them to profound insights and liberating deeds. They realize that some people stopped searching simply because they were convinced this forest was in fact a hopeless labyrinth without any real way out. The child of the pluralist society resembles not so much an alpinist who, after a successful climb has a magnificent panorama spread out before him as far as the eye can see, while he can put a name on all the surrounding peaks. They are more like ramblers who can no longer rely on well-trodden pathways and are consequently obliged to find their own bearings, relying perhaps on a guide, but never feeling totally happy or at ease.

One striking feature of all those who are "searching" within the context of a pluralist society where many possibilities are on offer is a certain resentment. They experience not only chronic doubts but even a certain aggression when they think of the old watertight truths in which people once had such blind faith. They have become allergic to cast-iron truths. They feel like children who has been peremptorily disabused of their belief in the fascinating fairy-tale figures, Santa Claus or Father Christmas, dismissed now as pure fictions which naturally "are not true." They wonder where all this demythologization will end. An accusation of naivete and credulity is the worst indignity a modern person can suffer. This is also true for adolescents going through puberty. The Anglican bishop John A. T. Robinson was quite correct in his characterization of our time as a crisis period for maturity or "coming of age," with all the features typical of that stage in a person's life: allergy to authority, a jaundiced view of days gone by and tradition, insecurity about the future and an energetic affirmation of personal freedom.

Their resentment against articles of faith does not in any way prevent modern pluralists from feeling deeply insecure internally and even guilty about their scepticism. Psychology furnishes spiritual tranquilizers to alleviate that guilt: that uncomfortable feeling is dismissed as the last residue of an out-of-date process of internalization from which enlightened persons must courageously set themselves free.

Modern humanity feels not only aggression vis-à-vis "the old days" but also "a metaphysical angst." This latter is a weighty term used by Kierkegaard by which he wishes to imply that nobody searches for light more than those who find themselves in the dark, or that a cul-de-sac is the best preliminary step towards discovery. For two hundred years now the Enlightenment has promised that, once it had shuffled off religious myths and superstitions, humanity would feel free and happy. In reality, humanity has ended up in a position of senseless gloom. "The old garments have been cast off, yet instead of feeling relief and emancipation he is disgruntled to the point of rebellion." It is this situation which in Kierkegaard's view represents the necessary springboard for what, using somewhat ambiguous language, he terms "the leap of faith." It is not an irrational leap in the dark but rather a premeditated answer to the Word's message. Kierkegaard believed that it was only in our day that it became completely clear that there was no other way out but Christianity. Thanks to pluralism it becomes obvious that Christianity is not an emergency exit (one among many) from a cramped and ultimately intolerable situation. Christianity is rather the door which persons will never find so long as they fail to see clearly that they are incarcerated in an inner court.

When Kierkegaard claimed that "truth is subjective," what he means is that our faith is born out of a dual personal experience. On the negative side we are in the grip of anxiety when faced with a growing realization that everything is absurd (Sartre and Camus claim that there is no escape from this anxiety and that consequently heroic courage is required to accept and live with this burden of absurdity). On the positive side there is the meaningful Word of God. This Word is neither an idea nor an objective doctrine. What this Word has managed to achieve during the course of history becomes obvious when we look at the lives of the great Christians who pledged themselves totally to the Word. What refusal of the Word implies is equally clear, e.g., in the attainments of atheism. While for many the modern angst is a dead-end street, for Kierkegaard it represents a purifying blessing.

The history of Christianity shows that fresh insight is only possible through letting go of straws which are manifestly unsafe and, after an enriching search, clutching at a more secure handhold. It was heretics and "dissidents" who posed ever greater challenges to spirituality and theology and stimulated developments in dogma, clarified our insights and deepened our understanding. What is remarkable in the case of modern humanity is that it let everything go all at once and ended up on the shifting sands of Cartesian "methodic universal doubt." What was originally "methodic doubt" has developed into existential angst and a deep-seated insecurity in our day.

And yet there is a glimmer of hope in all this open, honest self-interrogation about why one is actually a Christian. To the extent that the setting which makes someone automatically a Christian disintegrates, faith on the basis of personal conviction becomes not only possible but also necessary. The conventional Christianity of yesteryear developed either into an increase of personal faith, or into a growing dissatisfaction with aimless window-shopping in the shopping arcade with its cornucopia of "new" spiritual consumer goods.

A mature and responsible personal faith does not mean that one has to construct a new world view on one's own, independent of any social context, a feat which would in any case be impossible. On the other hand religious renewal is not simply the result of a change of environment. The question which always arises is: "Why does someone change his environment?" True conversions are not the result of mutations of the sociology of knowledge but rather of a personal encounter. In a letter addressed to the English novelist Lawrence Durrell, Anaïs Nin wrote: "There are no solutions, there are displacements. Something in you helped me to displace myself and I breathe better, thank you. Perhaps the old idea of faith."[6]

It is indeed true that the difference between faith and unbelief is a difference of point of view. Believers and unbelievers contemplate the same reality but from a different angle. One does not improve one's way of looking at things by closing one's eyes just because suddenly everything is cast in doubt. One corrects one's point of view by turning to someone who clearly sees more, and sees it more clearly. If this new way of looking at things renders possible a more adequate interpretation of my own experiences with God, with the world and with myself, only then have I good reason to review my position and be won round to the viewpoint of my friend. Only when an experienced person whom I hear or whose work I read offers me deeper insight will I make his or her beliefs my own. Such a process always signifies growth. Even if it should later transpire—and this is inevitable—that that person, too, is partisan of a particular (and thus limited) sociology of knowledge, then it becomes clear to me that no single perspective confers vision without a living, personal view. The danger for modern humanity is that it moves in an intellectual terrain where so little mountain landscape comes within one's visual range (on account of its own empirical and technological constructs) that it no longer even believes that mountains exist. It is true, of course, that the best vantage point from which to see a "mountain" is not necessarily the sociological spot where one happens to have been born. Pursuing the search for a better "viewpoint" so as to have the mountains within one's field of vision does not imply that one has to become a spiritual butterfly. Even less does one have to become an

6. Anaïs Nin, *The Diary of Anaïs Nin*, II, New York, 1966, 255–256.

intellectual defeatist who opts to admire the undeniably exquisite carpet of flowers on the valley floor rather than set his or her sights on the mountains which the normal person will in any case never manage to scale.

Even the most personal insight ultimately supposes a social context. I will only ever be really sure when my experience is confirmed by others. Every single vision of life, no matter how personal, lacks what H. Sullivan termed "consensual validation." That is precisely why Whitehead's affirmation that "religion is what a man does with his solitude" simply does not wash. The other is necessary to my faith. Moreover, this is the fundamental reason why the Church exists and is necessary. Whitehead even admits as much. For him a church community is "a group of people with the same intuition." A group of people, thus, who find their view of life and reality best articulated and interpreted in the teaching of the Church to which they belong. Even when all of these people cannot boast of a rich treasury of accumulated personal experience, the Church's tradition (i.e., the articulation, in terms of dogmatic pronouncements, of the experiences of the apostles, saints, mystics and reformers) evokes in them an affirmative response. "Mothers can keep many things in their hearts, which they simply cannot put into words."[7] The religious language used by the Church provides them with the concepts they need to give verbal expression to their personal experience. Herein lies the enormous importance of ecclesiastical doctrine and tradition.

In former days most Christians saw little distinction between Church and world. For them the world they knew was identical with the Church. It is only in our pluralistic world that Christ's words really strike home: "Where two or three are gathered in my name, there I am in the midst of them" (Matt 18:20). The primary task of the ministers of the Church is to confirm their brothers and sisters in their faith. This is a mandatory responsibility. It is up to them to fortify the budding faith and the often tentative commitment of their charges, in fidelity to the Lord's words to Peter: "Strengthen your brothers in the faith" (Luke 22:32).

When it comes to the fortification of his faith believers are not thrown entirely on their fellow Christians who are still alive. There is such a thing as the spiritual communion of saints. In the tradition of the Church, too, ordinary Christians find confirmation of what they

---

7. See A. Whitehead, *Religion in the Making*, London, 1926, 65, 128–129.

themselves, however unpretentious their claims, believe and feel. Tradition is experience translated into language. Christian tradition is a treasure chest of memories, i.e., of experiences, which those who have died not only had in their own lifetime but interpreted into language and placed on record. It can happen that when we read or hear about what Christians from an earlier age experienced and recognized as true it finds an echo in our hearts and spurs us to acknowledge, "Yes, there's a lot of truth in that. Even if I could never have quite put it that way myself, that's the way I see it too."

Does this mean that my faith is but the conclusion I draw from my own experience after comparing it with that of others? Is it not true of many Christians that they confess relative poverty in the area of personal insights and personal contact with God, although in the meantime they remain faithful to what they have received or inherited from others? For most converts and mystics, the strength of their faith lies in profound and even shocking experiences. Christians who received their faith at mother's knee will easily recognize themselves in the observation of Flannery O'Connor: "If you live today you breathe in nihilism. In or out of the Church, it's the gas you breathe. If I hadn't had the Church to fight it with or to tell me the necessity of fighting it, I would be the stinkingest logical positivist you ever saw right now. . . . What one has as a born Catholic is something given and accepted before it is experienced. I am only slowly coming to experience things that I have all along accepted. I suppose the fullest writing comes from what has been accepted and experienced both and that I have just not got that far yet all the time. Conviction without experience makes for harshness."[8]

Dogmatic truths emanating from the Christian tradition make it possible for us to experience certain realities. They draw our attention to aspects of reality which might otherwise have escaped us. In this respect the teaching of the Church plays an irreplaceable role in the individual Christian's assimilation of his or her personal experience. What persons experience for themselves is to a large extent determined by a series of suppositions, i.e., by what they already know and have learned under the guidance of the Church. This is not only true in the area of religious truths and values but also in every de-

8. Flannery O'Connor, *Letters, The Habit of Being,* New York, 1979, 97.

partment of human knowledge, even in the area of strictly scientific knowledge.[9]

The agnostic philosopher Karl Popper called it a "crazy superstition" that science should be based on observation and experience. Experience is in any case to a large extent selective. One's experience is not random. One turns one's attention first to certain objects because one supposes them to be in some way interesting. Experience already supposes a focused interest, or point of view, and a certain number of specific problems. Scientists investigate the link between lung cancer and nicotine or between sleeping sickness and the tsetse fly because on the basis of knowledge they already possess, it is assumed there is a link. In the same way the Church's doctrine draws our attention to certain connections and realities, even if on first inspection they strike us as odd, and in this way the teaching of the Church makes religious experience fully possible. The social context of the ecclesial community points the arrow towards the place where "the treasure buried in the field" is to be found, even if it is ultimately up to us to discover precisely where it is ourselves and dig it up. The Church does this in such a way that makes a lot of the hit or miss searching of the uncommitted "free-thinker" superfluous.

To sum up, it must be said that there is a dialectical affinity between tradition and experience, i.e., between the faith I confess and the experiences I have. "I believe, and then I reflect about the implication of this fact. I gather evidence about that which is the object of my faith, and this evidence provides a further motive to go on believing."[10] When intelligent insight and personal experience back one another up, confirm and supplement one another, then and only then do I make the transition from a childish faith which I have been spoonfed to a personally assimilated set of religious beliefs. Only the latter type of faith, however intensely assaulted by the inevitable "pollution of the spirit" (Roszak) which I inhale wherever I go, is strong enough to stand up to the determinism of the sociology of knowledge, in which the present age—in contrast with days gone by—pushes us towards atheism. The days of "conventional religion" are gone with the wind, forever. It is probably no exaggeration to say that contemporary "conventional unbelief" is already beginning to display signs of precocious senility.

---

9. J. Cobb and D. Griffin, *Process Theology*, Philadelphia, 1976, especially ch. "Doctrinal Beliefs and Christian Existence," 30–40.
10. P. Berger, *The Heretical Imperative*, New York, 1979, 141.

CHAPTER THREE

The Function of Religion and the Loss Thereof

1. The "Functionalist" Explanation of Religion

In his study *Les formes élémentaires de la vie religieuse,* the French sociologist Emile Durkheim claims that no society can survive without "collective propositions," i.e., without ideas, fixed values, commandments and prohibitions, all of which give meaning to daily life and as such guarantee order and solidarity. It was Durkheim's view that in primitive societies religion provided these "propositions." Were religion to disappear, society would slip into cultural chaos and a natural disintegration or "anomie." Consequently it was imperative never to abandon religious propositions before one came up with better and more convincing ideas to confer legitimacy on existing social institutions (such as, for example, science, philosophical ethics or humanitarian principles). A purely functional analysis of the religious phenomenon is always slightly shocking. If the social anthropologist tries to show that people bury or cremate their dead only in order to prevent infection, that Eastern cultures banned the consumption of pork in hot countries merely on account of the high risk of contamination associated with it at the time, or that the churches promoted monogamous marriage only with an eye to raising a large family, then it is easy to draw the conclusion that religion consequently is no more than a threadbare sociological cloak. Functionalism always undermines the value of that which becomes a "function" of something higher. If it can be demonstrated that religion was necessary to keep the people under control, then it is quite logical that the "freethinker" should attempt to get rid of this big stick. Religion's role in society is exposed; its time is up. Thanks to the functionalist sociologists, more and more people have come to think that religion was all eyewash or a moral soporific.

34

In *Les nouveaux possédés* the Christian sociologist J. Ellul attempts
to show that an atheistic culture can escape anarchy and immorality
only to the degree that a pseudo-religion (e.g. Nazism, Maoism, xen-
ophobic nationalism) takes over the place of religion. In other words,
if religion dies out, there is a serious risk of anarchy. Dostoevsky
never ceased warning of such a scenario. The moral confusion in
which such a large section of post-Christian society lives would at a
first glance tend to lend credence to the functionalists' views. Once a
people has lost its faith in its religious (or para-religious) leaders, it
automatically begins to doubt all that heretofore seemed self-
evidently true.

According to the functionalists, traditional religion performed a
four-fold role. First, it legitimated the existing social structures. It
made, for example, the caste system or monogamous marriage unas-
sailable and taken completely for granted. The archetypical question
"why must it be this way or that?" always received a religiously-
coloured answer: "It is the will of the gods," or "That is quite simply
the natural law." In fact such questions are rarely posed. Society or-
dains not only the behaviour of its members but also the way they
think and feel (e.g., by labeling certain feelings as sinful or perverted). In order to achieve this, "collectively accepted propositions"
are essential: epistemological systems or articles of faith which are
above and beyond all doubt. Sceptics or problematic cases are immediately referred to specialists or professional counsellors with an academic background in theology. These religious gurus will explain
why such and such is forbidden and why something else is absolutely indispensable. It was Durkheim's belief that religion was thus
reduced to a number of practices, conventions and self-evident propositions. In a traditional society, as yet "unenlightened" by the insights of detached scientists, religion is nothing more than the
"incensing and cement of the existing culture."[1] Traditions are kept
alive by showing that the gods intended them the way they were and
wanted them preserved.

Secondly, religion not only explains the reason for the prevailing
social order but also sanctions the strict observance of its norms. This
latter effect is achieved by means of internal and external control
mechanisms. On the internal level its method is the so-called "formation of conscience" i.e., by means of "spontaneous" arousal of guilt

---

1. W. Herberg, *Protestant, Catholic, Jew*, New York, 1955, 279.

feelings or anxiety (which, according to Durkheim, are in reality naturally acquired and internalized). Externally, it achieves its effect through juridical sanction (e.g., excommunication, refusal of the sacraments, inquisition, etc.).

Thirdly, religion also appears to be useful, if not irreplaceable, in life's "borderline" areas. In crises such as death, illness, war, natural disasters or domestic unhappiness, people spontaneously reach out for a Church. Up to now modern science has fallen short in this particular area. For that reason religion appeals even to modern man in this type of crisis situation. People still tend to turn to the Church on the occasion of "peak-experiences," e.g., birth, the initiation rites of the young adult or confirmation, weddings, funerals, etc. At these special moments people are prepared to see these religious customs as perhaps a little more than purely external forms or empty frills: "one never really can be sure."

Fourthly, the functionalists are prepared to admit that religion can be useful in guaranteeing the psychological stability of a large number of people. At some stage everyone feels the need for introspection, meditation, mystery (or the occult) and even for a "retreat" or a "weekend away from it all." Even modern people like to withdraw to a monastery in the heart of the countryside where in the cloistered silence they can "come to" again. Particularly in this hard, technological world, dizzy with frenetic activity, a growing number of psychiatrists view a mild form of religion as a benign medicine for the psychological well-being of their patients. The cynical advice, given by C. G. Jung to his atheist patients is well-known: try one way or other to pray on account of the beneficial effect it has on the human psyche. As early as 1932 Jung actually conceded: "Among all the patients who came to me in the second half of my career, there was hardly a single one whose problem was not linked in the final analysis to the search for a religious Weltanschauung. One can confidently say that they all felt sick, because they had lost what the living religions of all time had given to their adherents, and that whoever did not recover his religious Weltanschauung was never really cured."[2]

There are a number of critical objections which can be made against the reduction of religion to a pure societal function.

To begin with, the fact that it can be demonstrated that a certain institution happens to have a societal function is no proof that that is

2. C. G. Jung, *Psychologie und Religion*, Olten, 1971, 138.

all that can be said about it. It is undeniable that marriage fulfills an important function in all societies through stimulating reproduction, channeling sexuality, the education of children, etc. Is this a proof that marriage cannot be the fruit of disinterested love? Can one deduce from this fact that people marry only "so as to maintain the social order"? Or that people will cease marrying once, thanks to sociologists, they start to think that society has "invented" marriage so as to camouflage sinister aims and functions? Will people lose their taste for good food as soon as they "understand" that protein is necessary for a person's biological survival?

To those who see religion's principal function in the maintenance of traditional customs and the existing order, it is worth bearing in mind that Moses, Buddha and Jesus Christ attacked and changed the social structures of ancient Egypt, India and Israel in a pretty revolutionary way rather than give their stamp of approval to the existing order. Are not religious figures such as Francis of Assisi, Martin Luther or Helder Camara rather "meddlesome clerics" who threaten the established order rather than its puppets or collaborators? Is it really the case that the Roman emperors or modern dictators saw in Christianity such a useful ally that they welcomed it with open arms and worked hand-in-glove with the Church? How can we explain the episodes of cruel persecution? What was the origin then of the bitter power struggle between empire and papacy in the Middle Ages? And how can we explain away the phenomenon of "Christian dissidents" in the Eastern bloc, to say nothing of liberation theology in the West?

Those who see faith as nothing more than a means of achieving spiritual health or psychological equilibrium should remember that the Cross is both physically and psychologically very "unhealthy." It leads to death rather than to emotional stability. It is thus no accident that the modern "experience-makers" or promotors of experiential techniques which widen and enlarge awareness prefer to bring Eastern products on to the market (one has only to think of transcendental meditation, breathing control, astrology, etc.) rather than the Christian religion. This fact had dawned on such highly sensitive and talented thinkers such as Rilke, Herman Hesse and Fr. Van Eeden long before California hippies drew attention to the "Eastern renaissance." Anyone who has a modicum of feeling for poetry can understand that a poet can be moved by a "white waterlily." One needs somewhat more than a poetic sensitivity and an openness to the beautiful to understand how a poet like John of the Cross consciously opted to enter "the night of the senses" in order to discover there "the naked Christ."

In the meantime it is gratifying to note the number of psychiatrists, many of whom are schooled in philosophy and consequently see the person as a totality, who understand that persons can become ill and unbalanced when they eliminate or amputate from their lives so vital a dimension as religion. R.D. Laing had the following to say: "As this external human world is almost completely and totally estranged from the inner, any personal direct awareness of the inner world has already grave risk; . . . Among physicians and priests there should be some who are guides, who can educt the person from this world and induct him to the other. To guide him in it: and to lead him back again. . . ."[3]

What the functionalists rarely see is that certain things can be more than just "useful," particularly when they become the symbol of something deeper. A rose can be a sign of love when I offer it as a gift to my dear one. It thereby becomes more than just a decorative extra trinket. A father does not present his newly-ordained son with a gold watch because he is afraid that otherwise he would arrive too late to celebrate his Sunday Mass. Man transforms "functional things" into signs of love, affection and fidelity. Santayana commented that "every ideal expresses some natural function, and no natural function is incapable, in its free exercise, of evolving some ideal and finding justification. . . ."[4]

There is a great danger that modern humanity may indeed lose its sense of the symbolic. A growing number of people prefer "useful gifts" rather than presents "with which one really cannot do anything." "Silly" flowers are replaced by money, paid by credit transfer onto a registered charity's bank account. Religion is of its very essence creative of symbols because one can only speak of God in symbolic language just as one can only express one's feelings for another human being whom one loves in symbolic language. Can one effectively explain why one loves another person in cold, businesslike language? Sex plays a very important role in the animal kingdom, yet only humans can make sex into a "language" through which they communicate a much deeper reality, namely their exclusive love. There is no doubt but that they can keep sex purely functional and

3. R. Laing, *The Politics of Experience*, London, 1967, 114; 116.
4. G. Santayana, *Reason in Society*, New York, 1980, 9.

can "make use of it" for purposes of procreation or the arousal of physical pleasure, or "pour épater le bourgeois," a thing of which Breuer suspected of Freud and J. Ellul.

It follows from what we have been considering that a functionalist is incapable of thinking "sacramentally." Marriage raises up sex to become a language of love (even if the biological functions continue). Faith sees the Church and the breaking of the Eucharistic bread as sure places of encounter with God (even if the Church does not cease to be a human social institution, nor the host cease to contain calories). The Christians see in Christ more than "the son of a Jewish carpenter" (even if that was actually what he was on the social ladder of Palestinian society). The functionalist generally does not understand what is meant by thinking or operating with "ritual."

Viewed from the perspective of anthropology, a rite or ritual is a custom which emerged within a given cultural context but the original purpose (usually practical or "functional") of which has been forgotten only to be replaced by a new, symbolic significance. For example, such customs as offering someone one's right hand in greeting, tasting wine before offering it to guests, burying the dead, the use of incense or baptizing with water, were all originally "functional" usages. The purpose was to demonstrate that one had not a weapon concealed in one's fist, to show guests that the wine was not poisoned, to get rid of vermin, and to wash, etc. Most of what are generally considered good manners are actually "rites" i.e., actions whose original purely practical significance has been superseded and has slipped into oblivion. Incense is no longer actually used to chase away flies: they are far more effectively dealt with by spraying an aerosol. Would anyone in their right mind resolve never to extend their hand in friendship since they had discovered the trivial purpose (i.e., to remove suspicion of a disguised weapon) behind the original custom? Extending one's hand or shaking hands has had a far more human significance for a long time now. Are cultural anthropologists now to have praise heaped upon them for emancipating us from superstition just because they are able to provide us with the enlightening insight that desert folk were always "baptized" before each audience with a Bedouin king? Rites govern and civilize contacts between members of the same cultural group. Religious rites make contact between man and God possible. They ennoble that contact. They seem odd only in the eyes of people who have lost all sense of religion and who have "demythologized" symbolic language and gestures, i.e., reduced them to their original banal, businesslike and purely functional significance.

In any society in evolution there will necessarily be constant adjustment and renewal. A society which is split on matters of ritual and is lacking in symbolic creativity runs a serious risk of disintegration. This applies as much in the area of culture as that of religion. It is highly probable that the loss of a sense of the symbolic is one of the major reasons for the contemporary religious impasse. The fact that "useful practical things" have taken the place of symbolic gifts is, as has already been mentioned, an ominous cultural symptom.

There are many of course who will come up with the argument that the loss of the symbolic demonstrates all the more convincingly how right Durkheim and company were in interpreting the whole human cultural system in purely "functional" terms.

The functionalists do not deny that writers with poetic inspiration can see more than just their utility in things and structures. They would, however, claim that this happens only very rarely. It is J. Baudrillard's view, on the other hand, that the idea that modern human beings see everything as functional is old hat. In addition to losing their symbolic value, many things have now also lost their functional value. They are now but "signes différentiels."[5] In the eyes of a growing number of people, the value of things one possesses (e.g., *Encyclopedia Britannica*, a massive silver tea service, an antique dresser or a sports car) is measured by the degree they demonstrate who someone is. Things have become status symbols (instead of pure utility articles). Naturally, according to Baudrillard, there are few people fully aware of this. In reality everyone wants at all costs to show that he or she has a personal uniqueness and individuality. They achieve this end by surrounding themselves with objects which have a "social sign value," i.e., which command respect and confer prestige. It is striking how in our day "ideological things" are playing the role of "signes différentiels." Opinions are advanced to show who one is (i.e., différentiel). A docile faith comes across as old-fashioned and conformist. Marxist ideas are signs of a revolutionary, adventurous spirit. They sound good, they sound progressive. It is now only possible to profess an interest in religion and still be taken seriously as "personal" and "critical" by

5. J. Baudrillard, in *Pour une Critique politique du Signe*, Paris, 1976, and *L'Echange symbolique et la Mort*, Paris, 1976.

demonstrating a fluency in the vocabulary of Oriental religions and revisionist terminology. My faith expresses itself on the one hand in Asiatic concepts (my "true self," my "atma," "nirvana," "maya," etc.) and on the other hand in the modern panoply of personal doubts and mental restrictions. It has now become an arduous, if not completely impossible task, to enter into discussion with people who use their "convictions" as a shield against day-to-day reality and the self-evident.

2. Does Religion Still Have a Function Within Modern Society?

When we leave aside the primitive religions and theocracies (e.g., Iran or Saudi Arabia), then it would seem that in our day the influence which religion can still exert on society is of a dual significance. To borrow Teilhard's words, it can be "une force d'inspiration et de stabilisation." The religious convictions of a figure like Mother Teresa (and of her sociologically-structured disciples or "congregation") can cause a shock and make people sit up, not only in such a city as Calcutta but gradually throughout the world. On the other hand, the Church can defend a moral principle or ethical standard, such as, e.g., the life of the "unborn child" or the freedom of the Polish people. It is important to emphasize in this regard that the true significance of religion has nothing to do with society or social structure. Religious concern is with something much more real, namely with the personal encounter between God and human beings. Given that humans are social beings, this encounter often has a number of social implications. It is essential to consider these latter, however secondary their actual significance.

"Inspiration" is not essentially to be understood as a sort of idealistic activism under the standard of some powerful symbol or other (the cross, the red flag, or the tricolor). In order to make some sense of one's actions it is first necessary to have a vision of life. One has to have an idea of one's vocation in life which fires one with enthusiasm for a vision of one's personal future and which one can reasonably expect to realize. Humans are future-oriented beings. When the future is surrounded in darkness and mist, then everything becomes pointless, a person becomes despondent and his or her outlook on life becomes black indeed. And yet, for countless generations it has been religion's lot to cast light on that future, even if at the time the sky was somber and darkness hung like a curtain over the horizon.

Once religious inspiration disappears, one has to seek some alternative, otherwise the whole business of life becomes meaningless. One ends up in the type of situation Sartre repeatedly sketched, his pen dripping with the ink of cynicism. There are many psychiatrists and pedagogues who can testify that this vision of life is increasingly widespread, particularly among the young, "Nothing is worth dying for," to borrow the words of an American student slogan. These youngsters no longer know "Devotionsziele" (Schelsky), i.e., values which are sufficiently real and meaningful that they will devote themselves heart and soul to their realisation. There are no forms of social structure (e.g., a missionary congregation or a youth movement) which seem practicable to them or worthwhile. Or else people turn to "alternative" sources of inspiration or mediators of meaning which propose new forms of salvation or "utopias" (Bloch) which seem more acceptable.

The most succesful of these new preachers of salvation have undoubtedly been the Marxist radicals of all shapes and sizes and, to a lesser extent, the post-romantic nationalists, even though both groups recruited their supporters from various social classes. Their power lies above all in the fact that they offer "Devotionsziele" for the natural idealism that is peculiar to a balanced youth and at the present time, in that regard at least, they face little serious competition from the institutional Church.

It has largely been secularization and pluralism which robbed religion of the monopoly of "inspiration to a purposeful life." As a result, young people have been virtually obliged to look to extra-ecclesial, if not totally anti-Church organizations to be able to live a life which somehow transcends the banality of the consumer society. In days gone by the Church had no whole selection of structured possibilities on offer—either expert spiritual direction or "vocation retreats"—which confronted a young person with a concrete choice. Secularization and an unusually strong internal flight from the individual's confrontation with himself have made the ecclesiastical organizations less attractive, while pluralism saw to it that "neutral" or pluralistic organizations looked a lot more inviting.

The human being has been termed a "meaning giver" (Kruithof). They are surely that, even if not everyone is equally successful in answering this call. The believer knows only too well that a person does not get this sense of purpose out of thin air but rather receives it, or has it transmitted from others. In this way a mother's life receives purpose (or at least a deeper sense of purpose) through her child and the professional activities of husband and wife through their family. Humans have always sought the meaning of life, or perhaps more accurately "salvation" or ultimate happiness in the future which God held open for them. Believers see the world as a place of work where they try to refine, integrate and improve themselves, their natural environment and society, thanks to models, ideas and values which are ultimately religious in character. They do not offer a utopia but are underwritten by faith in God. They try to change the real world along the lines of the world they hope for and dream about. Their hope lies in the future which God has promised them and for which God has created and called them.

Throughout history attempts to solve the great social plagues such as racial inequality, assaults on life, the ostracism of lepers, pariahs or lunatics, illiteracy, etc., have drawn on religious inspiration. Missionary priests, nuns and religious brothers, as well as lay volunteers, devote themselves to these noble causes, usually in the footsteps of a prominent figure or "founder" fired by religious idealism. One has only to think of Gandhi, Martin Luther King, Las Casas, Father Damien of Molokai and the countless others.

In contrast with the Oriental and the Indian, who still conceive of nature as something holy, sacred and not to be tampered with, the Christian considers nature as an arena for scientific research, technological development and cultural expression. The Westerner transformed the impenetrable primeval forest into a pleasant wood, and the desolate marshes into a polder. Human beings sometimes have to play doctor to themselves by means of education, civilized standards, and self-mastery to subdue their often unruly natural instincts (a fact which anti-authoritarian educational theorists, with their idyllic negation of original sin, tend to forget all too often). In the Judeo-Christian perspective the world is changed, thanks to the intervention of human beings, although there is serious danger that the world can thereby sometimes be mutilated or even destroyed, especially when humans, thanks to a lack of true perspective on the future, perpetrate virtual rape on the natural world with a view to their own immediate pleasure. It is not surprising thus that people who have become aware of ecological problems will feel far more attracted to a more Oriental outlook on life which respects nature and leaves it alone. The "bonzai" is probably the most striking example of this. Let nature be, let it be itself! Let the tree alone, let it be itself, let it stand there a hundred, two hundred years if need be! We do not need growth, change and development. This naive attitude tends to make one forget that in order to maintain a harmony and stability in nature, pretty harsh and unnatural intervention is often necessary. The Japanese bonzai requires more cutting and pruning than the Western oak.

In the eyes of Christians God has gifted humans with a world, a body and a temperament so as to make something of them in a creative way themselves, i.e., to elevate nature into culture. Teilhard considered Christianity as ultimately the only source of inspiration enabling this process of "becoming human" to be effectively pursued on the level of society and culture as well as on the personal psychological level. The Christian faith, according to him, offered not only inspiration but also stability. Culture is posited against nature in the same way as cosmos against chaos. For that very reason Teilhard extolled a "cosmic Christianity." It is no "establishment religion" which preserves the status quo, but rather a religion which, often swimming against the popular ideas and received wisdom of the day, not only keeps certain beliefs alive but actually does something about putting them into effect.

Given that religion, suffering from a deep identity crisis on account of its waning credibility, is increasingly less capable of fulfilling this dual role of inspiration and stabilization, people today look for a more pragmatic legitimation on the basis of "pure science." "God" is whatever seems necessary for a person's psychological equilibrium, for economic progress or for the biological future of the human race. A hundred years after Dostoevsky's exclamation that "if God does not exist then everything is possible," there are still people who believe that a pure "lay ethical code" is, in the final analysis, impossible. The Jewish philosopher Emmanuel Lévinas wrote: "There is no morality without God. Without God morality is no match for immorality. God is the very principle of the triumph of the good,"[6] and many looking at today's world would tend to agree with him.

It is indeed true that "religion functions in society as a basis of morality, of law and order, of respectability, of a sound and sober way of life."[7] Christianity can never become the basis or the cement of fixed laws or moral systems, at least not if its observance is pure and it does not let itself be reduced to a state religion which then be-

6. E. Lévinas, *Difficile Liberté*, Paris, 1963, 107.
7. P. Berger, *The Precarious Vision*, New York, 1961, 173.

comes guarantor for the behaviour of a worthy citizenry. St. Paul never ceased reminding people that Christianity is "no new law." Even less does Christianity promise salvation on the basis of fidelity to norms, regardless of their nature. The Christian is not to be differentiated from the Jew or the heathen on account of his observance of a new sort of law or a more exacting standard of morality. Just like every other person the Christian, too, is obliged to trace as noble and ethical a path through the jungle of ever newer human problems. Their strength in these situations lies in their faith in and knowledge of Jesus Christ who makes it possible for them freely and without prejudice, to come up with fresh moral solutions to the new problems which keep arising. This in no way means that "Christianity is some sort of revolutionary doctrine which seeks the overthrow of existing social structures."[8] What it does mean is that Christ did not come to ratify or legitimize any particular established moral order and that, consequently, there is no Christian economy, Christian state constitution, or Christian revolution. There are however, thank God, a growing number of people who are striving to improve and humanize the existing economic, political and moral systems moved by Christian inspiration, i.e., by a believer's perspective on Christ who was himself given a sham trial and executed at the hands of moral purists.

To put it in the words of Henri Bergson, Christianity is a "dynamic source" ever productive of new impulses. This, of course, does not detract from the fact that no society and no Church can exist without a number of static or fixed laws and rules, so that Bergson is correct in speaking of "the twin sources of morality." On the one hand there are the necessary social conventions and laws, and on the other hand we have the renewed search for better solutions by people fired by a religious inspiration.

It is true that historically this static element has generally held the upper hand. It would be an error to measure the message and the essence of Christianity by what the average Christian has made of it, just as it would be wrong, if asked to define what a real pianist is, to compare him or her to the average amateur who can hammer out a few notes on the piano. It so happened that in the Middle Ages, following in the footsteps of classical Greek culture, a Christendom of balance and harmony was fashioned on the model of the cosmic

8. Ibid., 174.

"harmonia praestabilita." In this context morality was based on the order which prevailed in paradise until it later collapsed thanks to sin and the Fall. In contrast to this approach, a thinker like Teilhard de Chardin posited a Christian ethics shaped by creativity, conquest, risk, renewal and growth. Instead of balance and harmony, he posited improvement and refinement of civilization. Instead of a religion of order and law, he believed in a faith in continual evolution and progress, and instead of the preservation of pristine initial purity, he advocated the building up of a creative love.

For him, humanism is "une anthropogénèse continuée," a becoming of human beings which is far from complete. What is necessary is not so much the conservation of what one has but rather the discovery and practical realization of the destiny to which one is called. Christ did not come to rubber-stamp what already existed but rather to spur humans on to the realization of that full potential which God conferred on them when he created them in his own image and likeness.

The "Christian liberalism" of Paul's epistles to the Galatians and the Romans did not win easy acceptance in many Christian circles over the centuries and this is most probably due to the immaturity and absence of creativity which Kant had already observed at the end of the eighteenth century: "Laziness and lack of courage are the main reasons why so many people, after having been freed by nature from every foreign interference, keep however behaving their life long like half-growns. It is so comfortable indeed not to be fully grown. If I have a book at my disposal in which I find norms for my behaviour, a leader who takes over the task of my conscience, a doctor who decides about my diet, then I do not have any difficulties any more. I do not have to think, as long as I can pay."[9]

One is perhaps forced to conclude that the dual function attributed to religion in a modern, grown-up society (i.e., inspiration and stabilization) is essentially but one force of "inspiration." But then it must be an inspiration which is much more than an exotic or revolutionary caprice, out of whatever comprehensible disappointment. An inspiration which can offer stability and firm ground in the midst of a world of changing fashions, it finds its origin in the eternal God: "the Alpha and the Omega, he who is, who was and is to come" (Rev 1:8). From the point of view of redaction criticism, this phrase from the Book of Revelation is of great interest. The Christian author actu-

9. I. Kant, quoted by G. Morel in "Ouvertures" *Lumière et Vie*, XXIX, June 1980, 52.

ally quotes Homer (Zeus who is, who was and who always will be), although he amends the last member of the phrase. "Who always will be" (Homer) becomes "who is to come" (John). To the Greeks the gods were eternal and unchangeable. For that reason their moral code, just like the cosmos and the gods, was essentially stable. For the Christian God is rather he who is coming. Christianity is an "eschatological" religion. In this world Christ is not yet all that he will one day become, "All in all." His mystical body is still growing. Consequently the Christian way of living is still developing. What Teilhard said of the entire universe applies equally to the Church, her institutions and her norms: It is one single process of hominization or becoming human. The more the Christian leaven can do its work, the more human this world becomes. This is true, even if it must be conceded that many Christians repeatedly tried to turn this leaven into cement.

That terra firma which Christianity does indeed try to offer in the midst of the chaos of change and relativity is in our day eroded and put at risk by the growing pluralism and secularization already alluded to and which forms the subject of our next chapter.

CHAPTER FOUR

Pluralism and Secularization

1. Pluralism

A "pluralistic" society is generally understood as a culture in which various Weltanschauungen, sometimes widely divergent, exist side by side and even compete with one another. In a pluralistic society all perspectives on life are viewed as relative. Convictions are usually reduced to modest opinions or "a personal feeling." Life in a pluralistic society not only alters the social prestige enjoyed by the traditional teaching which once enjoyed a virtual monopoly, but also the way in which that teaching is now personally and consciously lived out by its adherents. Believing what everyone else believes offers a greater feeling of security than fidelity to a doctrine which is being challenged.

A "vision of life" involves a certain way of seeing things and of feeling and thinking which, like a pair of spectacles but without noticing it, we insert between reality and our experience of it. These spectacles simplify, classify and confer direction on our way of experiencing and our pattern of thought. All our opinions concerning world events, problems, people, groups, ideas, religion, etc., are coloured and shaped by our Weltanschauung. What we call "discussion" is usually confined to a crossing of ideological swords, just as innocent as a successful fencing match is unbloody. Most people are hardly aware of the a priori influence their Weltanschauung has on their whole thought process. In the same way a person who carefully examines a landscape is unaware of the glass of his own spectacles. And yet that very Weltanschauung is our guide when we develop theories, reason, perform actions, and believe or disbelieve, as the case may be. The reason why people in a pluralistic society differ so profoundly concerning views, convictions and faith is not that some are guilty of faulty reasoning. Nor is it that there would be discrepancies between the degree of their moral integrity or honesty. Their conceptions are deeply divergent because their "first principles" (Newman) are different. It is very difficult to look at a familiar landscape through someone else's glasses. A Weltanschauung comes about through the influence of three factors: personal experience, environment, and the spirit of the age, and then possibly the influence of some striking personality who opens up new perspectives for us.

A city curate who decides to go and live among immigrants as a worker-priest will probably get a slightly different perspective on a number of social problems. He will even view the Church's mission more generally in a new light. One can see that when it comes to their environment and the spirit of the age, the average members of the consumer society in our day generally have a rather one-sided, not to say simplistic view of reality. (They themselves consider this view "matter-of-fact" or "realistic"). D. Riesman characterizes modern humans as having a strikingly large dependence on their immediate environment, i.e., on "public opinion" or simply on "the other persons" with whom they are keen to remain "in touch." "What is common to all the other-directed people is that their contemporaries are the source of direction for the individual." This simply means that teenagers look to what other teenagers are doing where hairstyle, jargon and clothes are concerned as well as ideas (and thus not to their parents or teachers); "either those known to him or those with whom he is indirectly acquainted, through friends and through the mass-media. This mode of keeping in touch with others permits a close behavioral conformity."[1] The difference in thought and behaviour between the students in Paris and the hippies in Berkeley is consequently less than that between the average Parisian student and his or her father. Both father and teacher wear a tie. Students wear jeans the world over, hair that is a little long and scraggy, and preferably desert boots, sneakers or tennis shoes. What is decisive in this pattern of behaviour and conscious choice is no longer the education an individual received at home or at school, but rather the "peer group," i.e., the ideological climate prevailing in his world of leisure.

Where the third of our factors is concerned one has only to think of what people like Léon Bloy or Bergson meant in the intellectual development of such thinkers as Jacques Maritain, Charles Péguy or P. Van der Meer de Walcheren. Their contact with Bloy and Bergson

---

1. D. Riesman, *The Lonely Crowd*, New Haven, 1961, 21.

signified a fundamental reorientation or "conversion." It is not even necessary to have met such figures in the flesh. Through reading a book, watching a film or TV-interview, a person can also receive a spiritual shock and as a result become fascinated by, e.g., Mandel, Guevara, Schutz or Helder Camara.

In a pluralistic society believers and nonbelievers find themselves face-to-face with the same reality, often having received the same intellectual formation, possessing the same degree of honesty and an identical intelligence quotient, and yet they will have totally different convictions, thanks largely to their "Weltanschauung."

And yet the different Weltanschauungen which enjoy popularity in our day decidedly do not enjoy an equal chance. Marx's contention seen above, that "the ideas of the powerful are the reigning ideas in every age," applies here too. To quote Schelsky, it must be said "that class which rules the roost is the class which supplies and manages the ideological superstructure." In this view these are "the new leftist teachers of salvation," i.e., the new "intellectual clergy who control the mass communications media and the entire modern consciousness." The old religious rites were replaced by new political symbols: protest marches, mass demonstrations or sit-ins, revolutionary liturgies with rhythmic slogans and communitarian ecstasies, and democratic election scenarios with whistle-stop tours. Even the old fire-and-brimstone sermons have been replaced by interminable whining about social ills and the old heretics and dissidents have been replaced by the "establishment," the technocrats, the conservative churches and the academic pipe-smoking philosophers who won't stand for anyone else getting a word in edgeways. What was formerly known as salvation is now called "social justice," and redemption is translated as "revolution."[2]

The principal cause of pluralism is unquestionably the spectacular inflation of the communications media. E. Hall is quite correct when he states that "culture as a whole is a form of communication."[3] We

---

2. Cf. H. Schelsky, *Die Arbeit tun die Anderen. Klassenkampf und Priesterherrschaft der Intellektuellen*, Munich, 1977, 16; 201; 205; 246. For the functional take-over of religion by various modern parareligious creeds such as Marxism, Nationalism, hippy culture, etc., see: Th. Luckmann, *Das Problem der Religion in der modernen Gesellschaft*, Freiburg i. Br., 1963. See also: J. Ellul, *Les nouveaux possédés*, Paris, 1973.

3. E. Hall, *The Silent Language: An Anthropologist Reveals How We Communicate by Our Manners and Behaviour*, New York, 1973, 28. See also R. D. Laing's warning jibe: "More and more concern about communication, less and less to communicate," *The Politics of Experience*, 34.

"make a statement" with our clothes, make-up, posters, grand piano and garden furniture, even if the one generation does not always understand the other, and even if the younger generation "speaks" in shriller tones than the older. The media, technologically ever more sophisticated and ever more widely available, change not only the material appearance of the world (the world's great cities are growing in height, breadth and depth thanks to pollution, noise and redtape). People's behaviour is also changing. As the pace of life becomes faster, they are becoming more jittery, mobile and superficial. People travel more, move more frequently, change more. And yet above all it is people's awareness and mentality which is most subject to change. Marshall McLuhan hit the nail on the head when he pointed out that the media moulds, models, and massages the human spirit. The person who uses the telephone talks (and thinks) differently from the person who prefers to take pen-in-hand and write a letter. Telephone addicts end up in fact not even being able to write a letter. When put to it they can at best manage to send a "message" or a few polite clichés. The traveller who crossed the Atlantic by steamer arrived in America relaxed and refreshed; the passenger who now takes the Concorde, a little less so.

This over-used word "modern" means more than anything else a new sort of consciousness. Modern and old-fashioned people actually use the same automobiles, detergents, and telephones; and yet there is a big difference deep inside. Modern people not only change their place of residence, holiday resort and high-fashion clothes more quickly and more frequently, but also their general outlook on life, their value judgement and their beliefs. Everything for them has become more mobile, relative and less sacrosanct. Social and geographical mobility go hand-in-hand with flux and inconstancy in the area of Weltanschauung. Youngsters in particular are keen to travel, to experiment and to change.

In *Understanding Media*, Marshall McLuhan has looked into the influence which the media have had on both the body and spirit of modern people. Back in the 1950's, he points out, the American student did not for one moment protest against the war in Korea. Vietnam was a completely different story: the new generation took to the barricades. Were the students of 1975 better informed than their predecessors in the Fifties? No way. They were simply "differently" informed. It was no longer banner headlines on the front pages of the newspapers but photo-clip pages of screaming children, or an emaciated mother on the TV screen. It was a different type of intellectual massage with a different type of effect. It is perfectly possible that the student of the Fifties actually knew more about what was going on in the front-line in Korea than his 1968 counterpart ever knew about the drama in Vietnam. A printed map showing infantry movements can never have the same effect as an electronic film clip of the agonized eyes of a child in pain.

On any given evening the average faithful TV-watchers get a whole range of opinions, lifestyles, and protest actions served up for them to digest.

The superficiality of the impressions left by these images is the only thing which saves the modern persons from overwrought nerves and being caught in an ideological tail spin. It comes thus as no surprise that his spontaneous reaction is "Everything is relative and tomorrow, it is to be hoped, we will have something new." Monotony must be avoided at all costs: people have become used to their beloved "pluralism."

A mind which has been shaped and massaged in this way is bound to have greater difficulty in coming to grips with stable values, to say nothing of "absolute" values. And yet it is only through a belief in the supernatural and the transcendent that these bewildering intellectual and emotional collages can be correctly situated and set in a relative context. Only thus can one avoid becoming dizzy on this intellectual treadmill.

What is quite remarkable is the fact that it is actually the theologians and religious experts of the present day who have adapted the Christian message to the sensibilities of modern human beings in a grandiose effort at "aggiornamento," working on the assumption that modern consciousness is without doubt more scientifically based and internally balanced than older ways of thinking. This working hypothesis is no longer actually accepted by the average young person. No one adopts a more critical stance vis-à-vis modern society and the prevailing establishment mentality than our young people. It is thus a supreme irony and paradox that at the moment when our religious experts have completed their translation of the message into contemporary jargon, their young auditor no longer wants to listen to that type of language and turns rather to the age-old tradition of the Orient.

In his remarkable study *Facing up to Modernity,* P. Berger has pointed out that precisely among the young, for too long and too intensively massaged by the media, an almost fearsome anti-modern, anti-technological and anti-scientific resentment has broken out. Their spiritual hunger—in itself a healthy reaction and a sign of vitality—leads them to look for more exotic forms of religion and sources of intellectual security. These are called upon to furnish an antidote to what Roszak called "the contemporary pollution of the spirit."

Pluralism has succeeded in making many peoples' heads spin. More than ever people feel the need for some sort of absolute security. In the present climate it would seem indeed a foolhardy undertaking to make the doctrinal content of Christian faith so vague and open to a wide variety of interpretations that it can collapse like a house of cards with the first wind that blows, especially as the most enlightened of our contemporaries are looking for a refuge from the maelstrom of intellectual confusion.

2. Secularization

The main reason why theologians and those whose avocation is the propagation of the faith have set about translating and adjusting the traditional Christian message is the phenomenon of contemporary secularization. Secularization is a very complex concept which in a paradoxical way combines two seemingly contradictory phenomena. The term on the one hand means keeping the profane and the secular strictly separate from and independent of all religious influence or religious interference. On the other hand a person is considered secularized who opts to live out his or her faith in the context of ordinary, everyday life in the world (and thus not in a separate, sacral, or otherworldly setting). On the one hand separation, on the other alliance.

To start with the separation, secularization is a unique historical process, gradually getting off to a start during the Enlightenment, in which more and more sectors of the life of society (e.g., politics, education, science, art, ethics, etc.) were withdrawn from all attempts of religious interference. This is known as "external" secularization. The religious dimension of externals disappears. To put it in simpler terms—there is a radical separation of Church and state. All that happens outside the church building is laicized. Religious convictions are only tolerated as long as they are kept as private beliefs. It still remains an open question as to whether one can disinfect external structures of all religious contamination effectively without also at the same time weakening the inner consciousness of every direct contact with God. (This latter phenomenon is known as "internal secularization.")

Secularized human beings live—to borrow a phrase from Bonhoeffer—"etsi Deus non daretur" i.e., as if no God existed, or at least as if God had at long last commanded humans to stand on their own two feet without constantly grabbing the emergency cord of divine intervention. The cure for cancer must be sought in a hospital and not in Lourdes. Success in an exam is a question of hard work and a bit of luck rather than votive candles or novenas. Worldly matters have got to be solved according to the world's rules and not "ab extra" by divine intervention. Politics has got to be kept separate from confessional sympathies, and science has nothing to do with religion (one has only to think of "delicate" sciences like genetics, sexology or biophysics).

Secularization is what Max Weber termed "the dissolution of the spell" (Entzauberung) of the world. For early hominoids the whole of reality (food, drink, procreation, natural phenomena, etc.) was shot through with religion. As Malinowski once said: In primitive societies everything had a religious nature. Primitive humans were immersed in a world of mysticism and ritualism. Religion for them was coextensive with life and with death. Religion included all their practical tasks. So much so that the question could be raised: was there anything in a primitive culture that one could call "profane"?[4]

The reason why modern human beings are anxious to push through this separation and circumscription of separate territories is twofold. Atheism can lie at the root of it. People simply want to separate the wheat from the chaff. Religion is thus an illusion and consequently must be kept out of important secular concerns. At best, by mustering a modicum of tolerance, one can put up with religion so long as it is kept firmly in the private domain of a person's leisure hours "where it will harm no one." Secularization can actually also be promoted and implemented in the name of progressive Christian thinking, thus backed up by theological rationale. Generally this occurs under the Bultmannian motto of "Entmythologizierung." "A two-storey Christianity" goes out the window: gone are the natural and the supernatural pairing (in which the latter, by some miraculous or providential means, regularly intervenes in the former). One can no

4. Cf. B. Malinowski, *Magic, Science and Religion*, Boston, 1948, 7.

longer turn up one's nose at this natural and secular ground floor or consider it in any way inferior. The question now is whether there is any point in even planning a modern house with two stories. What secularization means is that we purify the gospel message of all out-dated "mythical" elements. Miracles, devils or a heaven or hell sepa-rate from the present world are "no longer acceptable to modern humans" and are just dismissed as being nonexistent. The theolo-gians of secularization have obviously a very high idea of modern conceptual powers. Contemporary human beings obviously have a more complete and limpid view of reality than all the thinkers of for-mer ages. What is no longer feasible for modern conceptual powers is best forgotten about, unless of course one succeeds in "translating" it into modern categories. "Resurrection," for example, must not be conceived literally or viewed as a historical event. It is a "mythologi-cal" or "symbolic" way of talking which in reality only means . . . (usually there follows some pretty abstract, vague ideas admitting of a variety of interpretations).

What is truly paradoxical about this trend towards secularization is that, leaving aside those who want to keep Church and State strictly separate come what may, its advocates take a stance against every form of divorce between faith and world. One has to be a believer within the ordinary day-to-day world. Being a Christian means being a person of one's own time. While on the one hand they accuse the official Church of meddling in politics outside their own carefully de-termined area of competence, they demand of Christians that they manifest a "political commitment." There is a paradox here: the su-pernatural chaff is separated from the secular wheat, while then we are told that our faith must fertilize and transform the secular city. All cultures have drawn a clear distinction between the religious and the profane. There are holy days and ordinary working days. There are holy places (a temple, a monastery, a shrine) and profane places. There are consecrated people (bishops, monks, priests, etc., clearly recognizable by a uniform, collar, ring, tonsure or missionary's beard) and ordinary lay people. Secularization is opposed to this difference. The priest lives, dresses, and behaves in an ordinary way, and tries to have his home with and amongst the people. Secularization is op-posed to religious apartheid. Why could one not celebrate the Eucha-rist in an "ordinary" room with an "ordinary" glass and an "ordinary" piece of bread? Why could not an unordained lay person preach, dis-tribute Holy Communion and teach catechism? Why cannot a church be used for such profane activities as films, concerts, dances or conferences? Why do we have the Church here and the world there? It is quite paradoxical that once upon a time, when priests and monks were an integral part of society, their being different was much more obvious (thanks to their special garb, lifestyle, dwelling, language and mentality), than is now the case. To put it another way: in proportion to the increasing infrequency of priestly vocations in today's world, what priests there still are live in a much more ordinary and unobtrusive way than was ever imaginable in days gone by. Now that a monk's life has become a nine-day wonder for today's secularized man, these self-same monks who are so peculiar are much freer about letting ordinary lay people into their choir stalls, refectories and cloister garth. Monastery and enclosure are much more open to the world at a time when that world understands less and less what they stand for. Bad-minded people will claim naturally that this openness is nothing more than a final desperate attempt not to sink into total irrelevance to the modern world. The local squire, too, could afford to stay on his high horse as long as the peasantry were still prepared to doff their caps to him. When this is no longer the case he too will descend from his pedestal and open the doors of his stately home to interested day-trippers. "Now, what is emerging in our days, and what may be a 'hapax phenomenon,' a unique occurrence in the history of mankind, is—paradoxically—not secularism, but the sacred quality of secularism."[5] While on the one hand modern Christians seem to have lost their feeling for the sacred, on the other hand it would appear that they have cultivated a great respect for the secular and "the everyday." They are anxious to live out their faith "within" the world of their fellows and no longer in a privileged enclave cut off from it.

It is probably superfluous to point out that this trend towards secularization is running out of steam in more recent years. People today are actually a good deal more critical of "progress" as the modern world sees it. While the secularized Christian asked the Church to turn its attention more to the world, the average citizen had become convinced that things have gone badly wrong with developments in that world and felt a growing disquiet in the face of the technical, economic, military and democratic "progress" heralded with such enthusiasm in its early days.

5. R. Pannikar, *Worship and Secular Man*, London, 1973, 11.

Despite all of this it is impossible to deny that respect for the secular and the material is a true Christian value, even if many Christians have, alas, forgotten this fact. It is not only unchristian, it is also against common sense to see body and soul, matter and spirit, action and contemplation, and the secular and religious as two totally separate dimensions. They are dimensions of one and the same reality. Between these two dimensions there is a mutual influencing and dialectic, yet never is there an identity. Turning down one's nose at one or other dimension has always been the chronic seductive power of every cheap dualism. One can neither save the soul by scorning the body, nor can one safeguard spiritual values by disregarding the secular. It is certainly to secularization's credit that it has pulled the carpet from under the feet of such incipient heretical Manichaeism. And yet there are still some hotheads among the secularists who feel they want to reduce the whole of reality, lock, stock and barrel, to undiluted "Diesseitige."

If one wishes to reach some sort of assessment of secularization, the first thing to be realized is that we are dealing here with a typically Western phenomenon. Secularization is in fact a phenomenon inspired by Christianity. The Judeo-Christian religion broke the ground. Speaking of the kingdom of God, Christ himself said: "You cannot say, look, here it is, or, there it is. The kingdom of God is *in the midst* of you" (Luke 17:20-21). And when the Samaritan woman asked Jesus where was "the precise place" where God must be worshipped (was it on Mount Gerizim or in the Temple in Jerusalem?), the Lord pointed out that from now on God could and ought to be worshipped "everywhere" and not only in special, privileged places. "But the hour is coming, and now is (it was in fact introduced by Christ himself), when the true worshippers will worship the Father in spirit and truth" (John 4:23). Authentic Christian secularization can best be summed up by Paul Eluard's verse: "Il y a un autre monde, mais il est *en* celui-ci." The Christian avoids dualism not by seeing one of the two dimensions (e.g., the spiritual) as unreal or illusory, but rather by looking for it *within* the physical universe God has created. For the fanatical secularizer (i.e., the God-is-dead theologian), even the term "un autre monde" is too much. In his eyes the only world that exists is the visible one. He is what Marcuse termed a "one-dimensional man." Others avoid dualism (and by the same token, dialectic) through passing over one or other element in complete silence or at best making a discreet nod in the direction of the private domain. This world is taken seriously; the supernatural is left over as a matter of purely personal choice.

The English philosopher H. Spencer wrote the following about his father, a believer but secularized through and through: "I do not remember my father ever referring to anything as explicable by supernatural agency. I presume from other evidence that he must at that time have still accepted the current belief in miracles; but I never perceived any trace of it in his conversation. Certainly, his remarks about the surrounding world gave no sign of any other thought than that of uniform natural law."[6]

A second element in any Christian assessment of the phenomenon of secularization is the fact that its development so far has made abundantly clear that any conscious or unconscious mixing of religion and science has always had a damaging effect on both. European Jesuits, for example, at the Chinese imperial court in the seventeenth century mourned the fact, even though the Chinese knew a great deal about astronomy, that their scientific knowledge of the stars was hopelessly mixed up with religious superstition which they got from astrology. Not only ought religion and science not be mixed. One must not fall into the trap of seeing religion as a sort of policeman whose duty it is to keep a tight rein on scientific research; the tragic Galileo episode has taught us an important lesson.

The Bible message "demythologizes" or purifies earthly reality from pseudo-sacral elements. There are no such things as "sacred cows," nor for that matter "ritually impure" pariahs. "The transcendental God of the Bible created a profane world and called upon man to go forth and dominate it. . . . For him (i.e., Biblical man) the world can no longer be a world inhabited by gods and even less the object of pious adoration as was the case for other religions."[7]

However much the theologians of secularization may be opposed to religious interference in profane matters, here, too, these selfsame custodians of "profane integrity" come along and tell us in a somewhat paradoxical way that God must be sought *within* worldly reality (and thus not in those few neatly cordoned-off sacral reservations which, in its tolerant benevolence, the modern world has set aside for religious pursuits). To put it more simply and in more graphic terms, on the one hand they issue a warning: "Reverend Father,

6. H. Spencer, *An Autobiography*, I, London, 1904, 89.
7. W. Pannenberg, *Was ist der Mensch? Die Anthropologie der Gegenwart im Licht der Theologie*, Göttingen, 1968, 12.

please stay in your church and keep your nose out of matters which do not concern you." On the other hand the same parish priest is cautioned not to persist in the illusion that God can be found only in his church: "Reverend Father, you mustn't think that Christianity begins and ends within the four walls of your church! Modern Christianity means social and political commitment and action!" Woe the parish priest who would try to offer the seculariser advice about finding his "identity." He will be sent from pillar to post, or—to borrow R. Laing's words—he will be caught in a "double bind." He will find himself caught on the horns of an impossible dilemma. The situation could be summed up simply as follows: "Old Indians" are quietly put into a reservation, while the younger generation make the best of it and adapt. They are integrated into modern society (i.e., culturally and even biologically they disappear into the melting pot which is the "modern way of life").

From the theological point of view, the secularization movement opposes Luther's theory of the Two Kingdoms that separated the world into two realms which were totally independent of one another.

It was Teilhard de Chardin's purpose throughout his work to avoid this kind of dualism. He insisted on finding God within the world and on refusing to conceive of the world as the antipodes of God. Love of God and awe-inspired admiration for his creation go hand in hand. Teilhard did not look for God in a separate religious enclave after having withdrawn from a pernicious and dangerous world. He preferred to encounter God within the cosmic unity of the universe.

"The kernel of my 'gospel' is not so much a new, individualistic conception of the God-cosmos relationship as a feeling of presence, of reality and of immediacy which it is extremely difficult to express in words. How often, alas, are attempts made to do just this with old-fashioned or banal formulae!"

"It so happens that this bond (between God and the world) came about gradually, in a sort of bewitching process. I have the strong impression that God reveals Himself to me through the Universe . . . I feel His presence everywhere. Through my religious experience I have reached the stage where I cannot but see Christ as the equivalent of the world and co-extensive with the universe; otherwise Christ would be less than reality. God reveals Himself to me EX UNIVERSO." (1918)[8]

8. P. Teilhard de Chardin, *Journal 1915–1919*, Paris, 1971, 304 and 306. Where the

What Teilhard experienced was "a communion with God through the cosmos. . . . It is my specific vocation to reveal God, to make Him loved, to make Him tangible (*toucher*) in the world. We have got to see God as being cosmically bound to the world."[9] To put it in a word: we reach God from our being at one with the world (and not "in the spirit" after one has withdrawn from the world or written it off).

One positive thing about the secularization theology is that it does emphasize that all of reality bears the imprint of God: "La nature est un temple" to use Baudelaire's words. In that respect the secularization theologians and Teilhard are in the same boat. The only difference is that modern theologians, when they employ the phrase "the whole of reality" generally mean the socio-political system. Teilhard, on the other hand, has a wider vision of "the whole of reality." It also embraces the cosmic dimension of the positive sciences, of poetry and of what he liked to call "l'éternel féminin."

It so happens that, aside entirely from Teilhard, the secularization school got a helping hand from another, rather unexpected, source, i.e., the world of cultural anthropology. Here is not the place to review or even attempt to summarize R. Girard's masterly study, *Des Choses cachées depuis l'Origine du Monde.* The reason why it needs to be mentioned at all in this context is that the author, an anthropologist who converted to Christianity on the basis of his study of non-Christian religions, saw the uniqueness of Jesus Christ in his radical refusal to have religion used as a sedative in a turbulent society. With the exception of Christianity in its purest form, for Girard all religions are a "sublimation mechanism" or a cover on the pot of human aggression. Whenever an attempt is made to keep this assertiveness in check, then there is no telling what the frustrated individual may do. It is at this stage that religion makes its appearance. In all cultures it is religious laws and customs which attempt not so much to put some restraints on that violence as to give it the chance to let off steam in a harmless way (i.e., under religious tabs). Generally this is achieved through the offering of bloody but ritual sacrificial oblations. The victim is either a human being (viz., Caiphas' remark "It is better that one man should die for the people") or a whole nation (viz., the anti-Semitic Holocaust), or an ani-

pantheistic-sounding terminology is concerned one must remember that here we are dealing with notes in a private diary which was never intended for publication.

9. Ibid., 242–244. In these extracts Teilhard is writing as a mystic rather than a philosopher or theologian.

mal, or some item of great value. The specifically sacral (i.e., that which is clearly distinguished from the profane and has a special status conferred on it) in Girard's view was the fruit of crises in society when there was a threat of internal violence. The sacral provides a solution. Instead of categorically condemning violence as Christ did in the Sermon on the Mount, religions came up with ritual safety valves: The people are thirsty for blood? Well then, blood will flow, even if it is to be kept neatly within liturgical rubrics and "feasts." The three pillars on which all sacral (i.e. non-secularized) religions were built were condemned and thrown out of court by Christ, i.e., mythical tales, ritual taboos and blood sacrifices. It was Girard's belief that Christ shows us what religions truly are: beautiful cultural structures of veiled violence. He did this by condemning in the strongest possible terms any sacrifice offered on behalf of a society, regardless of which society was concerned. He himself did not go to the cross as an "offering for his people." That is what Buddhist monks who set fire to themselves do. Christ was put to death, just like all the prophets of the Old Testament, by the political-religious leaders of his day. And yet through his resurrection, claims Girard, Christ demonstrated that ritual death never benefits the sacral murderers. In His Sermon on the Mount Jesus condemned once and for all the root of all violence, namely the scramble to possess ("la mimèsis de l'acquisition").

It must be said that J. Guillet is right when he pointed out that Girard failed to grasp the full potential richness of religious sacrifices.[10] A sacrifice cannot always and in all circumstances just be reduced to the elimination of a scapegoat in order to keep the group in check. A sacrifice can be more than a sociological sedative. An authentic sacrifice is "religious" in the etymological sense that one normally confers on that word ("re-lier"): it brings about a "relationship" or communion between God and human beings. And yet Girard has rendered an important service in drawing attention to how easily religious practices and sacral ideas (or myths) can be misused to serve the interests of society. Christ was a virulent opponent of such tendency. He tore the mask of these mechanisms by systematically demythologizing them. Even if it does not quite fit the bill, one can legitimately term this Christian secularization.

10. J. Guillet, *René Girard et le Sacrifice* in: *Etudes* 351, July 1974, 91–102.

The observant reader will already have noticed that the so-called "paradox" of secularization is essentially something more than a mere "apparent contradiction." What we have here is a very real contradiction with which all secularization theologians have had to come to grips. On the one hand they argue for a separation: the religious and the profane must be kept carefully apart. They do not want any religious contamination or interference. On the other hand they are opposed to all forms of dualism, and thus are against any splitting up or division. They are looking for a "secular Christianity" and a "committed" religiosity. One tends to say: look, it's the one thing or the other! If not then secularization ends up in the "principium contradictionis." In the meantime there is plenty of evidence to show that radically secularized Christians start searching for oases of religious life in the Orient, far from the madding crowd and the hurly-burly of technology, science, economics and politics. It would appear as if the radical separation was insupportable in the long term.

The rub of the issue in this contradictory contortion is the eternal problem of God's transcendence and immanence. Is God the "totally other," outside, above and beyond the affairs of the world? Does he, in some ethereal-transcendental way rise above all of this? Or is God on the other hand the ubiquitous one, close to us, here even among us and in everything around us? The answer to these questions cannot be a mere matter of personal sensibilities or preference, nor of culturally determined thought patterns. God himself has supplied the answer in his revelation, first to the Jews and then to Christians in the Old and New Testaments, and through them bit by bit to all peoples.

In contrast with Tertullian's contention that "the human soul is by nature Christian," Teilhard's assertion that the human spirit, abandoned to its natural fate, "thinks naturally in pantheistic terms"[11] rings a lot truer. Just like the most primitive of animists, a distinguished and accomplished scholar such as Aldous Huxley and a pious Buddhist like Suzuki discovered God "in the great Everything" or in nature.

From the very first chapter of the biblical creation narrative Jahweh makes it crystal clear to his people that he is not to be found in either the moon, the sea or any living animal. None of

11. Teilhard de Chardin, *Journal 1915–1919*, 304. *"Une sorte de révélation naturelle de la 'divinité' du Réel."* ("A sort of natural revelation of the 'divinity' of the Real.")

these beings, which are after all mere creatures, is divine. Or to put it more poetically, they are all mere "dust and ashes." Flying in the face of received beliefs of Babylonian and Mesopotamian "natural" religions (which surrounded the Jews and regularly infected their ideas), Jahweh imprinted his total transcendence on the heart and mind of his people. There was no point in their looking for him in a rock, a constellation of stars, a "holy" river or in any of their sacred animals. He lives so close to his people, invisible to them, behind the folds of the Tabernacle tent and later within the walls of the Jerusalem Temple. The world is profane, yet "this place here is holy," were the first sentiments Moses heard Jahweh express. And yet revelation does not just stop here. The divine pedagogy unfolds itself gradually, opening up like the petals of a flower. One of the first steps was the conversion of a vague and naturalistic pantheism to an insight into God's infinite transcendence. That was essentially the message of the Old Testament. God reveals himself first in the history of one people (to wit, the Jews) after centuries of searching for him in all sorts of ways and approaching him only through nature. And then finally he reveals himself in the life of one man, Jesus Christ. Revelation is an historical process and not the sudden, overpowering appearance of a "deus ex machina." With Christ God walked into human history. He took on "flesh," i.e., he became immanent in matter.

While the Jews found God within the sacred precincts of their Temple at certain periods of the year (the great feast days) and while they brought him sacrificial offerings, even before Christ ever appeared on the scene, there were prophetic voices which point beyond this religious ritual. "Your sacred libations mean nothing so long as in your daily life you do not pay your labourers a just wage, you do not honour your neighbour nor do you lend a helping hand to the widow and the orphan." In other words, God is not totally indifferent to worldly concerns. The secular domain, too, involves God. In a sense it was the great prophets who inaugurated the divine, Judaeo-Christian, "secularization process." The transcendent God reveals himself as being also immanent. Following in a line of great prophets, it was finally Christ who provided the definitive answer to the age-old question as to transcendence or immanence.

This does not mean to say of course that the early Church immediately understood this answer or grasped its full meaning. The full elucidation of this answer required centuries of "Church history" and

"development of dogma" and even yet a great deal more religious reflection and awakening is necessary. It is moreover more "natural" to
look for the eternal God in a timeless "Everything" than in a historical person. It also seems more probable that he is to be found
"among people of good will" without distinction or preference than
in the history of one chosen people. Consequently pantheism is a
much more obvious solution to the question of God than is historical
revelation. God's wisdom does seem, as Paul puts it, "folly in the
eyes of the world."

The hitherto unheard and improbable element in the answer provided by Christ reached us not as a dogmatic idea but rather as an
historical fact. In the incarnation God became human. As a result,
matter, the historically contingent, the human, the everyday and the
cosmic suddenly became holy. To put it in theological terms, the cosmos received sacramental value. God was now to be found everywhere, but especially in the very "mundane" events of birth (baptism), initiation (confirmation), human conflict (confession), suffering
and death. God is to be found particularly in the unusual encounter
of the Eucharistic meal. In this latter event God "touches" humanity
not only "in the spirit" but also through bread, which earth has given
and human hands have made, and wine, fruit of the vine and again
work of human hands. Since the time of Christ it has now become
possible for us to look for God in everything: "ut in omnibus
quaerant Deum" (which does *not* mean, everything is God).

Christ's incarnation is no mere contingent rescue operation by
which God wants to put his creation again in order after the rather
unfortunate sin which upset the apple cart of paradise. God actually
created the world with the incarnation very much in mind. Only in
the incarnation will it become apparent that the transcendent God is
also immanent. To put it more directly, God "dwells" not only in the
beauty of nature, in the great Everything, or in the poetry of a Buddhist monastery garden, but also in the most repulsive and ignomini-
ous suffering (the Cross), in the most unsightly coincidences of life
(Providence) and in the hard daily struggle (the everyday moral obli-
gations of a state in life or vocation).

Since the divine Word has become flesh, it has become possible to
speak about God's contemporaneous infinite transcendence and most
intimate immanence in a more adequate fashion. And yet the often
contradictory language used by the secularist theologians as well as
the clumsy abstractions employed in this chapter demonstrate how

difficult a task this is. God's closest friends on this earth, the mystics and the saints, show that intimate commerce with God in prayer leads to less paradoxical statements than result from some of the abstract mental contortions in "the language of today."

CHAPTER FIVE

Faith: Is It a Purely Psychological Phenomenon?

1. Freud's objections

Ever since the end of the nineteenth century, and in particular since the appearance of Freud's publications, it has been the repeated contention of psychologists that the phenomenon of religion can be explained as a pure fiction or as an illusory perception devoid of any real object. Religion is dismissed as either an infantile "fixation," a "projection," a "sublimation" of concealed sexual tendencies or as the principal cause of "self-alienation".

"Mode-psychology often tried to point out which kind of human weakness made the human spirit create 'religious illusions.' Particularly depth-psychology and Freudian psychoanalysis seem to have been rather successful in this iconoclastic enterprise." Therefore R. Catell could call psychology "the last nail in God's coffin."[1]

It is well known that Freud, who called himself an atheist and most probably was one, was at the same time virtually obsessed by religion. He wrote no less than five books on the subject, including his very last publication *Der Mann Moses und die monotheïstische Religion* (1939). The acerbic observation made by the Rumanian historian of religion Mircea Eliade concerning many intellectuals who had abandoned religious belief is very appropriate in the case of Freud. According to Eliade many Western intellectuals are deeply dissatisfied with the obsolete norms of the historically developed Christian Churches. They want to get rid of the faith of their parents, often even in a violent way. Yet at the same time they feel in themselves a strange kind of guilt, as though they themselves had killed the God

---

1. V. White, *God and the Unconscious*, Chicago, 1953, 3.

in whom they pretend not to believe anymore, but whose absence they seem unable to bear.[2]

Freud was particularly fascinated by two questions concerning religion: What is the origin of religion? How does it come about that people imagine the existence of deities? In other words, what is the "psychogenesis" of faith and how do we explain the origin of the "religious illusion"? The second question he poses concerns the nature of religion. Wherein lies the difference between a believer and an unbeliever? By what psychological mechanism is the "illusion" kept alive in an otherwise "enlightened" world?

The reason why an entire chapter of the present study is devoted to Freud's antireligious invective is not so much because his insights in this area are particularly brilliant or sound. Anyone knows that Freud's ideas concerning the origin and evolution of religion are completely old hat. It is certain that in his day he had read the first important publications in the area of comparative religion, a science then in its infancy. He was familiar with the works of E. J. Tylor, R. Marett and J. Frazer. His study of these works was approached from a somewhat unusual angle: "I am reading thick books (about the origin of religion) without being very much interested, however, because I already know the result: my instinct tells me so."[3] Once Freud moved away from clinical psychiatry and into the field of anthropology his imagination always became alarmingly fertile. No ethnologist in his right mind could take seriously Freud's theory of "the murder of the 'Patriarch' of the human race" as the starting point of totemism and, by the same token, of religion.

There are, however, four good reasons why Freud's antireligious tracts deserve close scrutiny and indeed are imperative. The first, and by far the most important reason, is that Freud was the first scholar who saw clearly that virtually all specific, concrete problems of faith (including his own!) were psychological. The shift from faith to agnosticism is rarely attributable to philosophical or theological factors, even if the individual who has abandoned the faith evokes them as rationalizations, if only to make the change of position acceptable (primarily for himself or herself, and in the second instance for others). In other words the modern persons who today lose their faith rarely do so on account of new philosophical insights they have ar-

2. M. Eliade in: *The History of Religions,* J. Kitagawa, ed. Chicago, 1967, 25.
3. E. Jones, *Sigmund Freud, Life and Work,* II, London, 1958, 394.

rived at in their own intellectual quest. Their new philosophical outlook is rather an a posteriori effect. It is the intellectual superstructure which readily fits their psychological evolution. Just as Marx explains a person's ideas on the basis of the socio-economic circumstances in which they live, Freud sees them in the light of the unconscious psychological conflicts with which the individual struggles.

Becoming an unbeliever is for Freud the result of a necessary psychological casting-off of naivete. From our perspective we often see it rather as the result of a crisis of puberty gone wrong. (This does not mean that teenagers who abandon their faith should turn their backs on it permanently. Believers and unbelievers have both gone through the natural process of maturity, have both grown up after, it is to be hoped, a "crisis." In the two cases, however, the crisis has evolved differently and is solved and "classified" in a different way). For Freud religious faith and unbelief represent different stages in human psychological development. We can follow Freud this far. As the child of his own day Freud was a convinced disciple of Darwin's and shared his optimism. He believed very firmly that human evolution always represented a forward movement and was a positive development. In his eyes people grew in intelligence and became increasingly "enlightened." There are few modern realists who would share this rosy view.

The psychological causes which lie at the root of faith and agnosticism are, in Freud's view, rather banal and virtually always can be traced back to the relationship an individual had with his father during childhood. There are few who will readily admit (even to themselves) that they have lost their faith on account of a problematic relationship with their father. It is for that reason that a person who "transfers" his or her allegiance and opts for a new life-vision as a result of family problems or attempts at self-emancipation, generally disguises this process in shrewd trumped-up arguments. And yet it must be repeated and emphasized: They do all this in good faith. They are genuinely convinced that they have intellectually grounded reasons for changing direction. It was Freud's contention that the human psyche is largely influenced by an unconscious sexual reservoir. There is always something slightly distasteful about reducing great principles to mere commonplace frustrations. No one enjoys hearing others explain why they arrived at a particular worldview or at none, particularly when this explanation sinks from the philosophical summits to the psychological "underworld." When E. Mounier claims that "many forms of political and religious quibble" are basically nothing more than "a delayed rebellion against one's family history" or that "the lurch to the left (le gauchissement)" can usually be traced back to early set-backs in affective contact with the community, on account of an upbringing which was excessively strict or rigid, or too sheltered or too lax,[4] it is easy to see why so many progressive thinkers set themselves resolutely against such explanations as being too simplistic and reactionary. None of this, however, takes away from Freud's brilliant insight that at the basis of conscious opinions or "philosophies" there can often lie unconscious psychological causes.

Freud of course was largely concerned to provide a psychological explanation of why some intellectual *minus habentes* still persisted in religious faith. He was only dimly aware of the fact that his great discovery was a two-edged sword or surgical scalpel with which one could also perform useful subcutaneous operations on the average atheist. In other words Freud discovered that the tender bud of faith as well as the flourishing flower of modern unbelief both have roots in the human psyche, and that these roots call for close examination if one wants to understand anything about their life on the surface of human experience.

The second reason why Freud's writings need to be considered in this context is the fact that no modern psychologist discusses the phenomenon of religion without instinctively turning to Freud's conceptual apparatus. Freud was after all not only a great clinical thinker, he was also a wizard with language and a literary genius. So many of the concepts he launched (one only needs to think of repression, sublimation, consciousness-awaking, trauma, complexes or frustration) have become an integral part and parcel of psychological jargon. What is actually at issue are not words and terms alone, but also patterns of thought and categories of experience. Since the time of Freud every psychologist who cares to examine the phenomenon of religion reaches for the Freudian binoculars (or microscope).

A third reason for studying Freud is that in post-Freudian psychoanalysis a number of revisionist psychiatrists appear on the scene (e.g., Adler, Jung, Frankl, Laing, Van den Berg, etc.) who fortunately had a more scientifically sound perspective on religion than their master, yet which was unthinkable without the pioneering work of Freud.

4. E. Mounier, *Le Personnalisme*, Paris, 1950, 66 and 122.

Their writings make no sense so long as one has not at least some familiarity with Freud's antireligious tracts.

A fourth and final reason why Freud's insights merit our attention is the following: Freud was neither mystic, nor theologian, nor even believer. For that reason he never discusses God. He was a doctor of the mind and confines himself to discussing "the image of God which some people posit or imagine." Now there can be no doubt that many people have a totally false image of God. It can be useful to learn from a brilliant psychiatrist how such people come to have such a perverted, unbiblical and mistaken picture of the divine. Why did the Jansenists happen to picture God as a harsh and punctilious judge? Can psychology provide any clues as to the answer? An important task of any prophet is what V. White has called "image breaking" and "new image making." With regard to the first task, Freud, (along with so many atheists) has had a purifying function. He has quite unceremoniously demonstrated that so many mistaken images of God and idols have feet of clay. Where the true God was concerned, however, he was pretty clueless.

Whenever Freud discusses religion he always proceeds from two basic axioms. To begin with, for him people's image of God is always intimately linked with the image they have from their father. It is undeniable this was true in the case of Freud himself. Freud extrapolated his own personal experience onto everyone (or at least all men). Just as he sat despondently trapped in an almost infantile love-hate relationship with his father, he assumed that everybody went through the throes of a struggle for personal emancipation. To begin with, everyone wants to be free of an authoritarian father, and then they want to be set free of the Judaeo-Christian God.

"Psychoanalysis of an individual reveals with a high degree of certainty that in each case the image of God is formed on that of his own father and that our relationship with God depends on our relationship with our physical father."[5] Elsewhere Freud wrote: "Psychoanalysis has exposed the intimate connection between father-complex and belief in God. It has made it obvious that a personal God is nothing more than an exalted father. It demonstrates clearly every day how young people lose their faith as soon as paternal authority is on the wane. Religious need is consequently rooted in the parental com-

5. S. Freud, *Totem und Tabu*, Ges. Werke, IX, London, 1940, 177.

plex."[6] What he exactly meant by this "parental complex" Freud never makes entirely clear. It is striking how, in this regard at least, Freud draws virtually no distinction between boy and girl. His only problem is the constant disturbance of the father-son relationship. Freud is noncommittal on whether an analogous relationship exists between mother and daughter or between father and daughter. One would gather the impression from Freud's hypothesis that girls are likely to have fewer problems with the faith than their brothers. How wrong he was the history of atheism amply demonstrates.

What does Freud actually understand by this concept "complex" so often misunderstood and misused in the post-Freudian era? A complex is an unconscious negative impulse. A feeling of inferiority is not a complex precisely because it is a conscious reaction. The person who genuinely suffers from an inferiority complex does not feel in any way inferior. The contrary is more often the case: Such is usually a bluffer and is constantly blowing one's own trumpet. They have the feeling that others unjustly underestimate them and leave them out in the cold. They never manage to get full justice, they would claim, on account of the blindness of others. Furthermore, a complex is a form of illness because its effects are always negative. An inferiority complex incites a person to jealousy and aggression vis-à-vis his or her friends and acquaintances who are visibly successful in life. A complex is thus a great deal more than just a wrong idea (e.g., in those who feel they have an IQ of 95 when they actually have an IQ of 135). A complex gives a person an acid tongue and provokes negative actions. For these reasons it needs to be handled clinically.

It was Freud's contention that persistence in religious belief in this "enlightened" day and age is nothing more than a retarded or entrenched Oedipus complex. Could we not draw a comparison between the overt sexual exhibitionism of our own day, which principally aims to shock the sensibilities of the respectable citizen, with certain forms of atheistic preening which make a frontal attack on seemingly infantile influences inherited from one's family background? Anyone who is still sceptical about the striking link which often comes to light between an overly authoritarian, weak, or absent father on the one hand and atheism or antireligious obsessions on the other ought to read a work such as Sartre's autobiography, *Les Mots,* or Anaïs Nin's diaries. This is not to suggest that all religious

---

6. S. Freud, *Eine Kindheitserrinerung des Leonardo da Vinci,* Ges. Werke, IX, 850.

problems can be reduced to pedagogical aberrations. It is perfectly natural that those who call God a "father" will distill this concept of fatherhood from experiences with their own father and with the fathers of other people in their circle of acquaintances.

The second of Freud's fundamental axioms—perturbing in its stark simplicity—is that faith is an "illness." Religious faith is for him "a universally widespread form of obsessional neurosis,"[7] from which psychoanalysis shall release the patient. In other words up until the eighteenth century (when atheism first emerged in the West) everyone was neurotic or mentally disturbed. It is easy to understand why Freud severed his relationship with his favourite disciple C. G. Jung when the latter discovered precisely the contrary in a growing number of his patients and wrote that "as religious faith declined the number of neuroses markedly increased."[8]

It remains to be seen how Freud explains the origin of religious propositions (or of this age-old "universal neurosis") both on the personal and the collective level.

Freud posits four neurotic mechanisms whenever individuals or cultures form for themselves an image of God: (1) infantile fixation; (2) projection of "wishful thinking"; (3) spiritual sublimation of trivial sexual desires which were repressed and (4) a destructive urge to self-alienating behaviour. After this brief discussion of what Freud understands by these four psychic mechanisms which are to be observed in a striking number of neurotics, a few critical observations are in order.

Freud always detects a "fixation" in an infantile manner of thinking and behaving out of anxiety or fear of the challenges of life. Just in the same way as a child rushes to his father for protection whenever it is confronted with a strange, dangerous or inexplicable phenomenon, so adults in a primitive stage of development seek refuge in an imaginary God. This always occurs whenever the burdens of life become too heavy, according to Freud. When this happens in a primitive culture the individual finds it perfectly natural and even to be recommended. This is no longer acceptable to the informed, critical modern person. In that sense religion is a childish nostalgia for the safe haven offered by a protective father who bore all responsibilities on his shoulders and laid down all the do's and don'ts. It is even

7. S. Freud, *Zwangshandlungen und Religionsübungen*, Ges Werke, VII, 139.
8. C. G. Jung, *Psychologie und Religion*, Olten, 1971, 139.

possible to flee back further still in a "regressive desire" to the mother's womb where one still lived as if in a natural "nirvana." This particular theme was elaborated by Freud's disciple O. Rank in his celebrated study *Der Trauma der Geburt*. Religion for Freud is thus a sort of daydream about a golden and happy past. Religion and dream are both no more than psychic mechanisms which are successful in making possible a temporary escape from a drab and dreary reality. People dream about a paradise because the world, in its present state at least, has turned out to be a disappointment.

People believe in God because life is so full of perils.[9] Freud is here repeating what Lucretius, whom someone once described as "the first atheist," said long ago: "Fear alone called the gods into being." The only remarkable thing here is that Freud's analysis paid so little attention to the anxiety about death. All religions seem to have initially grown out of a meditation about death. Human beings are the only biological creatures which are conscious of the fact that they must die. Consequently death is central to the life of each person, at least at the moment when he or she is mature enough to engage in a bit of reflective thinking. Outside the context of religious faith death is an insoluble problem. It is well known that Freud himself had an almost obsessional anxiety about death. He could not bear any of his friends making the slightest allusion to death. Death and old age were strictly taboo subjects. According to his physician Freud took refuge in the most infantile superstitions whenever anxieties concerning these matters began to plague him.[10] It is highly probable that Freud's agnosticism originated in a terrible fear, e.g., the fear of never being able to break loose from his father so long as he did not cut once and for all the gordian knot which was the faith of his fathers.

Following on the trail blazed by Feuerbach, in the company of Marx and Nietzsche, Freud saw religion as an illusory "projection." A projection is the product of the human imagination. What starts out as something existing purely in the mind (e.g., a dragon or a ghost) becomes something which the persons are convinced has an objective existence outside themselves. God, in reality a fictitious creation of my imagination, comes to be understood as an objective reality whom I then "project" in heaven. It was Feuerbach's view that religious believers still feel the childish need to transfer their own great-

9. Freud contended that the safer a child feels when it is young, the greater the danger that it will continue to believe later on.
10. Cf. Max Schur, *Freud: Living and Dying*, London, 1972.

ness and responsibility (which in their "humility" actually frighten them) onto this God who is the product of their fantasy. They say that God is in an eminent fashion all that humanity is not yet, but earnestly desires to be: happy, good, powerful, creative and succesful. Where self-development and self-realization were imperative, humanity in its "humility" took refuge in religion. Feuerbach sees theology as "une anthropologie qui s'ignore." Freud wanted to share theology with self-awareness. For him religion is nothing more than a process of the human imagination which psychology can easily explain. Freud claimed that he could retrace this process step by step on the basis of what he had observed in clinical analysis of his neurotic patients and their phobias.

Freud also saw religion as a typical example of "sublimation." What sublimation involves is the transfer of unharnessed (or repressed) sexual energy into an alternative, more socially prestigious or more "sublime" form of activity, i.e., what I cannot realize, am forbidden to do or simply do not dare to attempt in the sexual domain, I "work off" in my job or in some "sublime" cultural activity. Acts of altruism or religious piety (prayer or charitable works) are essentially nothing more than unconscious, camouflaged sexual urges. Behind devotion to the Blessed Virgin lurks an unconscious desire for an earthly virgin. Lurking behind the mystic marriage of the celibate nun is the need for compensation and thus spiritualized eroticism. Behind social commitment and care for the sick lies the unconscious desire to play a paternal or maternal role. Whatever believers cannot find in the material world they look for in the world of sublime fictions. The only particularly useful purpose served by that religion is that it gives a clear picture of the imaginative world of believers, lets us into what they feel they have and what they still miss. Their "religious obsessions" will reveal that believers miss intimacy, love, security or hope. On the other hand religion manages to harness dangerous tendencies, such as that to kill or spill blood, and channels them in acceptable directions (sacrifices, holy wars, etc.) This latter phenomenon is also to be found in the secular domain, too, with, e.g., sport or visual violence on television or in the cinema. Freud at once reduces our whole culture to a sort of travesty, i.e., to a series of sublime, disguised sexual passions. Cultural progress is best understood as a series of more neatly ordered and efficient channeling of the passions. All that exists is a search to realize libidinal desire. The aristocrat differs from the plebians only in the more refined way in which he or she pursues the same end. The sexual revolution of our own day only shows that we no longer have any way of disguising it.

Given that desire and pleasure would seem to be unmanageable without considerable work and effort, techniques have to be invented to allow people's desires to let off steam. What is needed is sublimation (and thus repression). Like a dam, repression keeps the passions under control and transforms them into cultural energy. One of the most powerful of all the repressive mechanisms or dams has been religion. It has been highly successful in transforming the desires fomented by the passions into ideas, principles and concrete work projects. The religious turbines worked as a giant transformer which transformed sexual steam into (rather naive) industry and self-sacrifice. Unfortunately the dam was too repressive (Marcuse spoke of "surplus repression") so that with pressure building up, fissures began to appear in its masonry. Religion no longer works. The result is that experimental science and psychology are urgently called upon to take over religion's role. The transfer of roles has not been all that successful as the sexual inflation and the decline in altruism and self-sacrifice amply demonstrate.

Finally, it was Freud's claim that, seen historically, religion was at the root of self-alienation on a massive scale. Yet, on this point, too, issue must be taken with the eminent psychiatrist. Freud actually rarely uses the Hegelian concept of self-alienation as such. And yet he originally termed the professional psychiatrist an "alienationist," i.e., someone who has to "reverse" an overdose of repression in his patient and direct it towards a sexual partner. Freud prefers to use such jargon of psychology as "an overly strong superego or über-ich," regarding which more will be said shortly. When we talk of self-alienation in this context this is only because virtually all Freudian epigones and psychoanalytic disciples made this concept their own, which Marxists made so popular, and because Freud, although studiously avoiding using the term, did adopt the idea.

Generally speaking self-alienation is understood as a feeling that one is no longer master over one's own actions. An "outsider" seems to have taken the pilot's seat in the cockpit of our own life. Freud goes even a step further. He claims that we have actually never been set in that pilot's seat. We have actually never been at the controls ourselves. It was our parents who taught us how to steer our way in life. At a later stage their role was taken over by what popular Marxism likes to call "the system," i.e., the accepted norms and principles of society in which I happen to live.

A distinction is drawn between an external and an internal alienation, depending on whether one becomes alienated in one's own external actions or in one's inner conscience. External alienation involves human beings conceiving the cultural achievements designed by themselves (e.g., the constitutional monarch, the caste system, or monogamous marriage) as external, natural and unchangeable divine institutions, which for that very reason cannot be tampered with and cannot be improved upon. Humans, themselves the creators and architects of culture, become servants of their own creations. And yet, instead of realizing that they are fruit of their own creative designs, they see them as the work of an "other" alien master. Sartre calls this "mauvaise foi," itself a variant of Marx's "falsches Bewusstsein."

Internal alienation, on the other hand, comes about when one's deeds are no longer the fruit of one's own insight, of the deliberation of one's own conscience or personal experiences, but rather the result of an alien will which one has transplanted into one's own heart. Freud speaks here of the "superego" which is "internalized or indoctrinated." That implanted superego is a moral censor or controlling power which rules my "I" with a whip hand even though I am not even aware of it. It was Freud's view that I wrongly assume that what I consider indecent actually depends on my personal insight. I have in fact been taught what I must consider unseemly. A four-year-old child does already know what it ought and ought not do, or what it ought to feel and not feel. In other words what persons consider beautiful, admirable or repulsive, Freud believed to be an appreciation which they in "empathy" took over from their parents. It might be worth pointing out in this context that this parental role has passed in the post-Victorian era to the influence of the "peer group," i.e., what an individual's contemporaries think and do and which is the air they breath, the "spirit of the age."

The super-ego is thus the sum-total of moral norms which my parents, my teachers and environment have taught me and which I have made my own, i.e., that I gradually come to see and accept as reasonable, normal, natural, and self-evident. Henceforth I will accept these norms as the "still voice" of my own conscience. Consequently what people call their "personal principles" are in fact convictions which are forced upon them by their parents or by other elements in society. I am thus "colonized" by foreign powers. They implant themselves in such a subtle and refined way that I do not even perceive their influence and remain convinced that my judgement is free and independent.

The origin of this self-alienation can generally be traced back to a fear of having to act according to the dictates of one's personal conscience. Freud sees religion as the most significant importer of the necessary underlying feelings of anxiety and guilt. Religion is thus a system designed to keep individuals docile and depersonalized with a view to social control and stability. In his famous story of the Grand Inquisitor Dostoevsky showed how, as an easy way out, people are inclined to want to be induced to leave "responsibility" over to others. As if butter would not melt in his mouth Goebbels was able to trot out his notorious slogan, "Der Führer denkt für euch" (Hitler does your thinking for you) precisely because he knew that so many people would feel liberated when this obligation to think for themselves was taken off their shoulders.

Alienated individuals do tend to seek protection from people who are more powerful than they are. They submit docilely when confronted with someone else's commands and with faits accomplis. They willingly join the silent majority. Because of an anxiety when it comes to personal decisions and free actions they allow a conscience-transplant to be carried out. They simply allow another's will (public opinion, the spirit of the age, the Church or any authoritative institution) to take them over. The individual who has become alienated in this way has become a "tele-operated" being: a marionette who dances to someone else's tune. Their most precious and most intimate possession, i.e., their personal conscience, they have simply allowed to be taken away from them by an unconscious amputation. This usually happens in the name of a misunderstood "obedience," "humility" or "subordination" which really is nothing more than an immature anxiety or angst for life.

It is quite undeniable that in both the area of external and internal alienation the Church has done a great deal of harm. Instead of encouraging people (who after all are created in the image and likeness of a creative God) on the one hand to be culturally inventive and to work for increasingly humane life structures, and on the other hand to follow their conscience (God's greatest gift to humanity), very often a wrongly conceived Christianity has valued a patient submission and resignation to the status quo, with "blind obedience" as the excuse.

2. Critical Reflections

After this somewhat complex journey through Freud's thought, it is time to pause and engage in a little critical reflection.

To begin with, a brief word is in order about an idea that enjoys wide currency, namely, that religious faith can be explained away by psychological factors. It is certainly true that the psyche or soul is the locus in which the religious experience is rooted. It is in the soul that God touches humans in the depths of their being (and not in their blood-circulation or their intestines). It is thus not surprising that one should try and explain religious experience in psychological terms. This does not, however, mean that psychology is at the same time the cause or explanation of their religious reality. Just because the only way I can hear a radio broadcast is thanks to my transistor, it cannot be claimed that my portable radio is the cause of the symphony concert I am listening to. Just because I can only follow the movements of aircraft on a radar screen in foggy weather does not mean that the radar is the cause of the flight whose trajectory I am watching on the screen. By the same token it is not because I experience God within my psyche that he is therefore necessarily the creation of my psychology. Description cannot always be reduced to explaining things in function of their causes, and a "conditio sine qua non" is not a cause. It is true, of course, that just as there are cheap and poorly made transistors which produce static and distort the radio signal, there are also people who suffer from mental disturbance who create religious obsessions or fictions. There are people who suffer from religious hallucinations just as there is chronic radio static. In the first case it is a good idea to go to a psychiatrist, in the second it is best to go along to a T.V. and radio repair shop and get the technician to clean out your set.

There are many who will probably concede that human psychology does not necessarily create experiences of God because they actually have never themselves lived such an experience. Here is not the place to engage in a phenomenological explanation of the religious experience nor to investigate the causes of contemporary humanity's experience of spiritual realities. We have already studied this particular subject in some depth[11] and it is sufficient here to refer to two factors which explain why the average person today does not

11. See H. Arts, *With Your Whole Soul: On the Christian Experience of God*, Paulist Press, Ramsey, 1983.

know what to do when confronted with religious phenomena, and why he or she seems to be blind to God's presence. The first cause is contemporary humanity itself. The second cause is explained by the fact that God will always remain essentially a Mystery.

In modern times the human spirit focuses all its attention on concrete things. It is focused on "the objective." God, of course, is neither a thing nor a concrete, empirical object which we can ever fix within the range of our physical vision. God always touches us "on the outer extremity" of our field of consciousness and he does this moreover in totally unexpected moments of grace. It is rare that we should experience God with overwhelming clarity, never with proofs, but always with signs which induce wonder. Perhaps if we use an image we can see the point more clearly: it is easier to photograph a concrete object than to capture an atmosphere of camaraderie or a mood. I can focus my lens on an object and get a sharp picture. God, however, touches us in a no man's land which lies somewhere between the world of concrete experience and the absolutely unknown. God is only to be found at "the mind's rugged shore, where the murmur breaks off abruptly, where we do not know any more how to be in awe. Only those who know how to live spiritually on edge will be able to go beyond the shore without longing for the certainties established on the artificial rock of our speculation."[12] God does not "pose" for the camera of our consciousness. It is just not possible to "conceive" or "nail down" God onto the sensitive photo-plate of our empirically oriented mind. Sensitivity to reality has been reduced to a very narrow field for the average modern person. What does not impose itself and almost brutally intrude on the modern consciousness is simply not experienced. Realism and reasonableness dare not transcend the limits of what is an immediate empirical fact. One has only to think in this context of Christ's warning when discussing the subject of how the Messiah makes himself known—"He will not argue or shout, or make loud speeches in the streets" (Matt 12:14), or to quote Rilke: "Du bist der Leiseste von allen die durch die leisen Häuser gehen."[13]

Only in a soul which can come to a state of chronic stillness will the mystery of God ever penetrate the field of consciousness. With the exception of the final moment of death, it is extremely rare for

12. A. Heschel, *Man is not Alone. A Philosophy of Religion*, New York, 1951, 58.
13. Rilke R. M., *Das Stundenbuch*, Wiesbaden, 1955, 38.

God to interrupt the normal flow of our lives to focus our attention on himself, even just for a moment. God respects our human busyness.

The second cause of our impression that it has become impossible to discover God or that we do not encounter him anywhere, lies in the fact that, wherever we do manage to track him down, he is shrouded in the mantle of Mystery. God does not come to meet us as the magical solution to all our problems but rather as the ever-new, infinite Mystery. Our scientifically trained spirit will always attempt to analyse prima facie mysteries (diseases, rare natural phenomena or unusual events) critically and thereby "solve" them. This is actually our job, at least when it comes to "things." A mystery is thus an enemy to be liquidated. A mystery is a challenge. The detective in us comes to grips with it first and then we subject it to the searchlight of our critical intellect. Whatever cannot be comprehended by our inquiring mind is not directly dismissed as non-existent but quietly slipped into the icebox of agnosticism.

A mind which has problems with a sense of wonder for the unapproachable is poorly prepared for the encounter with God. Heschel puts it this way: "It is not from experience but from our inability to experience what is given to our mind that certainty of the realness of God is derived. Our certainty is the result of wonder and radical amazement, of awe before the mystery and meaning of the totality of life beyond our rational discerning. Faith is the response to the mystery."[14]
mystery."[14]

Just because material things offer resistance to our physical impulses we decide that these things must be real. Our eye "runs into" an object in just the same way as our taste buds can "hone in" on a table in the dark. The fact that God offers resistance to our intellectual categories and thought systems ought logically bring us to the conclusion that he really exists. It is not so much the awareness of God's reality that is subjective. It is much more the idea of his unreality which goes together with the strikingly blind thought structures of the modern subject. His "mindscape" has become one-dimensional (Roszak).

It is consequently not so much the awareness of God but rather agnosticism which is a psychologically explicable phenomenon. It is a phenomenon which lies anchored in the shallow waters of a one-sided empirical disposition of the human spirit.

14. A. Heschel, *God in Search of Man, A Philosophy of Judaism*, New York, 1955, 117.

Now as to that objection that God is but a projection of the human spirit—it has to be admitted and emphasized that this is indeed the case and must be so. No one has ever seen God. Those many people who do develop an awareness that God is present within them consequently "project" him onto the screen of their imagination. One cannot form an image of the invisible God which can be compared with or readjusted in the light of another's experience of the invisible. One is thus just like a child who has never known his mother but who still tries to form an "image" of the woman who became invisible through untimely death. Mathematics and geometric "projective" sciences find themselves in an analogous situation. One does not begin with measuring already existing triangles to arrive at the subjective conclusion that the sum of their angles always adds up to 180°. The thought process works in the opposite way. A reasonable person who uses his or her intellect cannot but conclude that the sum will add up to 180°. For that reason they quite rightly project this conclusion onto reality. They can, of course, check out existing triangles as they inevitably will, to verify whether or not their "hypothesis" or "project" was in fact true.

The question is not whether the different images of God are not pure human invention. Normally that is what they are, even though every believer knows only too well that it is actually not possible to come up with an adequate image of God. It is for that very reason that they use symbols. Persons who make use of symbols always "project" what they actually experience in images, in the full awareness that these are images and not univocal concepts. The question that needs to be answered is why it is that people will always want to have images of God. The supposition that God could well be a "fata morgana" loses all its plausibility once we realize that no one travelling in the desert can be of the opinion that they have observed a glistening expanse of water unless they at some stage have seen real water which consequently must have real existence somewhere. To put it another way: the fact, in their naivete, people do construct illusions, demonstrates at least the fact that some fascinating realities exist which work on the human imagination. There is no one who mistakenly spots a deer on the edges of a forest unless they know that deer do happen to live in wooded areas. With the possible exception of people who are paranoid, no one projects non-existent things onto reality. Consequently no one in the full possession of their faculties is so naive that they are under the impression that they spied a dragon emerge from the forest. There are no such things as dragons. For that reason I never "see" them in reality, not even by mistake.

At the heart of this Freudian claim that religion is nothing more than the projection of a deformed paternal image or Oedipus complex onto a screen that spans the heavens lies a quite striking contradiction. If one asks Freud why exactly some people (i.e., those who have the faith) cannot free themselves of their obsessive father-image, he answers in the following terms: they are fettered by immature feelings of guilt and anxiety. In the Freudian scheme of things fathers are generally authoritarian and repressive. The consequence of this fact is that fretful people (i.e., people with a penchant for religion) discover a "father" at every hand's turn and are thus in a permanent state of fear. A little later on Freud informs us that fathers are usually experienced as a strong, secure protective hand against all dangers and difficulties. The consequence of this would once again be a projection: in this case an imaginary benevolent father who offers me permanent refuge. God is thus sometimes a projection motivated by anxiety and sometimes by hope: sometimes by immature rancor, then again by childish affection. If one were inclined to object that the Jansenistic idea of God as a harsh judge can hardly be the fruit of "wishful thinking," then Freud will point to immature anxiety and aggression vis-à-vis the father-figure in the Oedipus complex. Were one then to object that Bernard of Clairvaux's doctrine of divine love can hardly be explained away in terms of an Oedipus complex, Freud hits the ball right back into our court. This time the projection is a frustrated form of "wishful thinking." Of course the real question that needs to be asked is whether it is not rather the atheist who manifests the clear symptoms of an Oedipus complex. The atheist just cannot swallow this idea of a heteronomous "Father-God," who casts a long shadow over human autonomy. Voltaire's clarion call, "écrasons l'infâme" betrays an emotional repulsion from authority and dependence. Admittedly Voltaire was not an atheist. He was just about able to tolerate a distant and abstract Deity who was more like a technical architect of the universe than a father. Furthermore, it is not immediately obvious how the acceptance of the Cross as the central reality in this life can be reasonably explained in terms of "wishful thinking." Should one not rather say that the young atheists who are the heros of Dostoevsky's novels conceived of themselves as young gods who try to move through life in Feuerbach's footsteps, fired by an almost child-like exaltation so characteristic of the boy struggling through puberty? Atheism, far more than religious faith seems to admit of a "psychological explanation," especially as it is characterized by a distaste for anything that smells of authority and subservience. In that sense Freud was a typical case of what Dag Hammarskjöld liked to call "sophoclean or tragic irony." Freud made a categorical assertion which, although little did he know it, applied more to himself than to anyone else. While Freud's long, accusing finger pointed toward cases of infantile projection, he was blissfully unaware of the degree to which he himself was psychologically smothered. He projects his own impossible and unhappy relationship with his father onto his hateful image of God.

There is actually more to Freud's interpretation of religious faith than his view that it is pure human psychological projection. The way he sees it, projection and "wishful thinking" are actual symptoms of an illness. They are "products of fantasy." This Freudian contempt for the fruit of imagination is once again typical of his "businesslike" approach. It is undeniable of course that there is such a thing as a disturbed fantasy world. Psychically disturbed persons very often build up a fictitious world of their own in which they seek security. Complexes (persecution complex or egomania) and hallucinations (i.e., reception of sense impressions devoid of material object) are part and parcel of this type of condition. Long before the Parisian students came up with their famous slogan "L'imagination au pouvoir" in the heady days of 1968, Jung had pleaded the cause of an irreplaceable role for the healthy, creative imagination. Jung firmly rejected Freud's negative attitude on this point. In Freud's view the imagination is nothing more than a retarded and even sick emergency exit for frustrated sexual desires. Jung will certainly never deny that the human imagination can manifest symptoms of illness (e.g., he even believed Freud's own fantasy demonstrated suspicious symptoms).[15] And yet Jung chose to emphasize the positive role of the human imaginary powers, a role which is so easily overlooked in the "businesslike" West.

For Jung the imagination represents a particular mode of knowing by which the internal production of images plays an active role in supplementing poetic creativity. Thanks to the imagination it is possible to picture or make in some sense visible things which in principle

15. See C.G. Jung, *Herinneringen, Dromen, Gedachten,* Arnhem, 1963, 144–160.

are invisible (e.g., one's late mother, radioactivity, God, etc.). Possession of an imaginative flair consequently means having a spirit which thinks and works without constantly reaching anxiously back for the terra firma of pure material reality. Everyone knows that "the existing things are inexpressible" (Ionesco) unless persons attempt to express themselves with images or metaphors. The language of lovers, of fairy tales or of religion is always "rich in imagery." Their object, in any case, can never be captured in univocal concepts. Just as the sensual imagination plays an irreplaceable role in the sexual domain, so too the spiritual imagination plays an even more significant role in the domain of religious faith. Even nuclear physics is impossible to explain without a bit of imagination, i.e., without use of symbols.

Jung believed that Freud was unable to see how certain symbols and images appeal just as powerfully to the human imagination as certain physical objects titillate human instincts. To put it bluntly, the fact that a stag is excited by the odour of a doe demonstrates that they belong together, and the fact that people from all cultures feel attracted to and moved by certain sacral symbols does show that there exists a certain bond between humanity and the sacred. Naturally, both on the sexual as well as the religious level, there do exist fictions or "attrapes," i.e., deceptive or artificial stimulants which are pure human creations but which yet can arouse a certain response. One can think, for example, of pornography or "evil spirits" which can wind the human imagination up into a state of fever even though the beautiful woman or the evil spirit has no external reality. When Nietzsche uttered one of his famous paradoxes, "it is not the truth but rather the lie which is divine," he was not talking about the exact articulation of material reality but rather about the poetic suggestion of what is invisible, which touches and moves people.

Religion is indeed a projection of the human spirit, but in the sense that people project their inner experiences onto the screen of our imaginative language or symbolism. These concepts are no mere chimeras. In many cases these projections are the consequence of a preceding "injection," i.e., "an experience in which a meta-human reality is injected into human life."[16] To put it another way: Feuerbach was right when he claimed that gods are images which humans have created (a father, a shepherd, a judge, a king, etc). What he never managed to understand is the following, however: why it is that peo-

---

16. P. Berger, *The Heretical Imperative*, New York, 1980, 52.

ple have an "image" of God and why do they imagine that there is a
God who is "paternal," etc. The Freudian explanation by way of anxiety and wishful thinking is simply shoddy. People simply do not create or project an image of God just because they could not get on
with their Dad or because they need a guardian angel. People know
about God because they feel themselves spoken to or somehow
touched by God. Christians are capable of forming an image of God
because they know themselves to be, in the most literal sense, a divine project or creation. Humanity is created in the image and likeness of God. Given that since the time of Jesus Christ they know (or
are capable of knowing) that they are images of God, they can consequently "imagine" who that invisible God actually is. Even if in Old
Testament times Yahweh insisted that no images of God be made
precisely because humanity can so easily consider its own creations
as literally and adequately representative of the reality, ever since the
time of Jesus Christ it has been possible to make "icons" of God's
presence so long as one takes care to remember that icons are artistic
creations and not material photographs or magic "things." The evangelist calls Jesus Christ first of all "the Word" and "the Image" of the
Father. After turning their backs on images of God for centuries, in
the revelation of Christ human beings were able to find a language
and imagery which enabled them to explain, in Christian terms, how
one can best imagine God.

"What a sculptor does to a block of marble, the Bible does to our fin-
est intuitions. It is like raising the mystery to expression."[17] Or to put
it a little less poetically: the Bible makes it possible for us to articulate our most intimate divine "injections" into more or less successful
"projections." Since the time of Jesus Christ these human projections
are backed up by God, and have his guarantee so long at least as
they remain orthodox.

Where Freud's assertion that religion was "a mere sublimation of
repressed libidinal desires" is concerned, it must not be forgotten that
Freud views not only religion but the whole of human culture with
an eye jaundiced by pessimism. As a result of a series of painful personal experiences or traumas Freud grew up with a very melancholic
view of life which cast a long shadow over all his scientific theories.
According to him cultural progress is only possible as long as there is
systematic repression of sensual desire. Man's true, unconscious mo-

17. A. Heschel, *God in Search of Man,* 164.

tives are never particularly noble or idealistic, albeit regularly experienced and described as "sublime." Thus, for Freud, art is nothing more than the expression of a frustrated desire which has given up on ever attaining fulfillment with material reality. Artists consequently spend all their time on an illusory object (i.e., one that exists purely in their mind or imagination) which is designed to replace a real but unattainable object. Dante devotes some of his most beautiful verses to the young Beatrice precisely because she is physically out of reach. "On ne chante que les choses absentes," mused Valéry; Art is a *pis aller*.

Another thing Freud attempted to do was to debunk the rationalistic vision of the Aufklärungsmensch by demonstrating that humanity was nothing as "reasonable" as one liked to assume ever since the days of Renaissance humanism. For Freud, humans are rather a bundle of irrational passions which, far from being "enlightened," are repressed and unconscious. Religion is one of the many camouflages by which people attempt to keep hidden the brutal nakedness of their slavery to their passions from themselves and from others. Religion leads us off the scene of reality, i.e., sex. In the spiritual and intellectual correspondence between the unmarried writer Leontine Zanta and the Jesuit Teilhard, a Freudian would see nothing more than a well-intentioned, unconscious search of a woman for a man and vice versa. So, to put it plainly: since it was not acceptable for a priest to have a wife, he compensated for this lack with "sublime" letters and high-flown conversation. For once we have here puritanical propriety and Freudian exposure or unmasking hand in hand: neither of the two believe in the existence of spiritual friendship. For both, this latter phenomenon is but a naive camouflage for stunted sexual desires. It cannot be denied, of course, that where spiritual values are concerned it is absolutely essential to separate the wheat from the chaff and it is a happy coincidence that Freud developed a practical and useful control mechanism for the purpose. The only problem is that Freud actually believed that wheat was no more than up-graded chaff. For him all the world is a stage.

The brave soul who attempts to cast aside masks, make-up and type-cast roles in the name of undiluted truth and authentic openness will get a rude awakening when such a one discovers that all that remains is brutal, unbearable nakedness. Freud could not see the difference between dressing fashionably on the one hand and organizing a transvestite revue on the other hand. It is true that the whole of culture and religion can be termed a "sublimation" or an ennobling process. Just as is the case with "projection," sublimation does not necessarily have to be a pejorative process. To claim that religious activities are essentially no more than camouflaged eroticism, is just as stupid as to state that a park is no more than a stunted jungle or a field full of wild plants and weeds. Naturally a lot of work has to be done on a jungle before it is tamed so as to make it suitable for agriculture or forestry. It is obvious, too, that a great deal of asceticism and self-discipline is required before one can progress from a sexual-erotic love to a successful marriage, or from a life of devotion to one of profound religious faith. Wild plants have to be domesticated or processed if one is to engage in horticulture or agriculture. In the same way instincts and passions have to be channeled (and not killed, repressed or denied) if friendship is to become something more than instinctive physical bodily processes.

It is striking how Teilhard, without ever knowing Freud, also used this concept of "sublimation" in the context of a discussion of sexuality and religion. Teilhard was aware that there exists a whole range of naive and inauthentic sublimation processes. There are few things so often copied and faked as famous objets d'art and paintings. And yet Teilhard believed it was not only possible but also absolutely essential to separate the wheat from the chaff.

On 15 December 1918 Teilhard made the following jottings in his diary:

> Chastity is no frustration of passion (in any case an impossible and damaging exercise, and a hangover from primitive taboos), but rather an ennobling of this passion by a more or less direct divine action. . . . In the view of some the feminine is taken up (*résorbé*) into God who then steps directly into the vacant place. There are others who feel that God reveals Himself only in nature or in the female element in reality (sometimes initially in a disconcerting way, yet always inspiring and destined to be transformed into spiritual reality). You must not think that such a "platonic" love is pale derivative of the real thing or something anemic or hypocritical. Experience teaches that this love is totally real and extremely fruitful. Such a love is anything but milk and water, it is a *sublimated* love. Eros here took wings.[18]

Since Freud's day it has become a commonplace to view love poe-

18. P. Teilhard de Chardin, *Journal I*, 377.

try and the Christian bridal mysticism as erotic compensation mechanisms filling in the gap left by a missing partner in the life of an enclosed nun or a pious celibate. Pseudo-mysticism certainly exists as a form of unhealthy compensation, almost a necessary evil. And yet Henri Bergson, drawing on a wide knowledge of literary history, emphatically claimed: "Mysticism is accused of liking to speak the language of passionate love. One tends to forget that in reality it was very often the love lyric which plagiarized the language of mysticism so as to draw on its fire, its élan and its ecstasies."[19]

Finally, it must be stated that Freud's concept of sublimation is a clear example of reductionism. Complex and exalted truths are reduced to something common and banal.

If we press Freud and ask why people are so often inclined to take refuge in sublimations, then he will answer that it is to compensate for a deficiency which they feel and which has been caused by their education, culture, or a set of accidental circumstances. Patients, Freud would say, slip into sickness because they have neglected the real needs of their soul. These "real needs" are in Freud's eyes always sexual. It would be rather far-fetched to claim that the "psychological needs" which contemporary humanity is most easily inclined to overlook are all basically sexual. It is in no small degree thanks to the selfsame Freud that sex has again taken centre stage and so dominated day-to-day life that it is more appropriate to talk of saturation than repression. And yet psychiatrists have never had as many patients in their waiting rooms as at the present day. If, according to Freud, "the patient always suffers from what is absent" then that absent dimension is, to quote J. Van den Berg, "the life of the spirit rather than sex." Maybe this is why so many youngsters at the present time try to compensate for what they lack in the religious area with hyperactivity in the sexual domain. It is not so much a question of sexuality being sublimated as of spirituality being trivialized.

It never seems to have struck Freud that sublimation is not necessarily an unconscious process. Sublimation can actually be a conscious spiritual choice. Persons can freely deny themselves gratification of their baser instincts and desires with a view to attaining higher values which seem to them to be more meaningful. Freud was actually convinced that self-denial could only be the fruit of anxiety, inhibitions, taboos or indoctrination. It is in fact possible for a Trappist to deny

19. H. Bergson, *Les deux Sources de la Morale et de la Religion*, Paris, 1965, 39.

himself certain physical pleasures in the areas of gastronomy, tourism or eroticism because his mind is anxious to focus on something more exalted rather than out of anxiety or mere habit. It is impossible for a person to enjoy everything at once. Everyone has certain choices to make. With his essentially pessimistic view of things Freud believes people are always looking for immediate gratification of their passions, unless a (paranoid) anxiety or guilt complex act to restrain them. Here is a striking contrast between Freud's libertine theories and his own puritan lifestyle. In 1883, in a letter to his then fiancee who was later to become his wife Martha Bernays, he wrote as follows: "It is neither pleasant nor edifying to observe the masses at their amusements. We at least have little to do with such vulgar displays. The rabble indulges its passions while we deny ourselves things right, left and centre. And why do we deny ourselves so much? So as to preserve our unimpeachable integrity. We are preserving ourselves for a higher thing, even though we really do not know what it is."[20] The difference between Freud and the Trappist lies in the fact that the latter does happen to know "what this higher thing actually is" for the sake of which he is willing to deny himself so much.

Finally, it is important to consider briefly the claim that religion necessarily results in alienation. It is true that historically religion has often been at the root of self-alienation, although it would be outlandish to claim that there was a necessary or inevitable link between the two. If one understands alienation (literally "a process of change") as meaning that "an other" seriously begins to interfere in my life, then love and friendship are the most acute forms of alienation imaginable. The other party who influences my life does not necessarily have to be a strange tyrant or judge. Seen in religious terms, there is no reason to conceive of God as a wilful kill-joy. Christians at least do not see him in that light. The sentiment voiced in the Letter to the Hebrews, "how terrible it is to fall in the hands of the living God" is completely superseded. Such a thing exists as a positive alienation process, and this takes place in the name of authentic love. Just as the slavish, immature and timorous individuals will allow another's opinions and the will of another to take over their own hearts, and instead of following the still, small voice of their own conscience are attentive only to "their master's voice," so, too, persons who find themselves in love let the loved one take firm root in the

20. S. Freud, *Briefe (1873–1939)*, E. und L. Freud, eds., Frankfurt, 1968, 56–57.

affections of their heart. The former do this so as to avoid problems. The latter allow it to happen because in their eyes there is nothing more wonderful than to know that the persons they love are happy. The primordial object of a Christian's love is God. "Love God above all things" is the first and greatest Christian commandment.

One can, thus, term love "alienation." One allows oneself to be taken over by another, but not in the sense of being conquered by a stranger. In a loving relationship one opens up the most intimate depths of one's self and makes oneself available to the other. One does not act out of angst but rather out of passionate desire. There is no better way of describing love than in the words of Emmanuel Lévinas: "The calling in question of my own spontaneous desires for the sake of the encounter with the other."[21]

It was the disciples of Freud, psychiatrists such as Karen Horney, R. S. Laing and Erich Fromm, as well as certain philosophers like Herbert Marcuse, who gave this concept of alienation popular currency in the psychological literature. These writers attempted bit by bit to correct the rather bourgeois individualist in Freud by drawing on the insights of Marx. It is for that reason that the more orthodox Freudians labelled these prophets of alienation "revisionists."

From his reading of Hegel's *Philosophy of Law* (1821) the young Marx gained remarkable anthropological insights into the interconnection between specialization of labour, barter, money and exploitation. These were insights of which he was to make brilliant use later in his own socio-politically oriented philosophy. It was this Hegelian Weltanschauung which inspired Marx's philosophical broadside against capitalism. Hegel's concept of "self-alienation" was central to the Marxist critique. Before ever Marx put pen to paper, Hegel had already pointed out that the systematic impoverishment of the ordinary people would result in a growing deficiency of new markets and that an expansion of colonialism would follow. And yet Hegel was firmly opposed to any form of revolution because in his view it would inevitably bring cruel forms of terror in its wake. The French Revolution which had so fascinated the young Hegel taught him this lesson for once and for all.

Marx saw things a little differently. In his opinion the self-alienation of the impoverished working classes had taken such a catastrophic form that revolution was not only unavoidable but neces-

21. E. Lévinas, *Totalité et Infini, Essai sur l'Extériorité*, The Hague, 1971, 13.

sary. The young Marx's point of departure in his reflections was that work = exploiting oneself. He believed that every form of creative work in which workers express something of their own genius becomes impossible as long as systematic division of labour means that the individual worker sees the fruit of his or her own work disappear into the hands of wealthier consumers. As long as a person's work remains exclusively governed by the requirements, plans and interests of "aliens," then this work is no longer a source of self-realization but rather the cause of bitter self-alienation, emptiness and resentment. To put it plainly, the cause of this self-alienation lies in the type of work which the industrial labourer is forced to do. (Marx would call him the "capitalist labourer." It is a moot point whether thanks to the communist regime, the Polish miner did manage to establish a more creative and personal relationship with the coal mine than his colleague in capitalist Kentucky).

It is an undeniable fact that, thanks to the mindless work which they have to do, many people are forced to let their minds and their feelings wander off "elsewhere." Alienated by their work, they seek solace in a sterile world of daydreams. Certainly where labourers are concerned, especially those who work on an assembly line. This alienation can also hit the middle classes, i.e., the clergy, the liberal professions and business people. Because many of them experience deep alienation at the level of an interior or intimate life (their relationships with wife and children, with their parishioners and in their prayer life), they plunge into activity. Their work is the only thing that absorbs them: here they feel at home. Here they feel they are really themselves. Following on what A. Gehlen observed, P. Berger correctly points out: "While the individual may seek psychological refuge from the alienations of his work situation in private life, it is also possible that an individual may seek such refuge in the very anonymity of his work situation because he finds the non-anonymous relations of private life intolerable."[22] Alfred Weber takes it one step further. In his view it is wrong to measure a person's human work on the basis of achievements or activities. The criterion by which to assess someone's work is rather "the degree to which he remains spiritually detached from his work."[23]

In a religious context this phenomenon of alienation means that

22. P. and Br. Berger, H. Kellner, *The Homeless Mind, Modernization and Consciousness*, New York, 1974, 34–35.
23. Quoted by A. Gehlen, *Die Seele im technischen Zeitalter*, Hamburg, 1969, 111.

some of the faithful have so little intimate prayer life (i.e., they feel themselves so empty when at prayer, so ill at ease and so silly) that they throw themselves into social or political action, development aid work or some form of reformish-minded ideological activism. In other words they make the move from contemplation to action, from religion to moral reform, from a spiritual life to useful, productive work. Of course, the choice is not an either/or. Anyone who has a wife and children and loves them will work for them. And anyone who loves God will do everything possible to render service to God's children. It would be to fall prey to a dangerous delusion to think that hard work automatically leads to a meaningful life and true love. Work is a consequence of love. Love is never the result of a commitment to activity. Christian apostolate and philanthropic work are the consequence of prayer and flow from meditation on the gospel message. If this is not the case, they quickly become a sort of anaesthetic which reduces the pain which results from spiritual emptiness and a feeling of apparent meaninglessness. Work and feverish organizing are probably the most used drugs in Church circles to compensate for the gnawing feeling of God's absence which is always the result of inner or spiritual undernourishment. A feverish tempo of work transforms human beings into what R. Musil called "one of those many people who are always busy doing good. In their inner selves there is little goodness to be found anymore."[24] To put it another way one could do worse than repeat what the American Bucke said on observing the French Revolution: "They hated injustice with such a passion that they were no longer able to love man."

While according to Marx this process of self-alienation occurred in the workplace, Freud paid more attention to the area of moral decisions. His slogan was rather "boss of my own conscience" than "boss in my own factory." Or to put it in more Freudian language: "less über-ich and more personality." While Marx was an optimist with very high expectations of the revolution, Freud was a pessimist. In his opinion there was no one who escaped from alien indoctrination. One is weaned on the "alien" at one's mother's breast. The only thing people can do is make themselves aware of the unavoidable calamity of alienation. At a later period the South American Marxists did this with their notorious "conscientizatión."

Developing a sense of awareness is the first step on the road to

---

24. R. Musil, *Der Mann ohne Eigenschaften*, Hamburg, 1952, 745.

freedom and maturity. Even though Freud's insights into psycho-genesis are illuminating and startling, they are still defective. What he was not able to see was the difference between a childish super-ego and a mature ideal "I." As has already been pointed out, the su-perego is the Freudian equivalent of what the moral philosophers call the conscience. In Freud's opinion it is nothing more than the residue of parental indoctrination. It is the fall-out from what Mummy and Daddy found good, bad, proper, chancy or completely out of court, in the degree to which I have made these (alien) norms my own and consider them as my own personal convictions. A feeling of what is good or bad is, in Freud's view, in no way universal, natural or in-nate. A moral code is thus always relative, contingent, historical and socially circumscribed. In addition to this superego with all its learned behaviour patterns and habits there is also an "ideal-I" or a personal life plan that incites the mature personality to reach out be-yond the social impulses of the "Es," as well as above the conven-tions of the all-too-docile superego. This ideal-I, of which Freud is blissfully ignorant, puts things the way they could be or become. The ideal-I is a model or goal of the individual personality, suggesting the pattern along which it would like to grow or develop. The ideal-I of a mature free individual is capable of rising beyond a social context and social determinism. This is something which Freud's mechanistic positivism would never let him understand.

In the meantime the superego represents a necessary phase in the development of a child, even though it is far from always the prod-uct of indoctrination of principles and convictions. It comes about rather through a spontaneous "empathy" (Sullivan), first with the mother and father and later with those people from the child's envi-ronment whom he or she considers important and who consequently exert "influence" on him or her. In other words, my superego or con-science is gradually formed by a spontaneous and admiring looking-up to whatever my parents and my "significant others" do and feel to be important.

As I advance in maturity I come to have a certain view of the differ-ent influences which I have undergone. In this way I come to know myself better. By exploring a whole series of possibilities which my culture has on offer (and in a pluralistic society the range of possibili-ties is not exactly limited), I elaborate my own lifestyle. Were I to swal-low everything my immediate environment has to offer, I would end up being a conformist. Were I to kick over the traces and systematically reject everything, this, on the contrary, would make of me a dissatisfied rebel. Between these two extremes, a rigid superego on the one hand and an ego completely adrift on the other, it is possible to develop a personal lifestyle which has not so much made a clean break with the past but rather has grown out of it. The uniqueness and greatness of Mahatma Ghandi does not come from the fact that he was exemplary in his integral fidelity to the Hindu tradition. Even less so is his stature due to a revolutionary rejection of this tradition. Ghandi rather endorsed a large number of inherited Hindu traditions which he in turn faithfully passed on to his disciples. One has only to think here of Hindu piety, self-discipline taught through yoga, cottage industry based on an extended or nuclear family, an independent and tolerant state of India and other such things. He adamantly set himself against that same Indian culture when it set store by exaggerated aristocratic pomp and circumstance, the caste system and intellectual xenophobia. The mature person is observant, tries out a lot and keeps only what is good. The immature person is stuck in a reactionary phase, opposes a whole range of things and in this way tries—mistakenly as it so happens—to develop a sense of individuality or of being different. There was no one who recognized this complex interplay of unconscious influences as clearly as Freud. And yet Freud greatly overestimated the influence of family and tradition, while he underestimated the force of the spirit of the age and social trends.

The German economist Jungblut once said of Marx: "Marx provided a perfect forecast of the entire evolution of the capitalist system with the exception of one decisive factor in this process, namely the influence Marxism would have on capitalism." One can justifiably say the same thing about Freud. Freud was able to describe many of the characteristics of Western humanity exactly and he made us conscious of quite a number of things. He completely overlooked one factor, i.e., the degree to which Freudian thought would make modern human beings anti-family, anti-authoritarian and anti-religious. A lot of what Freud has to say to modern people is now old hat because they have imbibed more Freudian antibodies than the brilliant psychiatrist could ever have foretold. Whether modern persons feel better as a result remains an open question.

CHAPTER SIX

The Limits of Our Language and the Infinite God

1. Contemporary Language in an Impasse

What people see or fail to see, the areas in which they are sensitive and those in which they are not, the way they think, the feelings they repress, what interests them and what bores them, in a word, people's whole psychic disposition, depends to a very large extent on the society in which those people live. Each society develops its own way of feeling, observing and thinking. Societies are separated from one another by space and time, and thus differ on the basis of geographic and historical factors. The things a Zulu finds beautiful or agreeable, a Canadian may not, and citizens of nineteenth-century Vienna had different ideas concerning what was pleasant or moral from their late-twentieth century great grandchildren. A mentality is determined by factors of time and location. There are no aspects of life which people have *always* repressed, have condemned *everywhere* or *permanently* admired. There is no such thing as a general, universal or eternal psychology, at least not when this psychology bears the vaguest relationship to day-to-day life. There is no universal common vision of life, view of humanity or idea about God. Every psychology is "topographical" in this, that, in the one culture one reasoned this way and was sensitive to this aspect of life, but then almost completely ignored another side of life. There is no culture, however humane, refined or broadminded which has within its sights the whole horizon of reality: humanity is simply too limited to have such a vision. There is no Weltanschauung which is all-embracing. No matter how neutral or unprejudiced people may be, their consciousness (and thus their inner logic, their method of assimilating knowledge, their epistemology) is formed, fertilized and developed by the environment in which they grew up.

That mentality is above all the fruit of the *language* which one learned to speak in that environment. An Englishman thinks and feels differently from a Chinese. Furthermore the English used in *Newsweek* is concerned with other facets of reality than the language of Shakespeare's blank verse. The language of a Freudian psychiatrist is rather different from the professional jargon of a construction engineer. On the telephone one tends to structure one's sentences differently than when one is writing a letter.

A person's language is the pair of spectacles through which a person looks at reality. A given language tends to focus on certain facts. "Our language is our window on life. It determines for its speaker the dimensions, perspective, and horizon of a part of the total landscape of the world. Of a part. No speech, however ample its vocabulary, however refined and adventurous its grammar, can organize the entire potential of experience."[1] It follows thus that an individual's personal vision of life as well as the worldview of a particular culture group (e.g., of hippies or Marxists) is in the first instance a question of language. For that very reason it is not possible to speak of a believer's or an agnostic's epistemological or psychological disposition, without paying particular attention to the different linguistic devices which the believer and the agnostic spontaneously use. Given that no one invents their own language but takes over the language of their environment, it is essential here to consider the manner of expression of late twentieth-century humanity.

Something very peculiar is going on where the language of contemporary humanity is concerned. George Steiner has spoken even of a "linguistic revolution," which he traces back to the end of the nineteenth century. Two things have happened. First, reality has become so terrifically complicated that no one is capable of getting a completely global picture. What is worse, many aspects of reality (viz., nuclear physics, atonal music or radioactivity) can no longer be discussed in ordinary language. One has to resort rather to nonverbal symbols and mathematical formulae. Secondly, our ordinary language (i.e., the pithy phrases and fashionable jargon one takes over from glossy magazines, advertisements, T.V., the press, etc.) has become so impoverished that it is inadequate to express ideas concerning large parts of reality. One has only to think in this regard of the

1. G. Steiner, *Extraterritorial, Papers on Literature and the Language Revolution,* New York, 1971, 81.

phenomenon of religion, a person's intimate spiritual life, modern art, etc. It is virtually impossible to say a single meaningful thing about such things in contemporary jargon. As reality becomes more complex, our language becomes more impoverished.

Why does our modern language offer such a narrow window on the ever unfolding scientific knowledge of reality? "And the demand of mass culture and mass communication have made it perform tasks of ever increasing tawdriness. What save half-truths, gross simplifications, or trivia can, in fact, be communicated to that semi-literate mass audience which popular democracy has summoned into the marketplace? Only in a diminished or corrupted language can most such communication be made effective. . . . Motivation researchers, those gravediggers of literate speech, tell us that the perfect advertisement should neither contain words of more than two syllables nor sentences with dependent clauses."[2] If everyone has to understand everything then it is best to confine ourself to simple generalities which "come across" easily. Consequently modern language concerns itself with a limited segment of reality of which it is still possible to have an overview. Where the rest is concerned—and that rest is made up of an ever greater and more important part—the silence is deafening. How many women complain that their husbands have enormous difficulty in expressing what they really feel about them! This is even more so the case when a person attempts to articulate views about religion.

The language of the old penny catechism just does not work any more, while the new religious prophets seem to talk only of "diesseitige" things such as abortion, human rights, social commitment or the third world. The mass media are all too eager to supply them with the right terminology. When it comes to describing a "state of soul" (Bergson) such as religious faith, public opinion and the "milieu" are all but speechless. One prefers to conveniently forget and pass over in silence an experience about which one cannot or dare not speak. Pure platonic love has a short life. On the other hand the word possesses an enormous force. In the meantime the religious domain is discreetly covered over with the veil of silence (whereby it sinks quietly into oblivion). The moralizing preacher says nothing about God. Religious instruction likes to stick to familiar territory

2. G. Steiner, *Language and Silence, Essays on Language, Literature and the Inhuman,* New York, 1977, 26.

which there are still words to describe. Contemporary language is like a window that looks out on concrete things.

When Ionesco drew attention to the fact that "atheism is often nothing more than a misunderstanding of words" he did not mean to suggest that the atheist simply expresses himself differently from the believer while they both essentially meant the same thing. Himself a true artist with words, Ionesco knew and regretted rather that words such as spirit, devil, hell, God, sin, etc. were so often misused and so loaded with inherited infantile associations that these words *can* no longer be used without running the risk of being seriously misunderstood. Because people tend to studiously avoid the use of these words (without in the meantime finding new ones), they take refuge in vague abstractions or in temporary silence. The result is, says Ionesco, that this silence can be mistakenly interpreted as a sign of atheism.

2. Purely Operational Concepts

It must be admitted that any talk about the unexpressible is in itself a difficult enterprise. That enterprise has become a great deal more problematic in our own day because modern-day language is so ill suited to any discussion about God. Modern language is made up almost exclusively of "operational concepts." Analogous or symbolic concepts on the contrary are avoided. They are dismissed as being either too vague, too ambiguous or too far from the point. An operational concept is a word whose meaning is strictly limited to what one can *do* with the object referred to by the concept. A revolver, an automobile or a lamppost are clear examples of operational concepts. With these items one can shoot, drive or illuminate a street, respectively. When one starts considering such concepts as love, culture or faith as operational then things start going wrong. "Love" then becomes a question of performing a series of physiological operations (making love, or "faire l'amour"). Culture is then understood as having a certain number of concrete achievements on one's *curriculum vitae:* an impressive list of publications, fluency in five languages, an ability to play the piano well and being a wizard on the surfboard. In this context religious faith is considered to involve doing certain things (e.g., attending Sunday Mass) and not doing other things (e.g., not joining the local lodge of the Freemasons and coming out against abortion). With this greatly impoverished language it is very difficult to make it clear that love, culture and religious faith are not so much a question of performing certain operations and turning one's back on others. Love, culture and faith—to stick to the examples we have taken—are not "operations" but ways of experience.

The difference between a person who is in love and one who is not does not lie in the fact that their concrete actions or their behaviour as a whole are dissimilar. It lies rather in the way that both look at one particular girl. Both experience that girl in a different way. They experience a different feeling while they are contemplating her or talking with her. At a later stage in the manner of experience, one will approach her and help her, while the other will hardly bid her the time of day.

Anyone who wants to talk about God in contemporary language (i.e., in language that can be understood) is put on the horns of a sticky dilemma. Either they will use analogous, figurative or symbolic words, which then come across as "ambiguous" or "incomprehensible," or else they adapt, i.e., they are going to speak "operationally" and take on all the modern jargon. Consequently, they will no longer talk about God but about "current problems." These days Christian doctrine class is all about human rights, conscientious objection, abortion, sexual problems and other such subjects. Marcuse labelled this purely operational language devoid of a transcendental dimension "un univers du discours clos." The world becomes one-dimensional because its language is so limited and defective.

Goethe was well able to articulate the knowledge of his day in an understandable way. The everyday language of the time was adequate to describe the not very complex physical, astronomical, chemical and religious observations his era produced. Language was pretty much co-extensive with known reality. The knowledge one had, one could fairly easily put across in a way that it could be understood by the average person with a bit of education. This is no longer true in the modern world. "So far as the Western tradition goes, an underlying classicism, a pact negotiated between word and world, lasts until the second half of the nineteenth century. There it breaks down abruptly. Goethe and Victor Hugo were probably the last major poets to find that language was sufficient to their needs."[3]

A rift was created between things which words could describe and those for which no adequate words existed, between word and real-

3. G. Steiner, *After Babel, Aspects of Language and Translation*, London 1975, 171.

ity, between our language and our experience. As language became poorer, the real world became more complex. There are large sections of reality which consequently have to be expressed non-verbally (e.g., by figures, electronic signals, gestures, etc.). It was possible to explain and paraphrase in common language the classical works of art Breughel painted, the slaughter of the Holy Innocents for example, or in Beethoven's Pastoral Symphony it was possible to hear a babbling brook, birds chirping and a mounting storm. When faced with a painting by Rauschenberg or a musical composition by Stockhausen one is dumbfounded. This sort of art anyway "means" nothing. These colours and sounds are not intended as "signs" of one or other truth which could also be expressed in language if necessary. They are simply "compositions," a game of colours or sounds. No language is adequate to express what they are trying to communicate. To put it another way, the convertability between art and language has been abandoned. Language has lost a great deal of its value and prestige since it has had to be made comprehensible to everyone. As has already been suggested, the reason for this rift between language and reality is twofold. The reality of which humans are aware has become more complicated and that is something to be happy about. At the same time language has become poorer and more one-dimensional, and this is a regrettable development. Philosophers and artists have tried to remedy this situation. Wittgenstein saw that our thought problems had run aground in the shallow waters of "democratic" linguistic usage. He termed philosophy "language therapy." It was the philosopher's task to save the language, to heal and purify it. The poets did their bit by throwing the jargon of the day out the window but they were then immediately accused of total incomprehensibility. One held them for eccentric crackpots. What is striking is that all the great poets since Hölderlin, Rimbaud and Mallarmé have made language an issue. They do not compose verses about nightingales or sunsets, but rather about language.

In a similar way Fellini ("8½") and Woody Allen ("Stardust") made films about film-making. They are both concerned to highlight the banality of modern box-office successes. In his "Cantatrice chauve" Ionesco lets his audience hear a modern-day conversation that has neither shape nor content.

No one in one's sane senses will conclude that just because one cannot use plain language to talk about radioactivity or entropy (i.e., use the jargon of *Time* or the radio) that these realities are purely chimerical and have no real existence. People are apparently less ready to accept the fact that it is impossible to say something meaningful in our impoverished language of today. Boileau's (highly questionable) quip springs to mind here: "Ce que l'on conçoit bien s'énonce clairement." If one is not able to speak about God clearly and in businesslike fashion, this demonstrates that God's reality is confused and illusory. In other words one is very tolerant when it comes to the empirical sciences and allows the use of a lot of paralinguistic jargon. Theologians on the other hand are expected to speak about God clearly, unambiguously and in contemporary language. If they try to use symbolic or metaphorical language, then this is interpreted as a sign of camouflaged uncertainty of their ground or even of a mythological fairy-tale world.

It is of course easy to attack the impotence of contemporary language and in that way excuse one's own inability to speak intelligently about God. Why is that modern language so one-sided and why is consequently every attempt to use this language in discourse about God so terribly difficult? One reason has already been put forward, i.e., an almost "manic" preference which modern humanity has for "operational" concepts. The progress and success of the empirical sciences and technology have made their contribution. Using language correctly for them means the use of controllable, measurable and verifiable concepts. In their book psychology too is a "behavioural science," i.e., a pure science of behaviour. Being in love sounds sweet and poetic, yet it is vague, impossible to prove and thus nonscientific. If one has only an operational understanding of love, then it is possible to measure caresses, muscular reactions and glandular secretions and even draw them as a curve on a mathematical chart. A person's faith is too vague to measure: it is possible however to total up the number of communions or baptisms, and to make statistics about confessional practice and to forecast the regularity with which a given church will be visited.

3. The Youngsters Up in Arms Against the Right Word

In the Judeo-Christian religion, as we know, the Word occupies a central position: "In the beginning was the Word. The Word was with God and the Word *was God*" (John 1:1). Oriental religions like Buddhism and Taoism, on the other hand, are in search of a form of contemplation in which God is no longer praised, but in which thought, speech and feeling are absorbed in the general silence.

"The primacy of the word, of that which can be spoken and communicated in discourse, is characteristic of the Greek and Judaic genius and carried over into Christianity. The classic and the Christian sense of the world strive to order reality within the governance of language."[4] Language does indeed involve order and comprehension. It is only language which makes comprehension possible. The Jewish Torah, the biblical Word of God, the Justinian Code and Thomas Aquinas' *Summa Theologica* are eloquent examples of this general proposition. No culture has shown as great a respect for the exact, orthodox, dogmatic and efficient word as the Western. It is precisely against this culture that Western youngsters are up in arms. They spontaneously felt what sophisticated structuralists had come to discover, i.e., that there is an analogy between language (which is a structured system of rules, principles and laws) and the whole culture which produced it.

"Culture in its entirety (is) a form of communication" or "a complete system of signs and symbols."[5] Culture must consequently be understood "syntactically." Young people protested precisely against that order, that analogy and that complexity. To put it another way: "The classic speech-construct, the centrality of the word, are informed by and expressive of both a hierarchic value-system, and the trope of transcendence. These nodes of sensibility are interactive and mutually reinforcing at every point. (The tonalities of 'class,' 'classification' and 'classic' are, naturally, cognate)."[6]

It is against these established conventions, rules and laws that today's young people are rebelling. They generally do this under the cloak of spontaneity, "retour à la nature" and freedom. They give the impression of shrewd insight when they point the finger at the principal guilty parts of the "established order." That language has to suffer for it at the hands of a new generation, as the sociologist J. Duvignaud has so clearly shown in his work *La planète des Jeunes*. The youngster adopts an aggressive stance vis-à-vis the language and quite deliberately perpetrates linguistic rape. Sloppy spelling, deliberately wrong modes of expression, the systematic introduction of neologisms, the use of incomplete sentences and stereotypical jargon

4. G. Steiner, *Language and Silence*, 13.
5. E. Hall, *The Silent Language*, New York, 1973, 28.
6. G. Steiner, *In Bluebeard's Castle*, New Haven, 1971, 87.

words are all forms of protest against the language which they were taught by parents and schoolmasters. "The counter-culture is perfectly aware of where to begin the job of demolition. The violent illiteracies of the graffiti, the clenched silence of the adolescent, the nonsense-cries from the stage-happening, are resolutely strategic. The insurgent and the freakout have broken off discourse with a cultural system which they despise as a cruel, antiquated fraud. They will not bandy words with it. Accept, even momentarily, the conventions of literate linguistic exchange, and you are caught in the net of the old values, of the grammars that can condescend or enslave."[7]

Not that modern youngsters have themselves come up with a new creative language. Their language is rather reminiscent of the short TV commercial slogans or of the caption which *Time* delights in taking out of context and planking under its photographs: a commercial "flash" which actually says nothing but must suggest a lot in few but still "comprehensible" words. The language of today's youngsters reminds one of the bubbles which hover over the protagonists in comic strips. They are generally speaking parsimonious in their words. If one were to judge by their language, reality is disarmingly simple and above all pretty radical.

It is well known that there are certain cultures which use words lavishly and then other people who are very economic in their use of words and keep their language in their heart. Some nationalities, social classes, generations or professions talk more, others less. Swedes talk less than Italians. Lower social classes tend to speak more candidly and at greater length about sex than those further up the social ladder. Men were generally more used to speaking in public than women. Children were generally expected to keep quiet in the presence of adults while women generally made up for lost time in exclusively female company or hen parties. It is very striking that young people today use language a lot less (which is not to suggest that there is more silence in the world) and that in two respects.

Whenever youngsters get together the venue is filled with the sound of loud music which deliberately hinders conversation and makes it superfluous. And yet at these gatherings an intense form of "contact" is experienced, albeit a contact which is rather a transfusion of emotion or intoxication by the atmosphere rather than an exchange of views or ideas. Here everyone *feels* the same. Or, to put it

7. Ibid., 88.

more positively, people feel a sense of solidarity and fellowship. Within the acoustic walls of overpowering music one feels secure and protected against loneliness and futility. Music in this context is a mild form of spiritual anaesthetic. It is a drug which arouses feelings and brings on a state of ecstasy.

If young people do resort to communication by means of language then it is preferably through a speedy and erasable medium such as telephone or cassette recorder and seldom through such a time-consuming medium as a letter, which moreover can have consequences of its own. "A study of random samples of urban telephone calls suggests a drastic diminution and standardization of vocabulary and syntax accompanied by a formidable growth of actual speech-output. In the world of the telephone, we speak more to say less. It may be, correspondingly, that in that of radio, television, tape-recorder, and film, we hear more and listen less."[8]

It must be said that the teenager is not the only one who in this age of deflationary linguistic use takes refuge from a one-to-one conversation in electronically amplified prefabricated music. We are experiencing a striking trend across our entire culture whereby music is taking over, and always at the expense of the spoken and written word. Music enjoys many advantages in a pluralistic society: it cannot tell a lie because it asserts nothing. And yet it holds an increasingly strong appeal for people who seem to need the inexpressible. For a growing number of people classical music appears to be taking the place of prayer. Music is able to effect this compensation because it gives the music lover listening in silence the impression that he or she is suddenly transported into a totally different world, one which is spiritually more elevated and is almost transcendent. A melody in a Mahler symphony can reduce listeners to tears. They do not need to use any words to explain why this happens. The musical experience is transrational and inexpressible. Music just does something for them. It touches them in the very depths of their being where it awakens something within them.

Furthermore, music is very tolerant. It is always possible that someone may not be particularly enthusiastic about Wagner, for example. And yet one would hesitate to claim that Wagner was a subversive or mendacious musician. Someone reading a difficult sentence in a letter or book can look up for a moment and wonder what the words

8. G. Steiner, *Extraterritorial*, 103.

actually mean and puzzle over what the author may have actually meant. Music does not allow for such musings because the sound and the meaning here are contemporaneous. Consequently, music is not a language art for the very reason it is so rich in polyvalent effects. What music "means" or what it "says" is impossible for anyone to put into words. Music sparks off an echo in the complex maze of the human spirit and thoughts. And yet in its own way music, too, can lie. With his jolly cheerful waltz music Johann Strauss tried to distract the attention of the Viennese bourgeoisie from the tragic reality of the fin de siècle decadence. He did this by creating artificial oases of frivolity. It will thus surprise no one that it was precisely during the two world wars that this meretricious music was misused to the full, being passed off as pleasant "easy-listening music" so that it could hide the murderous reality.[9]

Music thus does have something to do with the transcendent precisely because neither can be captured by words. Moreover, there is no known religion which has not resorted to music in order to somehow give expression to the essentially inexpressible. "I cannot say what cannot be said, but sounds can make us listen to the silence."[10]

It may seem somewhat paradoxical but this tendency to relativize and even show disdain for the orthodox and exact Word in religion is strongest among the charismatics who nonetheless like to award a central role to "the gift of tongues." Looked at closely, this "gift of tongues" turns out not to be a language at all, but on the contrary a massive reaction against an encrusted, rigidly structured, traditional manner of expression (and prayer). A reaction, need it be repeated, in the name of spontaneity, authenticity and immediate expression of the religious emotions of the hour. It is not my insight which is here important but rather the fact that I feel myself driven or fixed (by the spirit) to express some of my feelings. Charismatics do not articulate something that they have learned from someone else; they spontaneously pour forth whatever is moving and touching them here and now. There is a danger that they may come to find the experience of being moved more important than he who touched or moved them.

One enjoys music simply because it is beautiful. The person who attempts to experience being touched by God as a sort of ointment

9. See F. Morton, *A Nervous Splendor, Vienna, 1888–1889*, New York, 1980, 143ff.
10. R. Laing, *The Politics of Experience*, 35.

for the soul, because it increases one's charity or heightens one's awareness, runs the risk of finding oneself on the same path as the man who smothers his wife with hugs and kisses only because he finds that it is a fabulous experience for himself. A kiss, like the whole of human sexuality in fact, is first of all a sign or a language by which an attempt is made to give expression to something deeper (unless one makes of it a pure physiological pleasure mechanism, just as in the way some people "perform their devotions" because it makes them feel holy!). In that sense the authentic love relationship between man and woman serves as a better model for describing the relationship between God and humanity than the bond between a music lover and his or her favorite composition.

4. Intimacy Made Something Vulgar or Promiscuity

In addition to the purely operational character of modern language and to the distaste which many young people have for correct language training, there are three other reasons which make it difficult to talk about God in contemporary language. To begin with there is the modern tendency to vulgarize what previously was intimate: they let it all hang out. As a result true intimacy is a scarce commodity. Then we have the inner word hushed, and thirdly the poetic word has been systematically replaced by the "businesslike communication."

In regard to the vulgarization of language Baudrillard speaks of "the cult of the so-called integrity" and of "the duty to engage in dialogue at all costs."[11] All cultures have subjects which are simply *not* discussed. This may be due to an exaggerated respect, awe or shame, or to the fact that it is thought that there are certain things which on principle should not be spoken of and that is that. People differ on this point. What one person holds to be of too intimate a nature to be the subject of public discussion, another person will not be bashful to explore in every detail because in their view "it must be possible to talk about everything." This latter approach is very typical of our culture. There is nothing which people ought really keep to themselves. Inhibitions must be overcome. Testimonies, honest and open dialogues, "mise en commun" and "sharing" will see to it. A flood of diaries and memoirs "reveal" discreet happenings behind the scenes. Television interviews with delicate and impertinent questions

11. J. Baudrillard, *La Société de Consommation*, Paris, 1970, 277–278.

being fired at the talk-show guest (which leave no stone unturned) are eagerly followed. On the other hand one can observe an increasing incapacity to express in words what it is precisely one is feeling, what one means or is experiencing, at least in that "direct" language which one likes to call "free, frank and uncomplicated." Modern persons like straight talking but are singularly inept when it comes to putting more intimate or deeper feelings into words. The problem as to what one ought to discuss and what not is solved in our day: one must talk about everything because that helps to liberate one. The question of *how* this should happen is also obvious: it must be honest and open, even at the expense of becoming brutal or crude since this is in any case a sign of candour and authenticity.

Our linguistic conventions are changed thus. We are now being asked to talk about things about which in the past we were asked to keep quiet. We are, namely, being advised to "come clean" about those facets of life which in most other cultures people cover with the veil of discretion. Think just of sex, the social taboos (and there are many of them, e.g., defecation, body odour or the most recent hospital bulletin of the king who has just had an operation) and those realities which particularly appeal to the archetypical unconscious (e.g., blood, destruction and other things "one does not like to have discussed at the dinner table"). It is interesting in this connection to compare the traditional use of the neutral colour white, symbol of hygiene and disinfection, in places one used to prefer to keep at a distance from the indiscreet eye (e.g., sanitary towels or bandages, underwear, sheets, pills and culinary dishes) with the blaze of colour which now decorates and makes attractive our bedroom and bathroom. Everything may and ought to be on display and seen. The greatest of all possible discretion had to be shown when it came to discussing religion. Here silence and diffidence were appropriate. The Jews were not even permitted to pronounce the name "Yahweh." And yet, this point too has become a subject for dialogue. No longer is it a case that one keeps quiet inside a church. The tourist guides take up where the sister "animating" the liturgy leaves off.

Are there any right-minded persons to be found, wonders G. Steiner, who will not feel themselves almost physically ill at all this verbal exhibitionism? Do people not realize that there is a total disparity between the unique character of my innermost feelings and the tired old clichés which are being used day by day? "It is almost intolerable that needs, affections, hatreds, introspections which we feel to be overwhelmingly our own, which shape our awareness of identity and the world, should have to be voiced—even and most absurdly when we speak to ourselves—in the vulgate."[12] As if this were even possible. Everyone knows that there are certain parts of another's anatomy that one simply does not touch, without at least running the risk of being considered extremely improper and shameless. One can also touch people with words. One can pry into a person's spiritual and religious intimacy by, for example, bringing up certain subjects and inducing too delicate answers. One encounters this type of effrontery generally in people who know absolutely no religious or spiritual intimacy. Pornography and spiritual exhibitionism often tend to run on parallel tracks in our culture. Only the materialist will tend to consider physical prostitution the worse of the two evils.

As a believer it is of course perfectly possible to demur when occasions for these public confessions arise. Language is—leaving aside the unconnected word-salad of the seriously mentally disturbed—a social phenomenon. No one invents one's own language. One learns to think in and speak an already existing language. There is no way one can undo the situation whereby, whether we like it or not, the language we are obliged to use in order to talk about religion is a language which is constantly being used in a profane context. There are no longer any words which are holy or exclusive. Words which in days of yore were reserved exclusively for the area of the most intimately personal and for such things as could not adequately be expressed (e.g., the sex life of a married couple or the sexuality of a celibate religious), these words have now become the common parlance of T.V. reporters and journalists thanks to a systematic and conscious promiscuity. Everyone has the right to use all the words in the dictionary if they want to. Everything has to be brought within everybody's reach. Whatever cannot be made perfectly clear to everyone is anachronistic or esoteric.

The difficulty is that by very definition God is completely beyond human "reach." Either one has consequently reduced all talk of God to the most generally understandable things (e.g., his moral exhortations to justice and neighbourly charity, or that "unforgettable person" that was Jesus Christ) or the curtain of silence and "the cloud of unknowing" falls over the religious domain.

It is no accident that the translation of the numinous Latin liturgy

12. G. Steiner, *After Babel*, 175.

into a comprehensible vernacular and the transformation of the solemn, stately language of the King James Bible into "Good News for Modern Man" was also felt to be required just at the same moment as all the sexual terminology (which for centuries was consciously kept shrouded in mystery by the use of Greek and Latin terms) was about to be translated into functional day-to-day language. Both sex educationalists and liturgical commentators are advocates of speaking a direct, sensible language everyone can understand and of calling a spade a spade. It goes without saying that an unprejudiced instruction of a child and the teaching of the gospel to a member of the faithful is not only a positive but also a necessary task. It is a matter of some considerable rejoicing that this can happen in our own day. And yet in reality a great deal more (or a great deal less) has happened than that.

One not only speaks in clear and direct language; one often tends to reduce a complex reality to something rather banal. It is correct to say that a crystal vase is basically no more than "a system of electrons which are separated from one another and inter-react with each other in a statistically quantifiable condition of motion." The question is, though, whether this description—however exact and scientific the terminology used may sound—is adequate to describe the beauty of an Empire vase.

We know that the friendship between Freud and Jung was seriously disrupted by a deep difference of opinion concerning "sexual instruction." According to Freud, an eight-year-old child ought to know everything. Jung believed this to be impossible. By "knowing everything" Freud understood an acquaintance with certain physical practices as well as with some specific glandular and muscular conditions. In other words, the complex and poetic reality that is love is here reduced to a few biological processes. By the same token one could ask oneself whether religion, as it is being brought closer to the life of everyday, has not in reality become little more than generous commitment to improving the lot of the poor and a moral code for social justice.

Those who brutally trivialize the first promptings of love in the heart of a young person by using such psychological labels as "puppy love" are comparable to certain professional evangelists who reduce religion to a certain number of moral principles which "say it all" and by which they smite the heart of the true believer. "It says it all" is unavoidably a lie. Moreover, the world is made up of much more than just sayable things. And certainly it is made up of more than those things which are scientifically quantifiable. (This is, in fact, the reason why science is constantly carrying out research). There is that whole area of reality to which reference can only be made with the help of sensitive symbols and figurative language. The visible and the sayable are but an allusion to the transcendental and inexpressible.

Even on the purely human level it is quite impossible to say everything. Why do self-respecting persons cover up certain parts of their anatomy as well as certain aspects of their interior life? Why is modesty not necessarily just a puritan inhibition? Physical modesty does not mean that certain parts of my body are impure, dangerous or somehow evil, but rather that I am a great deal more than this visible, tactile, naked body. Diffidence as to my feelings means that I cannot say everything. This indicates that I am more, that I feel more and carry within myself more than what I can express in comprehensible language. Consequently, I suggest the existence of that "more" by keeping quiet and by conscious discretion and reserve. I am not ashamed to show my nakedness, although I do find it a nuisance that I may thereby give the impression that now I have revealed all. I know in fact that that is impossible. Between my secret life and my public life lies the zone of my privacy, e.g., "that terrain in which I, however sociable I may be, conserve my deeper peace and my intimacy which I reveal to but one person."[13] What I say and show in public is but the tip of the iceberg. Since Freud appeared on the scene, of course, they would have us believe that there is little under the tips than a few repressed or unconscious desires. Modesty is the realization that a person is more than he or she can actually say, and than a psychologist can describe. It is the awareness that the visible and sayable do not cover the whole of reality. The positivist not only rejects the invisible God but laughs to scorn and makes little of the invisible dimension in humanity. In the best of cases the positivist leaves both areas to the symbolism of poets and romantics.

The result of this exhibitionism in its sexual as well as its religious form (to stick with our examples) is that in his intimate moments with his wife a man can hardly utter a word or make a gesture which he does not see a couple of times every evening on his TV screen performed by some worthless adulterer. The result of this is also that the liturgical words he now hears in the church sound very

13. E. Mounier, *Le Personnalisme*, Paris, 1959, 54–55.

similar to those "comprehensible" words which are being used every day in commercials, the world of show business or on the political hustings. These "ordinary" watered-down words allow one to make little clear beyond a few concrete practical banalities. The indirect suggestive language of poetry has been sacrificed on the altar of clarity. The result is that everything that is said is clear but that the most important dimension is passed over in silence and even its very existence is left hanging in the air. Love is no longer a unique experience since relationships are exchangeable and their expression has become as common as dirt. And religion, too, ceased to be "the most highly individual expression of the most highly individual emotion" since it became a communitarious and contemporary articulation of "something that is of equal concern to us all."

One regularly hears it asked how it is possible to term certain words obscene when after all they do refer to things which were created by God. A word does not sound obscene because God created perverse things but rather because the word or gesture at issue has a given function within a unique and intimate love relationship. Promiscuity is the mother of obscenity. Or to put it the way Simone Weil does: words only sound obscene and are that, too "when one forgets that the language of the bridal suite is not the language of the street." Prayers only sound banal when one forgets that the language of business is different from that used in intimate concourse with the loving God.

Now, where does the urge come from to express how one feels inside, or to tell what one is thinking or missing (instead of reserving this for moments of humble intimacy with the beloved)? To begin with, there is the influence exerted by Freudian psychoanalysis which is in any case a form of induced confession: the underlying conviction of which is that those things have got to be said. In many cases, Freud's method of making the patient conscious through "Aussprache" will have a liberating effect. Long before Freud came along to enlighten us it was well-known that an intimate chat with a friend, an understanding superior or a spiritual director could work wonders. It is only to be expected that the number of patients in psychiatrists' waiting rooms should grow at a time when growing loneliness in the inner city makes real friendship a scarce commodity and when mounting agnosticism reduces the number going to confession or seeking spiritual direction. And yet it would be a trifle naive to ascribe to Freud the achievement of breaking through the puritanic tight-lipped silence of the solid Victorian citizen. On the one hand, this puritan silence was not as widespread as one once thought, and on the other hand, where it existed it was not always just the result of anxiety and inhibitions.

In his work *l'Histoire de la Sexualité*, Michel Foucault rejects the hypothesis of Victorian repression (and mutatis mutandis of the so-called "religious individualism"). The author claims it is simply not true to say that before Freud those in the West did not dare to speak of sex; quite the contrary. They were characterized by an almost obsessional "mise en discours du sexe," "la littérature scandaleuse" and "le besoin de se dire."[14] One has only to think of the excessive sexual detail in the moral theology manuals, to say nothing of bellettrie. The only thing was that all of this took place in an atmosphere of secrecy and mystery. The reason was not so much anxiety as the wish to increase desire, to whet the appetite and stimulate passion. Those in the West were well aware that the secrecy of the forbidden apple was far more appealing to the senses than the "bare facts."

Modern film, literature and photography are becoming increasingly bold because "The collapse of taboos has led to a frenetic search for new shocks, for extremes of speech or behaviour as yet unexploited."[15] In days gone by even the most naive youngster knew that there was nothing which got people so worked up as an artificially heightened atmosphere of forbidden secrecy. In that respect the Byzantine iconostasis or liturgical rood-screen show more anthropological insight than the "house liturgies" so much in vogue among post-Vatican II priests. To say all, and to say it with the same words which everybody uses in public, means imagining less and diminishing the creative phantasy.

The almost rationalistic insistence on "explanation" which has become such a feature of modern-day liturgy has had much the same effect. The numinous mystery which characterized the liturgical action for generations has made way for a demythologized, matter-of-fact language. The whole of the Mass has become "the Liturgy of the Word." What has happened is that a "service of the word" had taken over from a pageant of music, mystery, incense, and ballet, punctuated by periods of silence and performed by principals in ornate vestments, assisted by altar servers in cassocks and surplices. The

14. M. Foucault, *Histoire de la Sexualité, 1, La Volonté de savoir*, Paris, 1976, 21 and 30.
15. G. Steiner, *Eros and Idiom*, in: *On Difficulty and other Essays*, Oxford, 1978, 136.

"celebrants" in many cases are turned into what Saul Bellow, speaking of modern intellectuals, has termed "explaining creatures." According to Denis de Rougemont there was one thing Freud failed to see. He did not appreciate that between the idealistic agapé and physical sexuality there is a third area which has engaged the interest of those in the West for centuries, i.e., poetic eroticism. Eroticism falls into the domain of passionate desire. Between the spirit and the flesh we have the heart. In the West that eroticism was protected and kept alive by a veil of secrecy and nonpermissiveness. Freud broke through this veil. De Rougemont points out that "passion becomes unthinkable in a world in which everything is permitted, because passion always assumes a third obstacle between subject and object, usually of a social or moral kind."[16] In simple terms, genuine love poetry becomes impossible in a permissive world, just the way religious language is completely out of order in a Marxist or Freudian "univers du discours."

The "Totale Aussprache" of intimacy leaves literature with three options. Literature can simply become an initially shocking litany of risky facts. On the other hand, it can repudiate a language which has become vulgar, i.e., it turns its back on the current trivial way of talking and searches for new forms, albeit at the risk of being accused of speaking double-Dutch or a "hermetic" language. Pushed to extremes, this language becomes an "idiolect" (i.e., if a "dialect" is a manner of speech peculiar to a particular, geographically localized group of people, an "idiolect" is the manner of expression peculiar to one individual). One has only to bring to mind the poetry of someone like Mallarmé, Stefan George or E. E. Cummings. The third option is to imitate Hölderlin: one just shuts up. One retreats into silence: "Wozu Dichten in dürftiger Zeit?" Concerning his philosophical writings Wittgenstein expressed the following sentiments to his friend L. Ficker in 1919: "my work consists of two parts: the one presented here plus all that I have not written. And it is precisely this second part which is the important one."[17]

If this pronouncement of Wittgenstein's is something more than a mere pleasantry it is because the tension between what a person knows and what a person says (or *can* say) has always been fruitful. Tolstoy did not waste his time in furnishing a naturalistic feature-by-

16. D. de Rougemont, *Les Mythes de l'Amour*, Paris, 1961, 52.
17. See G. Steiner, *After Babel*, 184.

feature account of his Natasia but by the suggestive power of his art as writer he managed to conjure up in his reader's mind an accurate picture of the girl. So accurate was the picture in the mind's eye that no matter what film actress later attempted to incarnate the role of Natasia later she always fell short, leaving the Tolstoy-fan disappointed that "this was not his Natasia" i.e., this actress is simply not Natasia as his creative imagination—inspired by Tolstoy's poetry—had pictured her. Nevertheless when Tolstoy was writing about his Natasia he had in mind one very specific girl, no one less than his sister-in-law whom he loved passionately. There is a buffer zone of discretion and reticence between what a poet feels in his innermost self and what he writes: "Between the urgent wealth of felt life and the actual idiom of the novel there is a zone of silence, an area of conventional selection in which the novelist's responses—material, psychologically informed, canny as are any of the moderns—are translated into the temperance and conventional indirection of Victorian public speech. But it is just this distance, this close presence of the known but unstated, that gives to the novel its intensity. . . . This effect derives, I believe, from a crucial notion of privacy. There are elements, particularly sexual elements, in their personages which the great novelists fully realize but do not verbalize. They seem to accord to their own imaginings a certain privilege of discretion."[18]

When Agatha Christie was asked in a TV interview what she thought of the mini-skirt as a fashion the old lady replied that she had only one reaction, namely, her regret that it was so unsexy. It was almost devoid of sexual appeal, at least when compared with the impression made upon her in India by the sari, that famous long garment which "revealed virtually nothing of the female body but managed to suggest everything" and thus fire the imagination. "Saying all means imagining less" was a tag of Steiner's. Or to quote McLuhan: a "cool" medium, i.e., "a medium in which a meager amount of information is given and much has to be filled in by the listener . . . . Cool media are high in participation or completions by the audience."[19]

The more explicit one tries to be, the less poetic. Only a person who has become immune to "understatements," poetic allusions and

---

18. G. Steiner, *On Difficulty*, 105, 106 and 133.
19. M. McLuhan, *Understanding Media, The Extensions of Man*, New York, 1964, 23. See also, *Hot and Cool Sex, Cultures in Conflict*, A. and R. Francoeur, New York, 1974, 38–61.

suggestion makes a beeline for the "naked facts." In this respect pornography is the diametrical opposite of poetry, and religious explicitness the opposite of mysticism. Once the Good News for Modern Man becomes translated into a universally accessible jargon, on that account it will virtually cease to make anything more than a superficial impression. In some respects a great writer actually says less and keeps his or her mouth shut more than an open-minded and frank psychologist. One can observe an analogous difference between a mystic and a theologian.

At the present time theologians tend to say a great deal and one can only rejoice in this fact. What they have to say is no longer expressed in esoteric Thomistic jargon, but rather there is a conscious effort to use a conceptual apparatus which is at once more modern and more comprehensive. The "univers du discours" which they generally select is either that of existentialism, depth psychology, Marxism or Oriental religions (unless, like Paul Tillich, they simultaneously pull out all the stops). Whatever changes may be made in the language used, it is essential that theology (and the liturgy which follows so closely in its footsteps) retains the necessary sense of mystery, i.e., the necessary respect and the necessary poetry for a reality which can only be hinted at or suggested indirectedly or symbolically.

Literature "is a setting apart of language from the requirements of immediate utility and communication. It raises discourse above common speech for purposes of invocation, adornment, or remembrance."[20] As it so happens, that is precisely what mystics and people moved by the Spirit have once again been attempting to do with language. The first step is to *withdraw* human words from everyday mundane usage. These words then receive a significance as it were "in the second degree": they become symbols or analogies. They are no longer used simply to communicate facts, but rather to suggest realities which neither human signs nor human language can adequately convey. The words have become poetic in the sense that they suggest to our imaginations that reality which simply defies all attempts to picture it accurately. Moreover, they keep alive the memory of what the invisible God has done for us in Christ.

20. G. Steiner, *The Death of Tragedy,* New York, 1961, 238–239.

5. The Inner Voice Hushed

Having looked at the generally purely operational character of modern linguistic usage as well as at the distaste shown by many of the young for correct orthography, syntax and choice of words, it is essential to draw attention to three other factors which make talking about God in "understandable" language very difficult at the present time. To begin with, there is the vulgarization or promiscuity of intimacy we have just been discussing. Secondly, there is that factor which we called the hushing of the language of inward thoughts or of the "discours intérieur" and thirdly, the reduction of language to pure means of communication. The latter two assertions require a further word of clarification.

People have a habit of talking to themselves (or on their own) and now and then they talk to other people. The only people we generally observe talking to themselves are children and the elderly. Average adults keep a discreet silence about the language of their inward thoughts. One does not hear them telling themselves to screw up their courage, making plans, daydreaming or deciding what they will shortly say to others. They do not tend to speak out loud about their fears, what they have to make a mental note of, their hopes or how they actually reason. This inner language is at least as important and statistically just as regularly resorted to as the language of social intercourse. In other words, language is not only a means of communication with others; language is principally "self-address." Before there is any dialogue there is usually a bit of monologue. The more thoughtful the person, the more intense the preliminary monologue. Before one ever talks to others one has always thought to oneself (in language) first. This is the reason why one can say so much more in a letter (N.B., not blurt out) than in a chat on the telephone. The letter-writer engages in a much longer monologue. One carefully weighs one's words before committing them to paper. Moreover, when writing a letter, one can correct, delete or begin again from scratch if necessary. The letter-writer actually keeps silence a lot, at least for all the outside world will ever know.

It is well-known that at the present time a growing number of people are put off by the time-wasting activity of letter-writing. The telephone is so much faster, easier and, above all, less compromising. A phone call leaves no traces (in every sense of that word). This rather banal phenomenon of our day betrays something much deeper. We experience a radical transition from internal to external use of language. We tend less and less to speak within ourselves or engage in self-reflection. We have increasing difficulty in filling our inner silence, let alone making use of it or simply enjoying it. We just kill it with transistors, with piped music, with work or with "social contacts." Our need to engage in dialogue becomes more and more urgent. Even retreats are now filled with conversation, workshops, exchanges of ideas, communal activities and "mise en commun." The balance between internal and external language has been changed; the balance has been upset. Nobody wants their child to be an introvert anymore. The first priority for children is that they learn how to express themselves. They must "dare" to speak up, to dance and draw. Their drawings are no longer stored in a drawer but are ostensively displayed on the walls of the schoolrooms or kitchen. The child is no longer taught to copy the design or picture which the teacher has drawn on the blackboard. Modern children are encouraged to show what they see, think and feel in their own way. Introspection, meditation, examination of conscience, etc., are considered dangerous. They lead all too easily to fruitless forms of worry and doubt. For that reason they have become replaced in many cases by more extrovert activities, such as collective evaluation and sensitivity-training (by which one learns not so much to develop a deeper or more sensitive conscience as learning to achieve a more adequate expression of our feelings vis-à-vis the outside world). This latter activity is designed to "emancipate humanity from its self-sufficiency" and furthermore to give it at least "a feeling" of contact and solidarity with others.

There is no ideal balance between internal and external linguistic usage. To some extent it is a question of temperament, culture and even vocation. There are certain types of character which can tolerate solitude or being alone more easily, need a greater degree of silence in their lives and actually chronically seek it. Other people need more background noise and atmosphere. A Trappist or a Carthusian is called to speak an internal language (and thus keep external silence) to a greater extent than the busy school chaplain or the kindergarten teacher. And yet there is something more going on. In our day the zone of silence has been radically reduced to a minimum in the same way as the domain of nature has been reduced to a modest strip of "green belt." The clearing of the forest of the inner life has been quite systematic. In contemporary literature, what have James

Joyce, Marcel Proust or Italo Svevo done other than expose the whole personal "stream of consciousness" in the light of public (and publishable) language? In these authors one no longer reads about what their characters did or told one another, but rather what their inner feelings, thoughts, fears and sensations were. Freud's psychoanalysis lent them a helping hand. Freud taught us how in the spoken word we bring to the surface these particular, shameful or confused sensations which we find so difficult to articulate. Freud furthermore warns us that this is salutary and necessary for our general psychological well-being.

But isn't language then actually an I-Thou relationship? (one may ask). Even in this internal language doesn't one usually speak in the second person? Doesn't language have an essentially "dialogical" structure? Does it not always require a partner? Does one not always address oneself to someone? Indeed one does. The structure of language itself leads automatically to the religious dimension. For centuries people have reflected, examined their consciences and given voice to their secret wishes "coram Deo" i.e., vis-à-vis their God. They knew that their silent prayers would be listened to and get a favourable hearing. People took prayer entirely for granted. Prayer made silence not only tolerable but even necessary. The old man's mutterings are seen less as a sign of senility than as a dialogue with the invisible God.

Even if one does not totally disbelieve in the existence of the invisible God, modern people certainly have difficulty in finding him and as a result one cannot cope with silence and fills it with background noise or with social chatter. Since the Enlightenment spiritual notebooks or "soliloquia cum Deo" (Gerlach Peters) have increasingly been replaced by "published" diaries or memoirs. For the religious person silence is anything but emptiness or a psychological vacuum. On the other hand, neither is it a Nirvana in which there is neither thought, desire nor feeling. Silence can be a moment of intense dialogue or conscious communion with Someone. Talking about monks, Rilke addressed these words to God:

Du bist der Zweite seiner Einsamkeit, die ruhige Mitte seiner Monologen.[21]

21. Cf. *Das Buch vom mönchischen Leben, Sämtliche Werke*, I, Wiesbaden, 1966, 19.

The great difficulty confronting modern human beings, including believers, is that they have been reared in an environment in which no one ever introduced them to "inner dialogue" or taught them how to engage in it. It is, of course, impossible to eliminate completely the language of internal speech, but it has lost more and more ground. What survives is easily dismissed as diseased or at least as a possible zone of psychiatric infection. The window to the soul has to be pried open come what may. It is daylight alone which can save us. Modern people find themselve completely at sea when the protective social walls of "contact" fall away. "Our fellow man becomes a scourge when we can't do without him. He becomes indispensible for whoever is lonely. It is this loneliness which thrusts people on one another."[22]

Kierkegaard pointed out that anxiety is that face-to-face confrontation with my empty self-awareness. Without a culture in which silence is an essential feature, (i.e., the silent word and prayer) our consciousness remains irreparably empty as long as the social partner and our fellow humans excuse themselves. The consequence is the celebrated modern duo which raises its head in every psychological desert which we find in today's world: *angst* and boredom. Sartre sums them both up in one word, "la nausée."

In cases where prayer is still discussed the emphasis is on its communitarian dimension. Prayer has to be audible, creative of community and even a charismatic outburst. Prayer is less a dialogue with God than a form of witness to one's fellow human beings. It is an open question as to whether the attention of persons who practice spontaneous prayer is not focused on the formative influence which they would hope to exert on their fellows rather than on the hidden presence of God.

6. Language Reduced to Mere Means of Communication

One final linguistic factor which makes it difficult for modern human beings to speak about God in contemporary language is the reduction of language to a mere communication system. Language is conceived as simply a means of communicating the things which we know to others. In reality, language achieves a great deal more, at least in the vast majority of cases. When a person speaks it is usually to comment on how things ought to be rather than on how they are.

22. H. H. Van den Berg, *Wat is Psychotherapie?*, Nijkerk, 41.

People make plans, discuss projects, express their hopes or articulate their fears, and put their convictions and doubts in words. Language is in the first case "fiction" or poetry. People do not always speak in the indicative mood: they often speak in the imperative, conditional or optative mood. "Statistically, the incidence of 'true statements'— definitional, demonstrative, tautological—in any given mass of discourse is probably small."[23] Generally speaking we do not spend our time discussing things as they are but rather things as they could or ought to be, things that we would like to achieve or things we would wish to avoid. We do not generally talk about what is *hic et nunc*, but rather about what is now past tense but which we want to keep alive in our memory. Words report or communicate not just what is, but they create, avoid, dream, stimulate and suggest a world gone by or one which has not yet come into being.

In our day-to-day use of language the amount of direct information or of "the truth and nothing but the truth" communicated is relatively limited. It is not that the truth is unimportant but rather that it is usually taken for granted. People generally use language in a "projective" fashion. In language they attempt to encapsulate the "not yet" of the future and the "no more" of the past. By means of their language they attempt to extend the parameters of reality, to confer on it an order and form. Through their language the poetic (i.e., creative and constructive) person breaks through the existing order. Language is consequently transcendental in essence. It reaches beyond the already existing to make possible the future or at least impose some sort of order on reality as it develops or comes into being. Language is not merely a snapshot or immediate representation of reality (although it is that, too, especially in the sciences which are concerned with existing "things"). Language creates alternatives. There is something utopian about language. It is creative in the sense that, for example, the words which two lovers speak to one another create the real relationship between them, develop it, injure it or destroy it completely. Starting by being smitten (by physically or psychologically attractive elements, or, to put it another way, by the so-called "coup de foudre"), they build up a more or less deep friendship by their language or by a number of paralanguages such as gestures or gifts. What matters is not so much an accurate representation of the immediate state of their feelings. What really matters is what the pair of

23. G. Steiner, *After Babel*, 220.

lovers actually mean, what they expect of one another and what they wish to spare one another. Conversation with friends will consequently be not so much a psychologically exact description of what one feels for them at the precise moment one is speaking to them, even though this may have its value. Speaking to one another will principally determine what will happen to the relationship in the future and how it will develop. Language has not only a communicative function but also an efficient or "performative" one.

Nowhere is this last fact truer than in prayer. Believers do not really need to inform God of their innermost thoughts and actions. What they actually want to tell God about are their hopes and fears, their desires and loves. The great problem with all of this is that average persons are so empirical and "dinglich" in their approach, are so lacking in imagination, poetic feeling and "insight," and are simply lost for words when it comes to prayer. For this very reason so much human conversation concerns tittle-tattle and contributes little to creating or building up relationships. This is particularly true when people find themselves confronted with God; they are tongue-tied and simply do not know what to say. They find it quite impossible to pray. "The school of prayer" (Guardini) is in many cases boarded up or else transformed into a workshop for social action or philanthropy. The school of inner experience makes way for a "workshop" for external action.

In the language of prayer humanity rejects the so-called fatalistic inevitability of what is currently going on and what already exists in the world about it. It can and must change and improve. As long as people keep that hope and that faith alive—however anxious and doubtful they may sometimes be—prayer is not only possible but even self-evident.

Paul Klee's aphorism that "becoming is better than being" means simply that creation, imagination, dreams, desires and prayer are ultimately more important than a reassuring, exact representation of what already exists. And because humanity knows this in its heart to be true, it keeps on "speaking" and praying.

CHAPTER SEVEN

One God, a Multiplicity of Religions

The apologist Ronald Knox, one of the most celebrated converts from Anglicanism to Catholicism, was of the view that the sharpest attack against Christian faith by its enemies came from the science of comparative religion. He accused that science of having reduced Christianity to no more than one of the many possible visions of God, and to seeing it as just as incomplete as any of its alternatives.[1] It is our view that a scientific comparison of different religions tends on the one hand to highlight the unique and original features of Christianity and on the other to expose possible points of contact between the various faiths. It is no accident, thus, that both R. Girard and R. Zaehner were led to convert to Christianity by their comparative studies of different religions.

The fact that different cultures have different concepts of God is a "scandalum" or a stumbling block in the eyes of many. One culture tends to see God as a stern judge while the other pictures him as a loving father. Some view him as the transcendental "totally other," while for others he is closer to us than we are to ourselves. We should not be surprised by these widely divergent views. Just as a woman is seen in a different light by her husband, her eldest son, her mother, her friends in the hen party, her colleagues or her mother-in-law, so, too, the one and only God is not seen or understood in the same light by all cultures (nor even by all the individuals within the same cultural group). The different people who know this woman see her personality from a different perspective. Their "image" of this woman varies greatly. They all essentially observe the same woman: the same dark hair, the same blue eyes, the same well-shaped figure. They all know this intelligent woman to be somewhat

1. R. Knox, *The Hidden Stream*, New York, 1983, 120.

of a polyglot and in possession of a university degree. And yet there are considerable differences in the way they see this woman, in the degree to which they find themselves on the same wavelength, like her or perhaps even love her. Furthermore, the woman herself is all too aware that some of her "acquaintances" have a totally false picture of her. It is a source of considerable pain to her that there is nothing she can do about this distorted image.

Who actually knows this good woman best? Without doubt those to whom she has made herself most intimately known. In the same way the people to whom God made himself most intimately known (i.e., the Jews, and especially those who were able to recognize in Christ the promised Messiah) are bound to have the most adequate image of God. People will always be understood, judged and responded to in a wide variety of ways. The reason for this stares one in the face: what people feel, think, desire, love and fear in their inner selves remains hidden to outside observers; they can only go on the basis of surmise or guess-work. Observers try to conclude what their inner feelings must be on the basis of a person's behaviour or what he or she says. People will sometimes explain themselves. They reveal themselves. Or at least they bare their breast to a friend or confidant. That is the moment of truth. "Truth comes into being at the moment when a person, separated as he is from the other, does not destroy himself by withdrawal inwards, but speaks to the other." [2]

The great Renaissance humanist Pico della Mirandola demonstrated as early as 1490 that all great religious figures from whatever religion enjoyed essentially the same sort of religious experience. They all drew on a personal view of the *same, one* and eternal God. The fact that their *images* of the *same* God were widely different was not attributable to an error in the religious experience itself (which was actually authentic) but rather to internal limitations in the thought systems of the various cultures in which they lived and the languages in which they had to express themselves. In other words, they simply did not possess a language which was an adequate vehicle for conveying their experience. It was Pico della Mirandola's contention that that "language" in which it was possible to engage in discourse about God was, after centuries of searching and experimen-

---

2. "La vérité surgit là ou un être séparé de l'autre ne s'abime pas en lui, mais lui parle." E. Lévinas, *Totalité et Infini, Essai sur l'Extériorité,* 32.

tation by human beings, actually historically revealed by God himself to the biblical "people of God." It became fully revealed in Jesus Christ. It is only since Christ's time that it has been possible to speak and think adequately about God, albeit by use of symbol and analogy. To put it more simply, in Christ God revealed who he is, how he wants to be called and where he can be found.

The fact that different religions have often gotten into violent and even savage conflicts with one another, however reprehensible it may be, should come as a surprise to no one. People are most ferocious in their defense of that which is most precious to them. The opposite of love is not hatred but indifference. Where tolerance is something more than weak patience it quickly slips into indifference or religious "Gleichgültigheit." Then, indeed, all religions have the same worth. As soon as a man is totally indifferent to what people may say or think about his wife (because as he sees it all opinions deserve a hearing), one thing is abundantly clear: he is no longer in love with his wife. A man who really loves his wife is convinced that nobody knows his wife as well as he does, quite simply on the basis that his love relationship over the years has borne fruit in a growing mutual "revelation" and a deepening intimacy.

All of this should help us to see that when it comes to our idea of God, not only do Muslims see things differently from Christians, but that even within the Catholic family the relationship which Thérèse of Lisieux had with the Lord and the way she spoke or wrote about him was strikingly different from that of the average Carmelite nun of her day. Within any particular religion there are different grades of intimacy with God, just as there are different grades of intimacy in the relationship between a mother and each of her three daughters. It is most probable that the mother loves each of her daughters equally. And yet she may feel that she can talk more openly to one than to the other, because the daughter in question is more understanding or has stronger family ties.

1. What common ground do all the major religions share?

Before plunging directly into an examination of the differences between the various religions, it is important first to determine what they basically have in common. When we speak of "major religions" there are two which do not fall within the compass of this study: the primitive and the perverse religions. Primitive religions are to be found among peoples who are still at a very elementary stage of cultural development. A three-year-old child will naturally know its mother. It enjoys a very intimate relationship with her. And yet no psychiatrist in his right mind would think of consulting the infant so as to arrive at a clinical profile of the woman who is his patient. It was certainly the case in the past that Westerners wrote off as backward or primitive many cultures which in reality were only "different" and very often highly developed, even if not very advanced technologically. Today the shoe is on the other foot. Thanks to a deep collective sense of guilt about his colonial past, those of the West have come to such a romantic glorification of "the noble savage" (Rousseau) that they simply will no longer admit that there are relatively underdeveloped and primitive civilizations. Despite this non judgemental attitude to other cultures we still do find that certain peoples do have such a naive picture of nature and of God that they really cannot qualify as having a scientific or orthodox image of the divinity. By "perverse" religions on the other hand we mean religious cultures which practice and even sanction actions which are manifestly inhuman and unnatural. For example, religions which appease their gods by the human sacrifice of children, ritual mutilation, etc. It is a fact that all religions can slip into excesses and aberrations. Cultures, just like religions, can break loose from their moorings to such an extent that—to borrow a phrase of Freud's—they can "sink into infantile regression." Cultures and religions which are so manifestly in a state of spiritual dissolution need not concern us further.

The experience of God which is to be found in the major religions boils down essentially to a totality of feelings and states of awareness experienced by individuals when they are convinced that they are relating to something "God-like" i.e., an invisible reality which goes completely beyond and transcends everyday human experience. From the phenomenological point of view a religious experience is one which leaves behind time and space and makes one feel the relativity of ordinary worldly experiences (like, for example, illness, success, marital difficulties, etc.). Above all this experience casts one's individual ego in a relative light, it being no longer the most important centre of interest. It dawns on a person, thus, that an eternal reality, unconditioned by time, which cannot be pinpointed on any ordinance survey map nor nailed down to a specific geographic location, really exists. The entire cosmos and the individual "ego" are experienced as relative, i.e., dependent on and pointing towards the absolute. At certain privileged moments of grace the religious individual experiences this absolute as reality and present to him or her. The absolute relativizes (in both senses of the word) earthly reality. The latter enjoys a link with and a relationship to this absolute. Most religions end up discovering that this transcendent or absolute takes the form of a "person." They will speak about God as a Person.

The result of all these experiences of God, be they genuine or illusory, is a particular religious outlook on life or spirituality. What we are dealing with is an attitude which has grown out of experiences with the transcendent, entailing respect for certain principles or particular objects which the religious person will conceive as of optimal importance for a meaningful life because it is this person's belief that they are of cardinal importance as eternal realities. They are matters which concern God.

What do we actually mean by transcending space and time? In contrast with aesthetic experience in which the individual's savouring of beauty is always accompanied by pain and sadness at its transitory nature, the experience of God is not accompanied by a fear that it will soon be over but rather by a serenity which goes beyond time. Goethe's Faust sighed, "Verweile doch, du bist so schön," and Lamartine, transfigured by rapturous contemplation of the beautiful Elvira: "Oh temps, suspends ton vol!" It would seem as if this despondent hope is actually realized, if only for a moment. Time seems to stand still or to lose momentarily its importance. Authentic religious experience is a foretaste of a world without time, i.e., of eternity.

People write about beauty only after their experience of it is over, and they describe it largely because it is so fragile and fleeting. It is for that reason that they try at least to recapture the original experience. In one's experience of God, on the other hand, a person realizes the existence of a fascinating reality, a reality which does not slip through one's fingers but which becomes more and more real and is, to put it in a nutshell, eternal. Consequently there is no danger that in the long term this reality will vanish into the mist for such a person. The religious person does not feel the frenetic urgency of the photographer who wants to get on film today what one can no longer observe tomorrow with the naked eye.

The Divine is at once experienced as something agreeable, fascinating (Rudolf Otto's "Fascinosum") and awesome (the "Tremendum"). The ratio of these components not only varies from religion to religion but also from person to person within the different religious families. For Muslims, Allah is the fearsome Ruler rather than the gentle Father he is for Christians. A Catholic like Julien Green who has a pronounced streak of Jansenism in his make-up is more sensitive to "The Tremendum" than Thérèse of Lisieux whose image of God encouraged total loving confidence and security.

Rudolf Otto's diptych of the sacred as something which exercises a fascination at the same time as instilling fear has won wide acceptance, yet for two reasons it represents an oversimplification. First, what he claims to be true of the sacred is actually a feature of every human relationship, at least if it has any depth to it. My friend possesses qualities which fascinate me. And yet in me there is also a feeling of awe in his regard: my friend is the last person in the world in whose eyes I would wish to make a fool of myself or to behave like a fool. There is too much at stake in the opinion which he holds of me. I hold his opinion as in a certain sense "sacred." Secondly, what people inwardly feel in regard to their friends as well as vis-à-vis God varies greatly from one person to the next and it is impossible to lump these highly individual feelings all together. Just as each individual friendship is unique, so too each relationship with God. The widest possible range of emotions has been involved in the way different people have related to God. There is virtually no feeling or emotion which the adherents of one or other religion have not felt or experienced in regard to their God. In most of the world's major religions we can thus discover a complex range of emotions which characterize the way their faithful have at some stage or other related to their God. "In any single life this sentiment is almost certain to be more complex, more subtle, and more personal in flavour, than any single definition of religion can possibly suggest. . . . It is sheer presumption to suppose that one formulation captures the completeness or precise emphasis of the sentiment as it exists in any single mature adult."[3]

The fact that God transcends space and cannot be localized means that his presence is impossible to pinpoint geographically (however much humans may tend to tie God to a particular place such as an icon, a holy mountain or a piece of broken bread). It was the mystic poet William Blake who said that God was always everywhere, even in the smallest and most imperceptible object, even in the most banal everyday reality:

3. Gordon Allport, *The Individual and his Religion*, New York, 1978, 65.

To see the World in a grain of sand
And a Heaven in a wild flower,
Hold Infinity in the palm of your hand
And Eternity in an hour.

All of this helps us get a clearer picture of what it is that makes Christianity unique. In the person of Christ God *enters* time and space. This happened "in the days of Herod the King" (Matt 2:1) and in the Promised Land of Israel. Through this event both history and matter, i.e., time and space, are endowed with religious significance. History can thereby become "salvation history" and material reality take on a sacramental meaning. God lets Himself be discovered *within* time and space. This meeting occurs in the day-to-day history of my personal fidelity and sinfulness in certain sacramental places and encounters.

Generally speaking we experience beauty in nature or in some cultural achievement such as a symphony, a Gothic Cathedral, or a painting. Where exactly does an individual experience God? To put it more bluntly, in what sort of objective situation or on the basis of what type of subjective disposition have the major religions generally tracked down God? *Where* did they meet him and how exactly did they feel or react to this encounter? We have here, clearly, two questions in one. First, in what type of situation or object does the religious person generally experience the transcendent? Secondly, what are the subjective needs or the psychological motivation which move them in their search for the divine?

Where the first question is concerned it is necessary to draw attention to four archetypal realities or human phenomena through which people of all religions seem to arrive at an experience of God.

To begin with, most people are inclined to discover the transcendent in the unusual, the extraordinary, or the inexplicable. One has only to think of illnesses suddenly cured, the birth of triplets, a lunar eclipse, an outbreak of plague or a prolonged drought, etc. Human beings who are generally keen to create order and regularity, [surveyability] in the cosmos are quick to notice that certain things and events are beyond their reach or at least so overwhelm them that they cannot quite "grasp" them. They do not quite "comprehend" them. They do not appear to be regular, "natural" phenomena. They therefore explain them as being of "supernatural" origin. They perceive the gods intervening in the normal business of day-to-day life.

The gods have their reasons for this intervention. It must be possible for people—in particular, priests and fortunetellers—somehow to decipher these reasons so that they can be borne in mind, and this is usually done through religious customs or rituals. For example, people fall on their knees and pray for rain or for the plague to cease. This is, in fact, the reason why contemporary humanity, whose control capacity and scientific insight has increased so enormously, is less and less inclined to resort to the "working hypothesis God" (Bonhoeffer), i.e., to detect the gods at work in day-to-day affairs. Cosmic events are by no means as mysterious and elusive of explanation as primitive human beings originally believed.

In the second instance, people tend to seek the transcendent in the high points of life: births, initiation into adulthood, marriage, illness or death. Even people who are not terribly religious are still inclined to believe that these great events in their and other's lives involve God some vague way. For that reason these occasions are enhanced by a sacral flavour and give some sense to religion. Even for those people who are not regular churchgoers there is nothing to lose in having a christening, a church wedding or a religious funeral. It would seem as if the shade of "le pari de Pascal" raises its head again here: one just never knows.

Thirdly, we have nature (e.g., stars or astrology, mountains, trees, the sea, etc.) as well as culture (e.g., the musical ecstasy in which music-lovers forget themselves so that their spirit can rise to loftier heights, regardless of whether we are thinking of a Woodstock-style pop festival, the throbbing rhythm of tribal Bantu dancing, or the melody line of Mahler's Eighth Symphony).

A final factor is that series of realities which psychoanalysis has shown appeals to the subconscious (and consequently the mysterious) dimension in humanity. In this regard, it suffices to think of, e.g., blood (whether of sacrificial offerings, menstruation or heroes slaughtered on the battlefield), fire, water, sex, unicorns, monsters, etc.

It deserves to be recalled that it is impossible to reduce Christianity to a type of naturalistic, purely human, archetypical path to God. Modern Christians whose outlook is humane and whose faith is mature could certainly make their own the Ignatian motto: "In omnibus quaerant Deum." They will search out God *everywhere* and will be able to find him. For them, God is no longer tied to spectacular moments or those which fire their imagination. Adult Christians will look for God in the "ordinary" events of their day-to-day lives. They even look for God in silence. If we look at the history of Christian spirituality, it is striking how we can discern a marked development from a stage of childish exteriorization (in pilgrimages, public penances, clothing or ornamentation of statues and icons, processions, etc.) to a more adult spiritualization or interiorization. In this way we see how external and material circumstances become less and less relevant. The God who reveals himself in Christ comes to us not to fulfill our chronic needs, to provide an answer to the questions which puzzle us, or to give a sacred stamp to our family feasts. He lets himself be found, to borrow Ruusbroec's words, "whenever He wants, by whomever He desires and in the way He wishes."

There was then a second question: in what subjective circumstances are people inclined to turn to God? What precisely moves them to shift their gaze from day-to-day life and fix it on the Transcendental? What psychological developments prompt an individual to pray? There are three factors which often tend to lead to piety in an individual. To begin with there is the problem of suffering and death. Then there is the natural aspiration to higher things of life, for example, beauty, truth, justice, holiness, etc. And then there is that perpetual gnawing question as to the meaning of life.

Furthermore, it is a characteristic of an adult faith that it is no longer tied to such psychological motives. Genuine prayer is not just a reaction to psychic stimuli but rather an answer to a moment of grace, even if the old Latin maxim "Gratia supponit naturam" still applies.

The adult thus develops "a religious sentiment that has thus become largely independent of its origin, functionally autonomous, and cannot be regarded as a servant of other desires, even though its initial function may have been of this order."[4] It is normal that a child should only pray for a white Christmas, the recovery of his hospitalized father or a nice present from Santa Claus. Adult faith is not just a palliative in the ups and downs of ordinary life, nor an added extra to increase our material or psychological comfort. Just like true friendships, a mature faith becomes more spiritual with the passage of the years. The person of prayer turns more and more towards God himself and craves less and less his gifts, help or intervention. The

4. Gordon Allport, *The Individual and his Religion*, New York, 1978, 72.

loved one wins the upper hand over my psychological need for a little friendship.

2. Different Types of Religion

How would one go about classifying the different world religions on the basis of their respective ways of experiencing the transcendent? To put it another way, what types of religion are there? In what different ways have various peoples and cultures down through the ages pictured God or the divine?

As we have already seen, the total absence of religion is a very rare phenomenon in the history of civilization. It was only when ancient Greek civilization was well on the wane, when the Roman empire was in its last days and then increasingly since the emergence of the Enlightenment (+ 1750) that one encounters cases of pronounced atheism. Widespread atheism is a very recent phenomenon.

The major world religions fall into two principal classes: those whose relationship with the transcendent is characterized by "magic" on the one hand, and on the other by "religion." The magical individual sees the divine as a power he can exploit if the necessary "know-how" is present, and yet as a power which deserves a healthy respect. This fact explains the combination of a series of magic rituals with a number of taboos or safety measures against the anger of evil spirits. The "religious" individual, on the other hand, wants to enter into a relationship with God (cf. Lactantius' etymology of the word "religio": "re-ligari" means a continually renewed bond with God).

The magical religions seek above all to influence the deity. They start with trying to put him in a good mood so that they can then use him and get him to realize human aims and grant such basic requirements as the cure of illness, rain, fertility, victory in war, etc. The next step is to distract the divinity's attention, divert his anger and neutralize his power to inflict punishment. This latter measure is generally taken by the offering of sacrifice or the performance of prophylactic rites. What magical individuals try to do is "wrap God round their little finger." They seek to manipulate the divinity (where favourable spirits are concerned) and to rock him to sleep or distract him (when it is a matter of evil spirits).

Given that what we are dealing with here is a primitive or even perverted form of religion, magical religion pops up with great regularity throughout history, albeit usually among tribes with a very low level of culture.

Positive magic is worked by magicians or shamans. They are especially selected intermediaries who can force or persuade the higher powers to grant salvation to the people of their tribe. With this end in view they have up their sleeves a range of esoteric tricks and rites. They are generally called upon to heal the sick, to see to it that such activities as the hunt, war and human reproduction have a favourable outcome, and to help the tribe come to terms with such unexpected developments as a prolonged drought or the death of a tribal chieftain. When performing their official functions magicians usually fall into a trance. They momentarily lose their own identity. This explains the widespread use of masks, vestments, leopardskin or eagle feathers, a secret language, etc. An external power or spirit rubs them. They are conscious of actually being "possessed."

In negative magic, on the other hand, the transcendent is conceived as dangerous, malicious and malevolent, impure and even contagious. It is quickly declared taboo (a term which in Polynesian signifies at the same time "sacred and forbidden"). The transcendent is no longer called God. It has become instead a diabolic power exercised by evil spirits. The magician thus resorts to rituals of purification, sacrifices and prohibitions so as to guarantee protection against these dangerous invisible forces.

It will by now be obvious that magical peoples treat the divine as a finite reality, i.e., as something which can be tamed and even manipulated on condition that the correct rituals are used. One can actually exercise control only over something of which one is ultimately independent. In contrast with "religious" peoples, those who work with magic through the magician do not, strictly speaking, seek contact with the divinity. The magician does not actually pray. Through application of a range of spells and ritualized practices they seek rather to create a secure, neatly arranged, comprehensible world which is free of unpleasant surprises and catastrophes, natural or man-made. They turn to the gods if suffering from a physical ailment, if their fields could do with rain or if they want to avert a "blight upon their house." Magical religion actually has a rather poor opinion of the gods. Thanks to a couple of ingenious little tricks, humanity is able to master the gods in much the same way as the fleet-footed toreador can mesmerize a raging bull. "The sacrifice (which was of enormous complexity) came to have efficacy of itself: it compelled the gods to accede to the will of man. Thus, through the sacrifice, man himself had become a god: given the correct performance of the ritual he could become the master of Nature."[5]

Magic plays the same role in primitive society that science plays in our modern culture: it looks for a safer world, where it is easier to forecast events, where unpleasant surprises and impenetrable mysteries are greatly reduced. While the magician resorts to rituals, the scientist works with hypotheses, experiments and the laws of physics.

Despite all the magician's best efforts there remains a whole range of phenomena and events which the magical individual finds odd, inexplicable and mysterious. For this reason, just like a child, they think along "animist" lines. What this means is that they conceive inanimate objects (such as thunder, a tree or poison) as persons, spirits or souls precisely because, like human beings, they are unpredictable. It is typical for children to rebuke "a naughty table" which "deliberately sets out to hurt someone," not realizing, of course, that a table is not a free agent and hence is incapable of doing either good or evil. The table is a purely predictable physical object without a "soul." The child sees the table in an "animist" light; the adult sees it from a purely "functional" perspective. "Realities whose behaviour it is impossible to predict we generally consider to be persons and treat them as such. That which is not totally transparent possesses an inner quality which is not completely penetrable to our stare, such as for example a soul. For that reason primitive man tends as a rule to see reality in "personal" (or animistic) terms. The sophisticated products of modern society tend to see things very differently. For them all terrestrial realities are, at least in principle, transparent and controllable."[6] There is even a danger that they will conceive of other human beings as "things" to be used, manipulated and controlled. The modern "homo technicus" is the diametrical opposite of the primitive animist.

All of this also helps explain the tendency of modern human beings to consider *all* religions as superfluous and illusory. When atheists talk about religion they immediately think of magic religions. By very definition for them religion is a magical perspective on reality. They would contend that the inexplicable, the incurable or the unattainable should not drive us to God as a refuge. It is much better to

5. R. C. Zaehner, *Concordant Discord, The Interdependence of Faiths*, Oxford, 1970, 62.
6. W. Pannenberg, *Was ist der Mensch?*, Göttingen, 1968, 25.

use a bit of horse sense and exercise patience by turning to science which will not only reduce bit by bit the realm of mystery, but is in principle capable of eliminating it altogether. There will simply be no more room left for gods. The only thing which the atheist has actually managed to demonstrate is that the magic religions are stillborn children and that a true faith in God will consequently have to be "religious" (see below) unless it wants to remain illusory, infantile and primitive.

What is really striking about modern human beings is that even if their attitude to God does not show symptoms of magic (in many cases there is no relationship with God to speak of) they make every effort to control, use and manipulate their *fellows*. Just like its magical forefather, modern humanity, too, cherishes and works for safety and security (e.g., in marriage, business affairs and in any relationship in which it is involved). The magical person deeply mistrusted the gods and therefore resorted to all these safety devices. As a result, he or she made a life of prayer or a relationship of love impossible. Because modern humanity is distrustful of the colleague, the partner or the superior, it develops a series of psychological defense mechanisms. "In their efforts to make themselves safe, people are by the same token making relationships with their most intimate human acquaintances virtually impossible."[7] In other words, just as magic makes genuine prayer impossible, so too the application of psychological techniques to one's fellows eliminates the possibility of true friendship. God and our fellows are not things but persons. At the heart of every person there lies a mystery. It is for that reason that a personality is so fascinating and is always able to surprise us. Religion and friendships do not serve any "purpose." Whenever we attempt to "use" one of the higher or more important of life's gifts, they are destroyed by our very touch and they slip away like water through our fingers.

Magic is in the blood in every generation. It keeps bobbing up, even in the great religions. Protestantism in the sixteenth century was in many respects a massive protest against the growth of magical practices within the late medieval Catholic Church. One has only to recall the pseudo-medical use of reliquaries or of certain sacred images, the touching or kissing of blessed objects, the beneficial effects of physical penances or pilgrimages, or of the spiritual banter in-

7. Ibid., 27.

volved in the careful mathematical totaling up of indulgences. What Protestantism tended to overlook in its reaction to medieval Catholicism was the true meaning of "incarnation," i.e., the presence of God within the world of matter. God, after all, "became flesh." It is thus that a purely spiritualized Christianity is impossible or at least very incomplete. Mozart dismissed Protestantism "because Protestantism was all in the head."[8]

The fact that there is a divine presence in material reality does not naturally imply that one ought to see sacred things or sacraments as "utilities" for spiritual or physical well-being. The person who goes to communion with a view to a cure or an intensification of the spiritual life does not yet fully understand what exactly a sacrament is. One does not make friends with someone just to receive presents, even though a friendship which never expresses itself in the exchange of gifts or in the occasional physical gesture of affection will eventually wither and die.

In "religious" religions humans attempt above all to enter into contact with God. They try to get a taste for that fascinating reality which transcends their ordinary day-to-day existence. In order to establish that desired contact or develop that taste they use symbolic words (prayers) and symbolic gestures (rites, sacraments, liturgy or cultic rituals). It is possible to distinguish two types or tendencies in religious experience, depending on whether the emphasis is placed on the moral (or behavioural) or on the mystical (or experiential) dimension.

Tolstoy, liberal Protestantism and liberation theology belong to the first type. They principally strive for a better and more just society in this world. For them God's will is a matter of a human life which is truly human, honest and committed in a spirit of openness. Their motto is "Action, not words!" Or, to paraphrase Marx, "We've talked enough about reality, it is now high time that we started to do something about changing it." For Christians this change should be modelled on the values of the gospel. With the gospel as their vade mecum, the committed Christian is extremely sensitive to the social dimension, while the Buddhist ethic, for example, will emphasize personal fulfilment, spiritual equilibrium and a state of harmony with one's natural environment and one's fellow human beings.

Persons inclined towards mysticism on the other hand seek "con-

8. Thomas Merton, *Conjectures of a Guilty Bystander*, New York, 1966, 11.

templation" in the etymological sense of the word: living together
with God in one and the same house or temple. Their spirituality is
one of prayer, asceticism, flight from the world, and abandonment to
Divine Providence. It goes without saying that what we have been
considering are actually two necessary aspects of the one, single
Christian and religious lifestyle. Both action and contemplation are
necessary. Both the humanistic and divine dimensions must be present. A better world here and now does not exclude eternal life in the
world to come.

A threefold distinction must be made within the "religious" faiths:
the third will transpire as the most important. To begin with, there
are national and universal (or supranational) religions. Then there are
the polytheistic and monotheistic religions, and finally the pantheistic
and dualistic (or relational) religions.

As far as our first distinction is concerned, primitive religions are
always national (and vice versa). Peoples have their own gods. They
conceive of their God as a sublimated collective projection to power,
e.g., in a totem or a sacred animal. The gods must above all protect
their people against their enemies. This deviant tendency pops up
again and again in all the great religions. One only has to think of
the Muslim *jihad* or "holy war," of Lepanto or the destruction of the
Aztec idols. And yet the great religions are genuinely supranational,
i.e., not bound by or confined to one particular people or culture. As
of the tenth century B.C., the Jews already venerated Yahweh as the
one, unique and universal God who—despite all nationalism, against
which Christ, too, had to take a stand—through Judaism reached out
to *all* peoples. Therein lay the root of Jewish proselytism. It goes without saying that an essential feature of the supranational religions
should be a sense of mission and conversion. Even if Hinduism, for
example, never felt any great need to spread itself beyond the bor-
ders of the Indian subcontinent, it does consider itself the most noble
response to the human experience of God and other religions as but
a pale imitation of Hinduism. Any Hindu missionary work or pro-
selytization which we find going on at the present time in the cities
of the West is usually carried out by white, ex-Christian converts to
Hinduism or by Indians who have become familiar with the customs
of Western civilization. Authentic Hinduism is blissfully unconcerned
about making converts.

Buddhism, Islam and Christianity from their very beginnings
spread to *different* cultures, races and language groups, even if they

made strenuous efforts to conserve one common cultic language (very often one which was not understood by their faithful, e.g., Arabic in Indonesia, Sanscrit in Japan or Latin in the West). Where the difference between polytheism and monotheism is concerned, it would seem that in most cases this difference is more apparent than real. All great religions are essentially monotheistic, i.e., they recognize only one transcendent Divinity of which the various "gods and godesses" are no more than popular representations, "incarnations" or images. So, too, the various "our Ladies" of Lourdes, Fatima, Czestochowa or Guadalupe are all historical and geographical variants of one and the same sacral person. Max Müller termed this phenomenon a "kathenotheistic tendency in all religions," i.e., the pull towards one God. Thus we read in the old Indian Rig-Veda: "They call that (ultimate reality): Indra, Mitra, Varuna, Agni or the heavenly Garutmat. All of this is but one reality which wise people invoke by a variety of names."[9]

Dag Hammarskjöld, whose idea it was to set aside a special room in the UN headquarters in New York as a place of prayer or meditation and stand a block of unworked stone in the centre of the room, explained his intention as follows: "We may see it (the stone) as an altar, empty not because there is no God, not because it is an altar to an unknown god, but because it is dedicated to the God whom man worships under many names and in many forms."[10]

Despite Hammarskjöld's noble intentions the fact remains that people have a natural tendency towards religious diversification. The pious can well consider our Lady of Lourdes a more powerful advocate than our Lady of Fatima. And yet no family of religions has so strongly defended the monism of God as the Judeo-Christian and the Muslim (which, as we know, contains Jewish, Christian and local pagan elements). In this respect one could supplement Hitler's famous quip that "conscience is a Jewish invention" (which, like all successful quips is strictly speaking, incorrect, yet contains an element of truth) with George Steiner's overstatement: "Radical monotheism is a Jewish invention." It is Steiner's belief that an animism with a panoply of Gods is "a natural human reflex." A monotheism with a divinity like Yahweh, of whom no carved or pictorial image can be made, entails a sacrifice which runs against humanity's most natural needs.

9. Rig-Veda, 1:164:46. Quoted by R. Zaehner, *Concordant Discord*, 62.
10. D. Hammarskjöld, *A Room of Quiet*, in: *Servant of Peace*, ed. Wilder Foote, New York, 1962, 160.

Steiner believes that it was simply asking too much of humanity and ended up driving many, Jew and Christian alike, into atheism. "No fiercer exigence has even been passed on the human spirit, with his compulsive, organically determined bias towards image, towards figured presence. How many human beings have even been capable, could be capable of, housing in themselves an inconceivable omnipresence? To all but a very few the Mosaic God has been from the outset, even when passionately involved, an immeasurable Absence."[11] According to Steiner this absence led to the situation where humans would actually declare that God "dead." Practical atheism is now carried right through to become the logical *terminus* of intellectual reflection. In other words, people start by conducting their daily lives as if no God existed even though one still claims to "believe" in all sorts of vague ideas and convictions. The second logical step is to abandon these hollow theories. The person who happily lived without God has now become a convinced atheist. Whatever cannot be expressed in terms of a concrete image simply cannot exist.

We know of course that in the Christian view of things God is in no way a faceless, monolithic abstraction to say nothing of an "immeasurable Absence," but rather a Trinitarian relationship of Persons united in love. Christ revealed the true face of God, even if it remains in many ways mysterious, in human words, images and symbols. The poet Rilke, whose vision of the divinity was un-christian, pantheistic and devoid of personality, wrote of his lonesome God as follows:

> Dir war das Nichts wie eine Wunde,
> du kühltest sie mit der Welt.

To put it in plainer terms: just because your loneliness had become unbearable, God, you created the world. Yet every Christian familiar with the doctrine of the Trinity knows that there was never a time when God was lonely and consequently he never "needed" the world. From all eternity he was a real relationship of Persons with Love as its bond. It is incorrect therefore to compare God to a woman who in her loneliness would "at least like to bring a child into the world" but rather we would compare him with a happy wife or partner in love who, in a superabundance of love, turns her mind

11. G. Steiner, *In Bluebeard's Castle*, 38.

to children (and has actually always had them at the back of her mind). "Even before the world was made, God has already chosen us to be his through our union with Christ, so that we could be holy and without fault before him. Because of his love God had already decided that through Jesus Christ he would make us his sons—this was his pleasure and purpose" (Eph 1:4-5).

A monolithic, non-Trinitarian deity such as Allah, for example, could not have been a person prior to creation because there was nothing or no one with whom he could have initiated a relationship. There was no one whom he could have known or loved. There was no one to whom he could have offered a gift or from whom he could have elicited a response. Nobody actually yet existed. Allah was a being existing in an infinite vacuum. In contrast we have "the concept of the Trinity which confronts us with the amazing view of a superior being within which persons enjoy a relationship of the deepest intimacy. A being which is by definition the negation of all loneliness."[12] Human beings were created by God in the image and likeness of this loving communication. Without love they just fall down and die.

We come now to a third and final distinction, i.e., the difference between a pantheistic and dualist vision of God. What makes Christianity unique is the fact that, as will be demonstrated in the next chapter, it is neither pantheistic nor dualistic, even though it does possess certain elements of these two extremes.

For the pantheist the unification of humanity with God is so total that the human being actually disappears into God (or into All-embracing Reality) like a raindrop in the ocean. Pantheists have a "cosmic consciousness": in their system God and the universe are coextensive. "The universe is God and . . . God is the universe; a great deal of this is, of course, from the point of view of self-consciousness, absurd; it is nevertheless undoubtedly true."[13] In the opinion of this successful pantheistic author our task on earth exists in raising our self-consciousness gradually to an awareness of unity with the universe and this is achieved by meditation, contemplation, exercise and finally enlightenment. An example of such conscious "disappearance into nature" was the American poet Walt Whitman, even if for him nature was predominantly a matter of sex.

12. E. Mounier, *Le Personnalisme*, 12. Cf. also in: H. Arts, *With your Whole Soul, On the Christian Experience of God*, Paulist Press, Ramsey, 1983, 125–138.
13. R. Bucke, *Cosmic Consciousness*, New York, 1966, 18.

For the pantheist, a human being is simply "a way of being God." Every pantheist could endorse Kloos' verse: "I am a God in my innermost thoughts," at least as long as the indefinite article "a" does not suggest that "yet other Gods" might exist in addition to or outside the universe. Authentic pantheists are thus always very positive about the world of nature. They express their enthusiasm by staring in contemplation at a mountain, a garden, a water lily or a rock. One has only to think of Chinese painting or Japanese gardens. The meditation garden in Buddhist monasteries is supposed to symbolize the universe. The grey gravel is supposed to represent the sea, while the rockery is designed to depict continents and islands in miniature. The famous Chinese floral arrangements, too, (in which diminutive human figures virtually melt away into the vast landscape) symbolize this same absorption of transitory humanity into everlasting, eternal nature. The "I" blends away into the greatness of the all-embracing universe. All that remains in the end is the totality. For that reason there are some who prefer the term "pan-en-henism" (all disappears in the one) rather than the term "pantheism" (all is God) which sounds a little too theistic.

In contrast with pantheism the dualistically oriented religions (e.g., Hinduism) divide existing reality in two, according to various elements: spirit and matter, eternal values and superficial considerations, God and World, soul and body etc. It is the first element in each of these pairs which in their view merits most attention. The second element is purely relative, not to say dangerous. For that reason abnegation is mandatory. In the view of Hindus, for example, individuals must first shed everything which is historic, transitory, material, sensible, earthly or physical before they can concentrate all their energies on the only true reality: the true Self. This "self" is actually God who is present in all in an identical way. For the Hindu, yoga is the ascetical technique which must help a person to arrive at total control over the physical and indifference vis-à-vis "worldly reality." Yoga concentrates the spirit on true reality, i.e., the divine in one. Once material reality has fallen away as in a sort of two-stage rocket, only one reality remains: the true self or God in me.

Finally, it must be said there is one thing pantheistic and dualistic religions have in common. While the human subject stands over against objective reality, the pantheist tends to allow this subject to discreetly disappear into the eternal objectivity by which one is absorbed. Dualists, on the other hand, turn their gaze more and more away from objective reality because in the final analysis only subjects themselves are eternal. For the pantheist the subject disappears (at the end of this earthly life). For the dualist, on the other hand, it is the object which disappears (if not in this life through the discipline of asceticism, then after the last migration of the soul).

It will emerge in the following chapter how it was that Christianity succeeded in a singular fashion in finding a *via media* between the Scylla of pantheism and the Charibdis of dualism. The central and eternal fixed point of reference is the relationship between humanity and God. At no stage is one of the partners integrated into or absorbed by the other. Love is in fact impossible without what Martin Buber called a permanent "I-Thou relationship."

CHAPTER EIGHT

Christianity between the Scylla of Pantheism and the Charybdis of Dualism

The one great question to which the different religions and spiritualities have always given contrasting answers has been: should true believers love the world or should they distance themselves from it as much as possible? Is earthly reality something positive which "God saw that it was good" (Gen 1:20) or should one take heed rather of John's warning in his first letter: "Little children, do not love the world or the things in the world." (1 John 2:15) Pantheists are generally dumbstruck in ecstatic awe of the cosmos. The whole wide universe is God's tangible presence. Dualists by contrast are full of suspicion of the snares and temptations of the world. As a consequence they turn their backs on the world as much as they can and strive to live in a spirit of ascetical detachment. The question which the present chapter seeks to examine is what attitude Christianity has taken to the cosmos down through the ages. Was it principally one of awe and contemplation or was it rather one of caution, detachment, or even rejection? Or was it perhaps an attitude of indifference?

1. Three Christian Attitudes to the World

Broadly speaking, it is possible to discern three major tendencies within Christianity when it comes to attitudes toward 'natural' values. There is first a suspicious and negative stance which we find in the desert fathers of Egypt and which is best summed up in Augustine's famous pronouncement: "Christus mundum de mundo liberavit" (Christ set the world free from all that was worldly). Concepts such as material, worldly, sensual or transitory are pejorative terms. The only worthwile realities are God and the soul. Or, to put

142

it as Plato did: the real world is the world of eternal ideas and not that of appearance or sensible things. The truth in this scheme of things is not found in created reality (which has in any case been tainted from the beginning thanks to the Fall). The truth is only to be found in the inner detachment of the purely spiritual. Life is "spiritual life." All the rest leads sooner or later to death. There is an almost Manichean rift between the good spirit and evil matter. This attitude can probably neatly be explained by the dissolute hedonism which was so characteristic of the last days of the Roman empire, or by the major influence which Stoicism and Neoplatonism exerted over early Christianity. Augustine was a convert who, as he admits in his *Confessions*, had gone from dualistic Manichaeism to a Neoplatonic monism which was sharply coloured by Stoicism. It is important not to forget that Stoicism, despite whatever other connotations it has gained in popular parlance, was a totally materialistic philosophical system. This possibly explains Augustine's later growth towards Plato's radical spiritualism or idealism.

By way of movements which advocated radical detachment this spiritualist vision continued to influence Christian thought and make its mark (one has only to think of the Cistercians, the Spiritual Franciscans and Dominican "idealists" such as Eckhart, Suso, Tauler), effecting the type of rationalism advocated by Descartes, Jansenism and even German idealism. In the longer term this radical spiritualism was to become one of the principal causes of the later reaction of positivism and materialism which are so characteristic of the late twentieth century.

Is it not quite astounding that a man like Francis de Sales should interpret "the beauty of the lilies of the field" as being "a symbolic description of the moral virtues which will decorate the human soul"? Does not one become aware of a strong antipathy to the world when reading Pascal's slightly chilling words: "If a God does exist then we must love Him alone and not creatures." For "all that brings us to attach ourselves to creatures is pernicious, because it prevents us from serving God if we know Him or from serving God if we do not yet know Him."[1] In other words, asceticism and detachment represent the first step towards faith. A writer like Surin was certainly not stepping out of line for his time when he gave the following piece of advice in one of his popular handbooks: "Hate na-

1. B. Pascal, *Pensées*, Paris, 1957, 1203, 1204.

ture, it is doomed to die." Finally when La Reveillière-Lépeaux noted
in his diary that "I perceive only two ideas which can genuinely be
called religious: God and the soul,"[2] not only is God's creation dismissed with a stroke of the pen but one observes to one's surprise
that God and soul are here termed ideas. Nothing could be more
spiritual and less cosmic. This school of thought sees the world as
nothing more than a cursed earthly valley of tears from which one
looks forward with a deep sigh to a heavenly hereafter. Right up to
the present day a lot of Christian devotional literature continues to
be characterized by antiworldly spirituality. In her autobiography the
English poetess Kathleen Raine described the religious attitude and
the outlook of her puritan father as follows: "My father looked for no
earthly happiness; he and his father, and his father's father, had
known that man in this world is 'a stranger and a sojourner'; all he
asked was to perform the task of his life and for him life was precisely that, a task to be performed—sure of the reward of the faithful
servant in another world."[3] Or, to put it another way in the words of
J. Veulemans: "You can easily betray life in the name of a cold God."[4]

The whole conceptual apparatus of the ascetic school strikes one as
very negative, although the etymology of the Greek word "askésis"
referred to a series of values which could hardly be more positive:
training, exercise and improvement. One can compare these ideas to
such Christian concepts as distancing oneself from, offering up, detachment, dying to self, self-abnegation, renunciation, etc. An exaggerated emphasis on such concepts can be misleading because love is
primarily a question of "attaching oneself to" and also because the
law of life involves a struggle against all that is killing or "death-
dealing." In itself renunciation is of course sterile. Very often it is
practiced in a way that is negative and leads to frustration, generally
in the name of a false notion of "altruism." Worse still, renunciation
can be practiced in the name of an egocentric self-pity. It is actually a
Christian's duty to relieve and minimize pain at every possible opportunity, whether it be one's own or another's. One's first duty is,
after all, "to love thy neighbour *as thyself*." Only in a case where suffering seems unavoidable ought it to be lovingly embraced as the
Lord's Cross. In the meanwhile no one is called upon to hammer together artificial crosses nor to knot one's own scourge. Our individual

2. *Mémoires de la Reveillière-Lépeaux*, published by his son, Paris, 1895, II, 166.
3. K. Raine, *Farewell Happy Fields, Memories of Childhood*, London, 1973, 23.
4. J. Veulemans, *Wachtend op een Wonder*, Leuven, 1973, 23.

Cross is placed on our shoulders by the providential action of God himself. Human attempts to imitate God in this regard seem pretty fruitless. Teilhard de Chardin greatly regretted that certain pagan and oriental influences again and again made their mark on Christian asceticism drawing their inspiration from a spirituality much more suited to fakirs than to the freedom of God's children. "The mystical history of the West might be described as a long attempt on the part of Christianity to recognize and separate within itself the two roads of spiritualization, the Eastern and the Western: *suppression* or *sublimation*? To divinize by sublimation—that was the side chosen, following the profound logic of the Incarnation, by the instinct of the nascent world. To divinize by suppression—it was in that oversimplified direction that the accustomed ways of the East exerted their pressure. Until our own day, the two currents can be recognized in the forms of expression adopted by the Christian world—if not in its fundamental, and correctly interpreted, attitude. Use and privation: Christ and the Baptist: attempts have been made to see in this duality two essential and reconcilable components of sanctity. . . . The Hindu saint closes in on himself and drains away his self in order to shake off his integument of matter; the Christian saint does so in order to transfigure matter and allow it to penetrate him (ṡuperindui'—to be 'super-enveloped'). The first seeks to isolate himself from the multiple, the second to concentrate and purify it. . . . If Christianity is to continue to live and be supreme, it must henceforth think and speak, unambiguously and exclusively, the language of the West: it must not resign itself passively, but attack; not ignore, but seek; not despise the tangible universe, but become enraptured by its contemplation and in its fulfilment."[5]

Teilhard affords us a second, and it must be said more positive, Christian view of the cosmos. We find traces of it as early as the dawn of the Middle Ages in the writings of a number of Christian authors. They drew to some extent on Greek philosophy. The pagan Greeks admired above all the perfect order, regularity and beauty of the cosmos. Initially the Greek patristic authors were hostile to this pagan cosmology. They found that the reality of original sin and evil was absent from this pagan admiration of the perfect order and harmony of the universe. Moreover, they warned against a temptation to

5. Pierre Teilhard de Chardin, *Toward the Future*. Trans. René Hague. New York: Harcourt Brace Jovanovich, 1975, 52–53.

make a god of this so-called order or confer a sacred character upon it. They refused to see God in this cosmos as it was only a creation or work of his. Once this pantheistic idolatry of nature ceased to pose a threat towards the end of the Middle Ages (because Christianity had made those in the West sufficiently aware of God's total transcendence), Christian thought began to devote more attention to the wondrous harmony of the universe, and that for two reasons.

To begin with Christian philosophy saw in this order a proof of the existence of a God who was creator as well as ruler of the universe: the so-called cosmological proof of God's existence. Secondly, this order had moral implications. In the area of ethics people had the solemn duty to mirror this natural order and harmony in their own lives or—as people are so fond of putting it in today's jargon—to realize this order in the social and psychological domain. In the social area it was deemed desirable that medieval society be as hierarchically structured as possible. The political system, it was felt, should mirror the cosmic harmony and stability. In the domain of individual psychology each person was expected to have such mastery of their own will, and their own character so well-adjusted that they could fight any irregular or chaotic passions head-on. Here, too, the cosmic order of nature was the ideal on which moral action should be modeled. What for the ancient Greek had been the object of respectful awe and contemplation (i.e., the harmony of the cosmos), became an ethical paradigm for Christians. "A good life" now equaled living according to the natural order. "Unnatural" activities or practices had to be rejected out of hand. The natural law was sacred. This idea was actually not far from the mind of Lao-Tse when he put forward the ideal of the "Tao" or of the attainment of the *via media* between the two principles of yin and yan (and not, e.g., a bitter struggle *against* the evil yan principle). This idea has made its way back into the modern world through Zen Buddhism, mostly in answer to Jean-Jacques Rousseau's call for a "retour à la nature." It is the contention of ecologists that human culture may never fly in the face of nature. On the contrary, it is essential for it to rediscover the natural order and harmony, and then learn to respect it.

On the issue of admiration of the marvelous order in the cosmos there are two pertinent observations. On the one hand there is a creeping danger of a radical conservatism in the religious and ethical domain: keep the beauty of creation in its original beautiful state! On the other hand modern humanity generally has problems in being edified by this so-called harmony. Instead it is puzzled by the amount of disharmony and seeming chaos in the natural world: earthquakes, floods, volcanic eruptions, failed harvests, plagues and diseases which strike down innocent victims, etc.

Where the first point is concerned a blind admiration for the harmonious state of the natural world has led to an ethical system which has the virtue of stability but is also characterized by rigidity and lack of creativity. God becomes a sort of "cosmic moralist" or universal policeman who would like to see the order of human affairs evolve according to laws predetermined by him and indelibly imprinted on human nature. It is forgotten that the universe is still evolving and is as yet in an unfinished state, that it is still in search of its authentic profile and destiny, and, even more importantly, that it still has to be formed by the creative intervention of human beings and culture. There is a danger, thus, that in the name of a sort of *harmonia prae-stabilita* an attempt is made to rule out all creativity and renewal, social or psychological. If the cosmic order is already stable and fixed then all one needs to do is to discover the moral norms contained in the natural law. Monogamous marriage which no one can put asunder becomes in this perspective "natural and self-evident." In reality, of course, the idea of monogamous marriage as the ideal is rather the fruit of culture than of nature, the fruit of humanism and of generations of human trial and error. Such a noble and dignified form of human coexistence is no mere natural datum, but is rather a supernatural task or vocation. Moreover, there is no built-in guarantee that in its present form this manner of human coexistence is in some sort of final state of realized perfection. There is no proof that we have reached the Omega point of Christian conjugal history.

It is generally accepted that the idea of an unchangeable "natural law" actually finds its origin in the Stoics and that it quickly found its way into the Christian thought system through the writings of the Greek Fathers. According to the Stoa a distinction had to be drawn between "civil laws" which were open to alteration and varied from culture to culture, and the "natural law" which was divine, universal and unchangeable. If, however, one cares to compare what Hugh of St. Victor considered to be the contents of the natural law with Seneca's understanding of it, one soon gets the impression that, even if the idea of a *lex naturalis* is not culturally relative, the commonly accepted view of its content and practical application certainly is.

To become truly human means becoming creative in the area of moral action. One does not do this following one's own fancy but rather inspired by a great humanistic paradigm. This paradigm is principally God's revelation through Christ the Lord. The treasure chest of revelation is so profound that we are as yet far from exhausting its riches.

Medieval ethics, based as they were on cosmological foundations saw things in a different light. In that system cultural norms were anchored in a supposed "natural order." The medievals had reached the mistaken conclusion that norms and standards which had been historically arrived at by human beings over many generations were in fact eternal, obvious and "natural" i.e., willed thus by God and thus laid down. What happened was that humanity became alienated from its own historical achievements by conceiving them as eternal, divine laws. A certain sense of insecurity may well lie at the root of the felt human need to act in this way. Humans want to "play safe" and avoid chaos or fluke.

While an animal finds a safe guide for its action within its biologically determined instincts, human beings have to search out their own way and "use their common sense." Different cultures and religions explored diverse paths. So as to confer a veneer of intangibility on these contingent, unstable, temporary and relative norms, the different cultures explained them as being the plan or will of the gods. Whoever dares to oppose this view or dissents from it is immediately guilty. "Religion legitimates social institutions by bestowing upon them an ultimately valid ontological status, that is, by locating them within a sacred and cosmic frame of reference. . . . Probably the most ancient form of this legitimation is the conception of the institutional order as directly reflecting or manifesting the divine structure of the cosmos, that is, the conception of the relationship between society and cosmos as one between microcosm and macrocosm."[6]

Once again we find Teilhard de Chardin taking up the cudgel against such a moral doctrine. Both microcosm and macrocosm, both my personal spiritual life and the whole universe are still in the full throes of a complex process of development. The perfect or ideal society still remains to be discovered. It does not exist even as a model or goal. The process of hominization is still underway. Humanity still has the duty to think up, explore and experiment with new forms of

6. P. Berger, *The Sacred Canopy*, New York, 1967, 33–34.

human living. There are few Christians who attach such importance to the cosmos as Teilhard did. What Teilhard marveled at in the cosmos was not at all that which the Greeks so admired: stable and predictable harmony. What so fascinated Teilhard in the universe was precisely the absence of statistical cast-iron predictability and the striking dynamism at work within it, i.e., the growth towards greater complexity, more life and greater perfection.

Furthermore, in the religious domain Teilhard opposed an image of God as "cosmic moralist" who was principally concerned with the maintenance of an already existing, established order. God, after all, did not create human beings "in the image and likeness of the harmony in the Universe" (a view the ancient Greeks held). God has created humanity "in his own image and likeness" (Gen 1). The book of Genesis presents God as principally reaching out to us in his "creative" activity. As a consequence, humans are also called upon to be "creative" in turn. In other words, humanity must begin to create order where chaos still prevails and to produce and fashion more perfect modes of living in situations where inhuman or barbarous ways of life exist. Teilhard is not alone in his criticism of an image of God which is a rubber stamp of the status quo. His insights on this topic are strikingly similar to the central ideas of process theology. "The notion of God as Unchangeable Absolute has suggested God's establishment of an unchangeable order for the world. And the notion of God as Controlling Power has suggested that the present order exists because God wills its existence. In that case, to be obedient to God is to preserve the status quo. Process theology denies the existence of this God. . . . God's creation activity is persuasion, not controlling, it is a love that takes risks. Hence, each divine creative impulse into the world is adventurous. . . . God (is) the source of adventure toward novel ideals."[7]

The second criticism which can be leveled against those mesmerized by the cosmic order is that the intuition which contemporary humanity has concerning its natural environment is, as has already been pointed out, in direct contradiction to the ancient Greek optimism about the beauty of created reality. Thanks to the influence of such recent intellectual luminaries as Marx, Freud, Spengler or Monod, modern humanity has come to the conclusion that society is nothing more than an ineluctable conflict between mutually exploita-

7. J. Cobb and D. Griffin, *Process Theology,* Philadelphia, 1976, 9, 57, 60.

tive classes or races, that the individual is no more than a bundle of irrational passions and instincts, that contemporary culture is on a slippery slide into pollution and self-destruction and that the entire cosmos is purely the result of accidents, coincidences and blind necessity. As a result of this gloomy pessimism many former cries of awe and wonder have made way for agonizing question marks. Human beings, once the centre of the cosmos, no longer feel that they are masters of creation but rather problematic freaks, buffeted and wounded by a degenerate environment and an increasingly heartless society. They know that their body is being harmed by pollution and stress. Psychologically they are suffering from meaninglessness and alienation. The shocking realism of modern art is poles apart from the brillant naturalism of the Renaissance. Goya was probably the first painter in whose work beauty and order gave way to images which were an indictment of brutality and ugliness.

This is far from the first time in history that this shift from admiring optimism to anxious pessimism took place in religious thought. One has only for example to compare the image of God projected by the prophets and the psalmist who praised the majesty and the splendor of his works with the tone of the later Wisdom books. The former discovered God's hand shaping both natural creation and the history of Israel. Ecclesiastes, on the other hand, is amazed at the chaos in creation and the unmerited pain which has to be suffered on earth.

Both this negative attitude toward earthly reality (i.e., the *contemptus mundi* spirituality) as well as the unsuspecting admiration for order in this world have practically speaking become untenable in our time. On the one hand, secularization has made us sensitive to the positive side of earthly values. On the other hand, the shock of two world wars, the end of the *belle époque* and the nightmare of both the Gulag archipelago and the holocaust have made us aware of the chaos which exists in politics, society and the inner sanctum of the individual psyche. Bearing in mind these two important phenomena of respect for earthly reality because it is God's creation and a revulsion against prevailing chaos because it is unjust and causes pain and suffering, a figure like Teilhard comes up with a third vision of the cosmos and of natural values.

Max Wildiers sees the novelty of Teilhard's vision as lying in the fact that he not only saw clearly how much the world vision of classical theology was out of date, but also that he was immediately able to provide Christian thought with a new vision of the universe which was rooted in the positive sciences. In his masterpiece which has not won the recognition it deserves, *Wereldbeeld en Theologie, van de Middeleeuwen tot vandaag*,[8] Wildiers was able to show that the relationship between worldview and theology—and consequently between cosmos and God—has been a constant source of preoccupation to Christian theology. This relationship was already a fundamental problem for Greek thought (and actually for all great religions). It is Wildiers' belief that many Christian thinkers were more in debt to Greek philosophy than to the gospel when it came to their view of the value, structure and significance of the cosmos. If what Wildiers is getting at is that in Christian thought there have been regular and regrettable infiltrations of Greek paganism (a claim liberal Protestantism keeps making since von Harnack's day), then we must agree with him. If on the other hand he is implying that before Teilhard there were no real evangelical Christian thinkers who knew how to treat "the worldly," then it is our view that he is greatly exaggerating. In many of the Christian mystics we find an evangelical purity which is in marked contrast to the chronic pagan deviations of their day.

It remains undeniable that medieval theology had elaborated an all-embracing, coherent Weltanschauung within which cosmology and anthropology (or worldview and image of humanity) were blended together in a harmonious way. This system which certainly owed a great deal to Greek philosophy became the substructure for a theological superstructure which fitted it like a glove. From the seventeenth century onwards this old cosmology was conceived of as naive if not downright wrong. People like Galileo and Newton put their fingers on the first cracks in the foundations. The immediate consequence of this was that the children of the Enlightenment began to articulate their doubts about the equally unstable theological *super*structure. The positive sciences broke loose from clerical meddling and pressure. The "profane" sciences left the rest to make a career of their own. They no longer wished to "serve" as the base for a theological monument. The gulf between the profane sciences and theology was only to widen with the years. Both now blazed their own trail. Henceforth knowledge of the cosmos and knowledge of God would be taught in different faculties. This spelled the end of

8. M. Wildiers, *Wereldbeeld en Theologie, Van de Middeleeuwen tot vandaag*, Antwerpen, 1973.

what had for generations been understood as a "university." To some extent one ended up with a godless science and an otherworldly theology, a scientism without values and an abstract dogmatics. It was against this intellectual divorce that Teilhard set himself with such vigour.

Long before Teilhard ever appeared on the scene Nicholas of Cusa had realized that a separation between cosmology or natural sciences on the one hand and theology or reflection on the supernatural on the other, would have damaging consequences. The papal legate prophesied that theology would suffer from this unnatural loneliness. Since the great divorce, heralded by Copernicus, Kepler and Galileo, the "worldly" was viewed by many Christian thinkers as, if not a religious danger, nothing more than an irrelevant detail. The "natural" domain was from now on left by the theologians to the profane scientists and artists. Speaking about God was consequently more "ethical" and alien. What was revolutionary—and for many theologians deeply worrying—in Teilhard's approach was his tireless effort to heal this Renaissance "divorzio al Italiano." In his view the cosmos was the point of departure in the attempt to understand God. God's being, that of the universe and of humanity are intimately connected with one another. Whoever dismisses one of these three areas in principle—whether it be for personal reasons or for scientific ones— condemns one's self to an inadequate and abstract view of reality. Theology, cosmology and anthropology must engage in dialogue. Teilhard was actually opposed to a theology which treats of a totally transcendent God who only touches humanity in its inner spirit or soul.

However much Teilhard attempted to reconcile theology and science and oblige them to engage in dialogue, his brave attempts did not meet with a sympathetic reception from the ecclesiastical authorities of his day. Rome kept putting pressure on him to stick to "pure scientific work." The divorce Teilhard was striving to heal was long since accepted in Rome as an irredeemable *fait accompli*. A fresh confrontation between the two sides was consequently deemed superfluous and pointless. In the meantime the powers had attempted to neutralize Teilhard and make him harmless by keeping him firmly within the bounds of his specialization, namely, paleontology. Teilhard was not kindly thanked for his "universal" approach.

Teilhard, however, continued his search for a more adequate cosmology, in which the concept of the "wondrous eternal order" would give way to that of "continuous dynamic evolution." Teilhard brought cosmos and religion together again. His spirituality was characterized by a "cosmic image of God." He never lost sight of the cosmic dimension of God and the religious significance of the universe. He issued stern warnings against all forms of antimaterialist dualism which sought to reduce Christianity to "une religion du pur esprit." Paraphrasing Wildiers, one could sum up Teilhard's message as follows: There is an unbreakable bond between our view of the world on the one hand and our view of God on the other. The classical view of the cosmos has been shown to be gravely defective. The classical evaluation of "earthly and worldly reality" was also seen to be essentially wrong. It was actually nothing short of Manichaean, Albigensian, Jansenistic or downright Puritan. A fresh perspective on the "Diesseitige" will also lead to a more adequate image of God. Teilhard's intellectual program takes this insight as its starting point. It was only after his death that the truth of his vision began to dawn on others.

2. Teilhard de Chardin Between Scylla and Charybdis

Teilhard's assertion that it was imperative for our image of God to have "cosmic dimensions" led certain of his opponents to consider him a thinly disguised pantheist. To what extent does this accusation of pantheism hold water?

Ethnologists and psychologists have provided more than enough evidence that a people's image of God is always very strongly coloured by its culture. Nomads worship a different sort of God than farmers. The gods of warriors like the Spartans will exemplify manly heroic daring and courage rather than womanly fertility. Initially the "political theologians" of the Roman empire tended to see less possibility of salvation in the Christian God of love, imported as it was from a rebellious peripheral country with no tradition of statesmanship to speak of, than in the image of a deified despot. As soon as a nomadic people puts down roots and starts farming plots or tracts of land, and consequently, after seed that has been sown, must endure the time until the coming harvest, we see such a people worshipping a mother goddess, a sort of Mother Earth, patroness of all fertility. The city dweller, by contrast, sees local deities as principally national protectors of law and order, of political identity and mutual solidarity. To begin with, religion was a matter of economic necessity. Then it turned into a civic duty.

Virtually all ethnologists agree that primitive humans never think of analysing or dissecting the world about them. The simple, naive individual still lives with a vague feeling of unity and identity with all reality. Teilhard's image of God has nothing to do with such a "pre-logical" feeling of cosmic unity. He actually terms this a childish pre-religion. Maturity in his view comes about through sober, detached analysis and differentiation: "It is necessary to have first discovered the divorce and the antagonisms which exist between the cosmic elements before then making the fascinating discovery that there is a mutual bond between them."[9] It is thus necessary to have suffered under the diversity and apparent contradictions and loose ends in existing reality before coming to realize that Baudelaire was right when he spoke of "une ténébreuse et profonde unité . . . ayant l'expansion des choses infinies."

Teilhard's perception of cosmic unity not only has nothing to do with a naive animistic cult of Mother Earth, but it also flies directly in the face of certain forms of Eastern monism or "pan-en-henism" (Zaehner). He was absolutely convinced that an authentic awareness of cosmic unity could only come about in our own day, and then only in the West. In contrast with the Orientals, those in the West have never denied the multiplicity of realities, the materiality, the antagonisms and the contradictions we find in this world, nor have they simply dismissed them as being of no consequence. On the contrary, they have had a very close look at them and only then discovered "que le multiple est de nature convergente."

Buddhists and Hindus believe that we will only discover "the One" when we gradually allow the "illusions" of a multiplicity of things to go up in smoke and when we shake loose our desires for concrete things or separate entities. Or to put it more poetically, the fundamental sound of the universe could only reach our ear once the clamorous cacaphony of all things is reduced to silence. Those in the West know, however, that a fundamental unique harmonious sound will only be achieved through a symphonic polyphony, i.e., by way of a "Bewältigung," a perfection and transformation of an original diversity. I only get an adequate view of the world once I refuse to allow the uncontrollable jungle to continue rampant in its "natural state"

9. P. Teilhard de Chardin, *Les Directions de l'Avenir*, 49.

but attempt rather to transform the jungle into a neatly manicured garden.

Teilhard essentially sees reality as one organism or one dynamic whole. If we are somehow to intellectually grasp this awesome unity, two things are necessary: scientific analysis and a historical perspective. Through such techniques as vivisection, splitting of the atom and other forms of analyses we have first to establish the diversity which is to be found at the heart of the cosmos. One then needs sufficient historical "recul" so as to discern the dynamic convergence of the evolution within the same cosmos. It is only in our own day that these conditions—even if not yet realized—are on the road to realization in principle.

When we use the term "cosmic" to describe Teilhard's image of God, we thereby mean three things.

To begin with, Teilhard sought God in nature (and not, for example, in a transcendental analysis of the human spirit or epistemological structure). It is not simply in a cognitive way that humanity acquires an awareness of God through contemplating the universe. Ontologically and sacramentally, too, there exists a real "communion" with God by way of earthly and cosmic realities. One has only to think of bread, wine, the majestic beauty of the mountains or the infinite expanse of the sea as they are described by Teilhard in his essay *La Messe sur le Monde*. The cosmic and the purely spiritual are here at opposite poles. For too long God has been discussed in psychological categories as if God and human beings were actors on some abstract stage without the world as a backdrop on the cosmos in the wings. In reality humanity is intimately bound up in the cosmos, is an actual component of cosmic reality. It is only in that context that we can make any sense of humanity. It follows that when it comes to God, in the image of whom humanity is created, we must not only apply to him spiritual or moral categories such as weakness, righteousness, understanding, etc., but also cosmic dimensions.

A second feature of Teilhard's approach is that he feels it necessary to emphasize the all-but-forgotten dimension of God's *immanence* even more than the divine transcendence. Thus, for him God is not so much the "Ganz Andere" (K. Barth) but rather he who "walks among us" but whom we apparently have such difficulty in recognizing.

Thirdly, for Teilhard cosmic means historically evolving. Cosmic thus is the opposite of eternal, timeless and unalterable. Here, as has been mentioned, Teilhard comes very close to the insights of process theology.

Thus, in the first instance humans come across God in the world of nature. It is important to emphasize that Teilhard is certainly sensitive to the poetry of nature, and yet with the important qualification that a microscopic analysis, the positive sciences and biological evolution are no less poetic than the nineteenth-century romantic's falling autumnal leaf or golden sunset. Teilhard's lyricism reminds one rather of the poetry of G. Achterberg when the latter, in a cool but religious, even mystical, poem describes his experience of God in terms which a romantic would have considered anything but poetic:

> The radio-angels are singing
> they awaken magnets inside me . . .
> I feel myself bloated
> from excess of space . . .
> Your being breaks over
> mine in a flash.

In his diary Teilhard writes about a sort of "natural revelation" of God in the cosmos and in its energies: "I have the impression that God has always revealed Himself to me through the Universe. I feel His presence in everything. There is no other way I can love Him."[10]

In Teilhard's case, his passion for the cosmic was always the expression of his deeply religious and Christian approach to life. One never gets the impression from his writings that the values derived from biblical revelation were slotted in or stuck on afterwards. According to him it was dogmatic Christianity which opened his eyes to reality. The "universal Christ" and "the Omega point" are for him a synthesis of the historical Christ and the evolving universe. Christ is the one human being who incorporates all of humanity into himself, assimilating into himself all generations, past, present and future.

What is most remarkable is that this perception of cosmic unity struck home in the least poetic circumstances imaginable: in the trenches during the Great War of 1914–18. There he felt himself forced "to seek out the divine that is hiding in the very matter which

10. Teilhard de Chardin, *Journal I* (26 août 1915-4 janvier 1919). Paris, Fayard, 1975, 304.

constitutes our cosmos, our humanity and our progress."[11] In what he termed "le goût de la terre" Teilhard tasted and felt a force at work, unifying the earth, however painfully. He regarded it as his particular vocation to teach people "to learn to discover and love God *in* the world." For him a Christian life did not mean cautiously negotiating one's way between the perils and dangers of the world. Even less does it involve a life full of anxiety lest one stains or spots one's pristine purity. Christian life is rather "becoming deeply involved in and committed to life" so as to ennoble it. It is gold ore which is still in need of purification in the furnace. Teilhard would probably have been able to endorse Kafka's laconic observation: "there are some who have survived the wail of the Sirens, but there is no one who has also survived their silence." Teilhard was opposed to all forms of religion which promoted inner purity but which dismissed externals and religiously inspired activity as meaningless, indifferent or irrelevant. He opposed what Hegel termed as "das unglückliche Bewusstsein der schönen Seele." In other words, he was against any human ideal which advocated that one should refrain at all costs from sullying one's hands with worldly affairs. For him, God is radically "concrete" in the etymological sense of the word: "concrescere" (Latin) or "growing together" towards Unity.

Teilhard refuses to see the universe as a "thing" which was fashioned by God and from which God then distanced himself much as a watchmaker does from a finished time-piece. Teilhard's search for God within the cosmos can perhaps best be summed up by paraphrasing Abraham Heschel: "The Ineffable cries out of all things. It is only the idea of a divine presence hidden within the rational order of nature which is compatible with our scientific view of nature and in accord with our sense of the Ineffable."[12]

Teilhard is also opposed to a psychologizing or anthropomorphic image of God. God is altogether more than a sublimated human being who is capable of experiencing love, sympathy, pain and joy. One does not discover who God actually is by confining one's view to one single part of the cosmos, even if it is the most perfect, i.e., the phenomenon of humankind, particularly its psychology. A human being is also possessed of a body which is deeply rooted in material reality. It is not only the structure of the human spirit or psy-

11. Ibid., 59.
12. A. Heschel, *Man is not alone*, New York, 1976, 150.

che which reveals something of God's being to us but also the entire universe. Teilhard attaches great importance to the classical distinction between God's "natural revelation" within the unfolding of natural-cosmic reality and "historical revelation" which culminates in the person of Jesus Christ.

It is important not to misunderstand Teilhard. It was not his intention, in using classical vocabulary to infiltrate the pantheistic Trojan horse within the walled citadel of Catholic theology so that by this devious maneuver he might make Christianity more acceptable to the liberal world of science. Teilhard hated all sorts of childish talk about God or the use of the language of fairy tales with such statements as "God is angry," "God is sad," or "God cannot put up with this any longer." This is indeed the type of language one can find in the earlier books of the Old Testament. Teilhard tried to discover less naive and less psychologizing forms of theism.

There is one fundamental truth which needs to be driven home urgently: it has to be impressed on people how great, how all-embracing and how immediately palpable God is within that universe which seems to exercise such a fascination on contemporary humanity. Sure, God is a Person. He is much more than simply a silent, benevolent Father-figure, more often than not absent. In Christ, God revealed how open to the world and how future-oriented those who are genuinely seeking God need to be.

In 1917 Teilhard made the following entry in his diary: "The world is large. . . . We Christians must speak with a voice that reflects that reality. All too often we have instead tried to anthropomorphize God and reduce Him to a human scale. To some degree at any rate God must be thought of and loved as a World, as *the* World." And, "The contemplation of the universal Energies alone is incomplete and simplistic, as long as we do not combine this with an acute awareness of the psychic consciousness (of God). Truth lies in the synthesis of the two elements: the center and the sphere, spiritual refinement and irrational immensity."[13]

In 1939 Teilhard realized that these youthful musings in his diary risked pushing God as person too much into the background. There is always a risk that when one is dazzled by the brightness of a new insight or revelation that one tends to forget about or even deny an older self-evident truth. A new insight will correct older ideas or set

13. P. Teilhard de Chardin, *Journal I*, 244.

them in a fresh perspective: "Modern reaction to anthropomorphism has gone too far, even to making people doubt the ultra-personality of God." Teilhard went on to warn of "the antipersonalist complex which paralyses us . . . God is a Person. We have to think of Him as a person. An impersonal God wouldn't be a God."[14]

All of the major religions have experienced great difficulty in putting into words the simultaneous realization that God is on the one hand very close to humanity, that he is even *in* humanity and *in* nature (by virtue of his immanence), and that he is infinitely greater than humanity and nature (by virtue of his transcendence). God is at one and the same time, to borrow Augustine's phraseology "closer to me than I am to myself" (immanence) while still remaining "infinitely other" than humans (transcendence). The most radical form of immanence is without doubt pantheism within which God and cosmos are fused or identified with one another. In contrast we find in Islam, for instance, an extreme form of transcendence. God's inaccessibility and exaltation above all that is human and natural is emphasized in Islam to such a degree that Allah seems to have but the most tenuous of links with time and space. Between these two extreme notions of God Teilhard set himself to find an orthodox *via media*. He worked within the dual perspective of his scientific research and his Catholic faith.

Teilhard regarded as one of his top priorities to emphasize the immanence of God because traditional Christianity all too often described God as a "being" who reigned "above" this world and even "warned against the perils and dangers of the world." Just in the same way as the Greeks of old held that the gods dwelt on the heights of the distant Mount Olympus, so too a certain brand of Christian theology preached a God who was too heavenly and "extrinsic," who just allowed the laws of nature to run their course and on occasion "intervened" miraculously in history. The same school of theology tended to view Christ too much as an "individual," a fragment of the universe who comes to us as a messenger from a remote father with news about a new moral code. It is not so much a question that God transcends time and space but rather that he makes them holy, he sanctifies them by the intimacy of his presence within them. Teilhard felt that what needed to be looked into more closely

14. Teilhard de Chardin, *Lettres intimes à Auguste Valensin, Bruno de Solages, Henri de Lubac, André Ravier. 1919–1955*. Intro. and notes by Henri de Lubac. Paris: Aubier Montaigne, 1974, 271, note 70:3.

was the "divine-cosmic links." God's most beautiful name is after all Emmanuel or "God with us."

We do not reach God by shuffling off the world and its toils. The world is not a barrier between humanity and God. We actually tend to feel and experience God's presence while fulfilling our worldly task. In this respect Teilhard exemplified the Ignatian ideal of "in actione contemplativus." Humans only gain access to God through the day-to-day tasks they perform in this concrete world. Involvement in the world is neither an obstacle nor a distraction, but rather a *conditio sine qua non* for prayer. Humanity reaches God in the process of its efforts to change, civilize and perfect itself and the world. To some extent one can even say that humanity reaches God in much the same way as God reached out to humanity, i.e., by authentically "becoming man."

For this reason every task undertaken in the world has something of eternal value for humankind and humanism is the only way to an authentic Christianity. To put it in Teilhardian terms, "hominization" and "amorization" are synonyms for "Christianization." By becoming more human and by loving with greater intensity we can only become more deeply Christian.

The cosmos actually plays a triple liturgical function. In the cosmos God's work and his presence to us is felt and effective. We actually ally ourselves with Christ in his "work of transformation" (a term Teilhard prefers to the rather negative and ambiguous term "work of salvation") through our involvement within the cosmos. We do this through the efforts we make to bring "order" out of "chaos." (The chaos of original sin is consequently just as indispensable to humanity as the unfashioned marble block is to the sculptor). Then again, humanity draws closer to the "omega point" the more it strives toward the realization of a deeper humanism. In a word, the cosmos is God's sacrament *par excellence*.

There is a third and final implication of Teilhard's "cosmic image of God." Given that the universe is still in the full throes of evolution it is quite impossible for our image of God which is deeply embedded in our view of the world to have reached its final state. God is not yet "all in all," at least not in a fully conscious way. To put it more theologically, there is such a thing as "l'historicité de Dieu" (Chenu) and "Gottes sein ist im Werden (Jüngel). Without actually realizing it, Teilhard was very close to process theology.

It was the basic idea of the Anglo-Saxon theologians who formed the process school that whatever is real is in a state of development, decay or "process." "Being real" consequently means not so much having taken on a fixed form or being a "thing." Reality is more a question of working, happening, moving or becoming. Both the ancient Greeks and theologians of the Greek school had a prejudice against such concepts as still-in-the-making, changing, or becoming. For the Greeks perfection inplied rest, eternity and immobility. The first qualities attributed to God were thus independence and timelessness. Both for the process theologians and for Teilhard the relationship between God and cosmos was a mutual and "real" relationship (and not just a "relatio rationis" as Thomas Aquinas maintained, so as to guarantee that the "first Mover" would himself remain "unmoved." For the Angelic Doctor, motion or change in God would imply that he was not yet perfect).

Surely the concept of "having a relationship with someone" implies a lot more than a relationship which is purely platonic or only spiritual. Isn't a *relatio realis* a great deal more mature and perfect than a *relatio rationis*? Is the Christian God not the God of the Covenant? Is he not the God who is authentic, palpable Love (and not only platonic or spiritual love, but also a sacramental love)? Is not the Trinity truly a relationship between Persons which deeply involves humankind? If God is love, does not this fact imply that he really is concerned with and committed to those whom he loves? Is he not consequently moved or touched by what those he loves do or fail to do? Would what happens to his loved ones leave God cold or indifferent? Do world developments not touch him in any way? These are all general questions raised by process theologians which also aroused Teilhard's curiosity and stimulated his inquiring mind. For him the universe was still in a state of becoming and cosmic development had not run its course. The future is still an open door.

Teilhard did not see the cosmos as a "vast substance" but rather as a complex reality growing towards organic unity. God is related to everything. While Hartshorne chose to speak of the "surrelativity of God," Teilhard spoke of "the Christian Pleroma or of the synthesis of the Uncreated with the created." God desires growing unity. He makes this not only possible in principle, he leaves the practical realization of his project to some extent to human ingenuity and creativity. In this sense human beings are, to borrow St. Paul's phrase, "God's co-workers."

The deft way in which a process theologian like Whitehead man-

aged to avoid slipping into pantheism makes one regret that Teilhard
was not a better theologian. Whitehead drew a distinction between
the growth process of the Universe on the one hand and God on the
other. The two are certainly related but not identical. God is actually
not what Aquinas and Tillich claim, "Being itself." Being after all in
addition to so many beautiful things also embraces failures, perver-
sion and evil.

For Whitehead the primeval chaos of the world possesses virtually
an infinite wealth of potential and possibilities. To get the show on
the road, so to speak, God sets the original goal or "initial aim." God
coaxes cosmic reality out of its shell. He stimulates it to become a
universe. In the meantime it is always possible for humanity to oppose God's plan by promoting its "subjective aims." Humanity can
stray from or totally abandon the path to the Omega point, to put it
in Teilhardian terms, and thus give up on its true vocation. God's
plan offers us a possibility but not an inevitable fate. What we are
confronted with is an invitation, an inspiration or a vocation, and not
determinism, *faits accomplis* or predestination. God's stimulating influence is one of order and equilibrium. One is totally free (from a
psychological but not moral point of view) to opt for particularism,
immediate satisfaction or disintegration. Process theology not only
manages to avoid the accusation of pantheism and determinism, it
also leaves the door open for a theological reflection on the mystery
of evil and the decadence of the world.

Teilhard's doctrine dovetails very nicely with this vision of the
God-cosmos relationship. His language is far more that of a visionary
or of a poet with fire in his blood rather than of an orthodox theologian. He only starts worrying about fine theological distinctions a
posteriori, i.e., after his writings were subjected to scrutiny, misunderstood and condemned by official ecclesiastical authorities.

The words uttered by Martin Nijhoff: "God, I think, is like a lonely
man who looks at the world and gives it his approval," would have
ruffled Teilhard's feathers in no uncertain terms. God is anything but
lonely: "The kingdom of God is in the midst of us." God does not
just look on from the sidelines. He is involved. He does not only nod
in approval, he also disapproves. When it comes to expressing in
philosophically and theologically precise language rather than in lyri-
cal or poetic phraseology how close the bond is between God and
the Cosmos—without of course slipping into a pantheistic fusion—
the Teilhardian vocabulary falls short.

He really meant it when he wrote as follows to a Jewish lady of his acquaintance: "Fundamentally, what I desire so greatly to share is not so much a theory, a system, a *Weltanschauung,* as a certain taste, a certain perception of the beauty, the pathos, and the unity of *being.* . . . These theories really matter to me only by their vibrations in a province of the soul which is not that of intellectualism. Fundamentally, it is not possible to transmit by words the perception of a quality, a taste. Once again, it would be more to my purpose to be a shadow of Wagner than a shadow of Darwin."[15]

To sum up, it has to be admitted that for many long years Christianity has been trying to find a *via media* between an alienating dualism and pagan pantheism. Any Christian attempt to address the issue of God, if it wishes to respect the canons of orthodoxy at least, must find words which effectively translate the ideas of God's immanence and transcendence. Before the revelation which took place in and through Jesus Christ this seemed a totally impossible task. Since the advent of Christ and through Christ, God trusts human intellectual creativity and ingenuity to proclaim and teach God's word anew as faithfully as possible. The evangelist who is sensitive to the signs of the times and the needs of his or her own day, will try to stress that aspect of God's inexpressible essence which runs the greatest risk of being conveniently forgotten about by the world. Just like psychiatrists, theologians and evangelists can also differ in their opinion, and then not only concerning the diagnosis but also regarding the more or less hazardous and sensitive business of awareness stimulation that is then required.

15. Teilhard de Chardin, *Letters to Two Friends, 1926–1952.* New York: New American Library, 1968, 58–59.

CHAPTER NINE

Religious Faith in a Climate of Scepticism

If, despite the various scientific and intellectual objections, it is still possible to engage in reasonable and meaningful discussion about God, as indeed we have tried to demonstrate in the preceding chapters, it is still up to us to make clear what precisely we mean by "belief in God." Faith, as a concept, has meant so many different things to different people throughout history, that it is essential to reflect critically on what faith basically entails. Before we launch into defining faith, in order to avoid misunderstandings it is important that we point out what we do not understand by faith.

Faith does not mean placing one's signature under a series of credal articles, nor giving one's assent in principle to dogmas or unsubstantiated declarations the inner logic or contents of which are not fully grasped by one. Faith cannot be reduced to accepting, without further ado, a number of statements issued by Church authorities as true.

Faith is even less a matter of voicing a hesitant opinion along the lines of "I believe I must have left my handkerchief on the bench in the park" or "I really believe that it will snow tomorrow." When we use the word "believe" in a religious context we mean neither a dumb acceptance of axiomatic dogmas nor some hesitant form of knowledge. Moreover, one does not believe in "things"; things are known, supposed or doubted. One always believes *in*, or has faith *in someone*. This "someone" says and does "things," it is true, and if I am to come to have faith in that one then I ought to be attentive to that one's words and deeds.

Faith means entering into a relationship with others because one observes and accepts their witness (i.e., their word and their deeds). Faith is in fact the only form of knowledge which is possible between people. Or to put it another way, if I *really* want to get to know other persons (i.e., not just the colour of their hair, the correct spelling of their name or their vital statistics) I actually only have one bridge open to me, namely, my faith in them. It is up to me to accept that all that they say and the way in which they behave and present themselves are authentic (and thus that they are not posing, acting, or engaging in hypocrisy or "impression management"). A naive person is generally too quick to have faith in another person. The sceptic is too slow and the agnostic will never do so.

Faith always has five essential components. To begin with, faith involves *persons* who *meet* one another. It does not concern things which do or do not exist, nor is it a matter of people manipulating one another or subjecting them to scientific analysis. As Luther so nicely put it: "Der Glaube geht allezeit auf eine Person." Thomas Aquinas does not mince his words either when he writes: "He who has faith, accepts another's word. In any act of faith it is the person whose word is accepted which is the decisive element. On the other hand the content to which one gives one's assent (i.e. his words and deeds) is in a certain sense secondary."

Secondly, faith will inevitably always involve an element of risk. Another's interventions, feelings, integrity and thoughts are always invisible. I am obliged to discern them from his or her outward behaviour.

Thirdly, faith keeps on searching, it is always partially incomplete. A person who believes in others does not do this on account of a cast-iron guarantee regarding their character or actions. Only *after* one has put one's faith and trust in someone (on the basis of a number of positive experiences with such a person) does one then begin to get to know that one. It is not because I've built a bridge that I immediately reach the opposite bank. A bridge makes it possible to explore the other side. I would never have bothered to build my bridge at all if I had known that all I would find on the other side was marsh and shifting sands.

Fourthly, faith always implies love. One has only to reflect an instant on the rich etymology of the Germanic word "Glaube" which one finds in various forms in such word as love, the "beloved" etc. To put it in theological terms, the three theological virtues of faith, hope and charity always go hand in hand.

Finally, faith always assumes freedom. One can, of course, force someone to give one's assent or affix one's signature to a painful text. Yet one cannot force someone to see what they do not see, nor to love the person that one distrusts. These five cornerstones of faith need to be examined more closely.

1. Faith Concerns a Person

When two people meet one another, their words and their actions "bear witness" to what they desire to be for one another. (The many human relationships which are not successful only demonstrate a lack of initial critical attention to those very words and deeds). It really does not make much difference whether the two persons involved in this encounter are human beings, or a human being and his or her God. From a phenomenological point of view the act of faith in both cases is analogous. In both relationships faith is the only bridge from the one party to the other. It is always possible to blow up that bridge, erect a barrier or simply after a while no longer bother to use it. As long as the bridge still stands, its piers will be the parties' words and actions (i.e., smiles, gifts, caresses, mutual favours, helping hands, etc.). These words and actions are never really a proof of anything. They can be lies, tactics, a game or simply misunderstanding. They are rather signs of what people feel for one another, of the esteem in which they hold one another and of their desire one for the other. These signs can at a certain stage become so plentiful, so harmonious and so convincing that I come to the firm conclusion that my friend or partner *really* is my friend. He or she really is sincere with me. I believe in their friendship. I have every reason to do so (i.e., the signs of their affection which they showed me). After knowing someone for a certain time I decide whether or not to put my faith in that one. I can pay no one a greater honour than by making an act of faith in one. The most beautiful thing I can ever say to anyone is "I put my faith in you."

My faith in others is based on two essential elements: their words and their actions. When it comes to God, of course, the natural question arises as to where it is we hear his word or are witness to his deeds. The answer is quite simple. We find God's word in his revelation to humanity. That means in the sacred Scriptures and in the way they have been historically explained within the Christian tradition. Where God's Word is concerned, Christianity has always made a distinction between internal and external evidence of God. The external

evidence is that publically articulated word of God we find in the
Bible and in the Church's dogmatic declarations. "Who hears you,
hears me" and "Whatsoever you shall bind upon earth will be bound
in heaven." (Matt 16:19)

The internal evidence, on the other hand, is the soft whisper of
God in the soul of the person at prayer. This revelation takes place
without the objective mediation of priests or any other links in an ecclesiastical chain. One is reminded of Paul's words: "Whoever has the
Spirit is able to judge the value of everything." (1 Cor 2:15) This divine speech to the heart obviously is not made up of words, concepts
or thoughts which are whispered by God into the inner ear and
grasped by the human intellect. The internal Word of God touches
and radically transforms the whole being of the one who prays. Such
persons are seized by God's Word in the sense that henceforth they
experience more deeply peace, joy, love, and even faith. These feelings well up so strongly that the person who experiences them becomes convinced that this new quality of being cannot simply be
explained by ordinary psychological factors. Given that in this area
there is so much illusion, subjectivism and projection, a "discernment
of spirits" is highly advisable. Throughout the history of the Church
the Christian giants, i.e., the mystics, saints and reformers, have with
some justice felt called upon to defend their inner evidence of communication with God against the clerical powers-that-be who live in
perpetual fear of an illuminism, unsoftened by the virtues of
meekness and humility. As often happens, those things which could
lead to misunderstanding or could be abused are conveniently swept
under the carpet of oblivion. The so-called "free interpretation of the
Bible" which the Catholic Counter-Reformation was only too eager to
fling in the face of Protestantism, had really nothing to do with libertine subjectivism. Protestants saw clearly that those who received
"the anointing of the Holy Spirit" through the waters of baptism can
be directly spoken to in their heart by God's Spirit. Protestantism
was thus a protest against a Catholic attempt to suppress God's
Word by the monopoly of the exclusively external (ecclesiastical)
evidence.

Quite independently of Luther such figures as Thomas à Kempis,
Erasmus and Ignatius of Loyola and many others had at an earlier
stage pointed out that God communicated not only through Church
structures but also immediately through personal prayer. The author
of the *Imitation of Christ* uses strong language, even if couching his

views in cautious terms, when he writes: "Let not Moses nor any of the prophets speak to me, but speak Thou rather, O Lord God, who are the inspirer and enlightener of all the prophets, for Thou alone without them canst perfectly instruct me, but they without Thee will avail me nothing. They may indeed sound forth words, but they give not the spirit. They speak well, but if Thou be silent they do not set the heart on fire. They deliver the letter, but thou discloseth the sense" (III, 2:5-11).

In what terms are we to understand God's actions and deeds? To begin with, our minds turn to God's creation which betrays something of the Creator's own inner nature. Then there is the double history of Israel, or the people of God on the one hand and of Jesus Christ and his disciples on the other. One has only to think of the closing verse of John's Gospel: "But there are also many other things which Jesus did, were every one of them to be written, I suppose that the world itself could not contain the books that would be written" (John 21:25). God's deeds are not just confined to those reported in the Bible. Furthermore, we also have the Church's tradition which is just the reflection of God's work in the life of his friends, saints, mystics and blessed ones. And then in the final instance there is my personal life on which I can look back and in which I can discern "signs" which we might call providential because they have determined or changed the direction of my life.

In addition to the salvation history of the people of God there is also such a thing as my "personal salvation history." This is made up of those facts or events in my life which only I can see as providential rather than pure chance. The things which I personally experienced make it clear to me on closer reflection that the Lord calls me closer to himself by a series of ordinary, unremarkable events. What we are dealing with are the sort of "saving events" that Dag Hammarskjöld refers to simply as "marking stones." These are events which turned out to be so important in his life that he felt obliged to make written note of them so as never to forget them. The words of the Bible are pertinent here: "Make certain that you do not forget, as long as you live, what you have seen with your own eyes. Tell your children and grandchildren." (Deut 4:9) "These notes?—they were signposts you began to set up after you had reached a point where you needed them, a fixed point that was on no account to be lost sight of." About these "markings" Hammarskjöld goes on to say that they were series of providential events, insights and experiences during his lifetime. "These entries provide the only true profile that can be drawn."[1]

In an analogous way Teilhard advised his niece Marguerite to make note of all the moments when she noticed Divine Providence operative in her life: "Are not those beams of light, which from time to time enable us to see more clearly or assimilate one or other fundamental truth, of great value? Have you never thought of noting them down whenever you experienced them? Bit by bit the physiognomy which the Lord desires to give to our spiritual life takes flesh. By making a little effort to note it down, that beam of light becomes clearer and more specific. It takes a shape which we might not be able to discern in it later. . . . In moments of darkness one can latch onto those words, which articulate for us insights of peace and clear vision."[2]

For those people who are short-sighted or suffer from a spiritual myopia, words and deeds attributed to God's revelation or providence are put down as purely human events or the result of coincidence. Only when I put my faith in the Invisible One who hides behind these events can these "words and actions" become revelation.

2. Faith Implies Risk

Given that signs are never cast-iron proof, faith must always involve an element of risk. Signs (e.g., of love) invite faith and trust; proofs on the other hand aim at scientific certainty. The road sign to Zurich is just a sign, it proves nothing. And yet since my experience has taught me that the technical staff of the Swiss ministry of transport generally place accurate signs on the highways, I confidently follow the road indicated. I travel through Switzerland by following the road signs. In fact our whole life follows much the same pattern. In ordinary life it is rare that one asks for scientific proofs; they belong to the research laboratory.

In our contact and relationships with other human beings we never have such things as proofs. A person's inner motives, thoughts and feelings will always remains invisible. One only finds proofs when it comes to concrete things. A judge presiding a court case will believe some witnesses only after listening for a long time and a searching cross-examination, while there are other witnesses in whom the judge has no confidence at all. The proof in a court case only con-

1. D. Hammarskjöld, *Markings*, New York, 144 and V.
2. P. Teilhard de Chardin, *Genèse d'une Pensée, Lettres (1914–1918)*, Paris, 1961, 139.

cerns things: revolvers, fingerprints, traces of blood or intercepted correspondence. People either believe one another or do not. It is impossible to prove someone's reliability or test it scientifically. This is not, of course, to imply that one ought to blindly trust another person or be cavalier about placing one's confidence. One puts one's faith in another person (be that a human being or God) on the basis of one's experience with that person to date. That experience may have confirmed that the person was serious, reliable and faithful, or may have suggested the contrary. What really makes a partner tick (i.e., inner motives, feelings etc.) remains invisible. And yet it is what makes one tick that so fascinates me.

> I would like to put my hand
> through your wide pupils
> so as to be able to feel
> the images you keep of me.
> I would then feel my own
> and then discover where it was I touched you;
> what part of me still makes you glow
> and what has gone cold.

The poet Adriaan Morriën who wrote this short poem rightly uses the conditional mood or the "irrealis." He would like certainty, tactile contact and self-assurance. Yet he knows he cannot have them. How the other person sees him is and must remain her secret. Through words and gestures she can, of course, show what her feelings are for him. And yet there is no scientific, cast-iron proof supplied. For that reason every relationship that delves beneath the surface involves an element of risk.

This risk element is increased by the fact that my partner transmits signs other than those of affection and trust. In all relationships— including my relationship with God—there are the occasional "brush-offs" which make me doubt. Every now and then we give a friend the cold shoulder or leave one in the stake. In retrospect their or our words seem hollow, incorrect, and sometimes either exaggerated if not downright lies. In my relationship with God, too, there are now and again signs that would seem to suggest that God is not quite what he appears in his revelation; he seems anything but infinite Love. Would not such phenomena as a handicapped child, the sudden death of a young wife and mother, a senseless natural disaster such as an earthquake, tidal wave or flood which leaves hundreds of innocent people homeless, etc., not suggest rather that God's love is a very relative concept?

Even more disconcerting is the fact that God's existence cannot be proved with absolute certainty. There are actually signs which would point rather to God's nonexistence or total absence. The mystic Simone Weil correctly writes about the "non-obviousness" of God and "the need for God to hide himself" so as "not to crush" his creatures. God waits for a free assent to his existence. "Our yes of affirmation would be of no value" writes the philosopher Schelling, "unless it were possible to contemplate a no." That rejection of God, that "no" to his existence, has never seemed so plausible nor seemed so utterly reasonable as in our own day. There are certain undeniable signs which point to the reality of God's existence. And there are also signs which suggest that no God exists. God does not want to force faith on people. He wants neither to trap nor to seduce people. He awaits our assent within a range of other possible responses. It is the fact that there is the possibility of free choice which confers an element of risk on authentic faith.

It may seem rather odd but in fact over the centuries this risk has been reduced. One often hears it said that the apostles who were able to see Jesus Christ in the flesh, hear him and touch him, were in a privileged position and had little "problem" in believing. And yet the contrary is true. The gospels prove pretty convincingly that these men were very reticent to turn their backs on trusted Jewish tradition for the sake of this unknown carpenter's son from Nazareth, put their faith in him and leave all to follow him. They were confronted with something totally new. They had not a clue how the adventure into which they were launching themselves would end. The contemporary Christian on the other hand can take a fairly detached view and discern where discipleship of Christ leads to. He knows lots of examples of deeply committed Christianity and sanctity, while also being familiar with examples of lapsed church practice and atheism. In Mother Teresa of Calcutta he can see clearly the consequences of her understanding of the gospel message and her Christian faith. It is even easier to come up with examples of notorious apostasy and its consequences. The Christian tradition enables us to make out in general terms what Christian faith involves and what it excludes a priori. One of the obvious objections that comes to mind here is the fact that in addition to a couple of saints one has an endless number of lukewarm nominal Christians. Generally speaking, today people experience greater difficulty in admiring a singular personality than in subjecting the great mass of humanity to critical analysis. Modern humanity is uneasy about expressing admiration. It is afraid of "personality cult." (It seems to completely miss the point that the only cult worthy of humankind is in fact that which honours a person, and not worship of a fetish, party, social structure or any inanimate "thing"). It is quick to claim that "we have seen it all." And yet, in fact, humanity probably was not attentive enough to reality to cultivate genuine admiration for it.

This incapacity for gratuitous admiration has a deeper cause. It lies in the "perverted mania of our day to reduce to banality all that is sublime or noble" by which "one attempts to explain Dostoevsky's genius through his *petit mal* or Nietzsche's philosophy through his syphilis."[3] The person who loses a feeling for the extraordinary, necessarily then opts for what is banal, common and stereotypical. It is easy to explain stereotypes. The reactions of the common person are not hard to forecast. Admiration is consequently very difficult because it always goes hand in hand with an awareness of our own limitations. Within a society based on ambition, competition and self-realization any comparison with those who have made it, with those who are greater than oneself, is painful. Comparisons of this kind lead rather to feelings of inferiority than to contentment. Whoever is constantly concerned with keeping one's own image "spick and span" has neither the time for, nor interest in, that which is singular and unique.

It must be admitted that we are still capable of admiring what some people do but no longer what they *are*. We admire achievements, but not people. We readily admit that a given Ingmar Bergman film is a great work of art, and yet we would insist that we consider the Swedish producer "as a person" as being banal, frustrated or one-sided.

Blake's quip "We become what we behold" can be loosely translated as "Tell me whom you admire and I will tell you what sort of person you are becoming." We must be careful not to misunderstand this sentiment. Authentic admiration is always gratuitous. It does not seek personal advantage. Admiration does not mean becoming a copycat. The genuine aesthete does not admire a masterpiece by Rembrandt so as to improve one's own painting technique. Venera-

3. D. de Rougemont, *L'Amour et l'Occident*, Paris, 1956, 46.

tion of the saints or respect for the Lord's intimate friends are not "means" for the attainment of a more intense religious life or a higher moral standard. Just the way true love desires and reaches out towards a friend (rather than to subjective erotic experiences), so too authentic admiration is directed toward the person admired (rather than to one's own spiritual progress). Charles du Bos pointed out that "le vol d'un oiseau s'admire, mais ne s'imite ni ne s'apprend."

While many people tend not to admire anyone but go through life without pretension, sober, critical and without nurturing many illusions, there are others who admire only details in the character of their fellows. Although Christians may know that the greatest richness a person possesses is a deep religious faith, they are also well aware that no one attains such depth of faith while at the same time disregarding humane values. They could include intellectual formation, a balanced emotional development, a social consciousness and an interest in culture and the arts. A holistic view of humanity is important to Christians. Christianity is radical humanism. It is impossible for someone who is mean and venal as a human being to be highly thought of as a religious figure. Profound Christianity and human backwardness and misery are mutually exclusive. It is quite impossible to put a magnificent roof on a derelict house. It is for that reason that admiration for the Christian in a given person goes hand in hand with respect for his human qualities. Veneration of a saint is rather different from idolatry of a pop singer or sports personality.

In conclusion, it is worth pointing out that those who discover the greatness in another are themselves ennobled by their admiration, even though they do not consciously seek this. Love makes people resemble one another, and without an element of admiration, love is quite impossible. The introduction which the son of the blessed Marie de l'Incarnation wrote in his biography of his mother opens most fittingly with the following words: "O God, I offer you this artwork of your grace without demanding any favours for myself, except that of being able to look with admiration on her and thank you for all the favours and privileges which you have so liberally bestowed, and to pray that they may to some extent flow over me, too."[4]

Even though authentic faith will always include an element of risk, that risk is reduced for those who are aware of the great things that God has realized in those who are consistent in their discipleship of

4. Cf. G. Oury, *Marie de l'Incarnation (1599–1672),* II Québec, 1973, 584.

Christ. This risk is not an irrational venture, nor is it a bold leap in the dark. By "risk" we only mean an attitude which not only holds caution and circumspection to be important virtues, but also daring and fidelity.

3. Faith Never Gives Up Searching

One does not embrace faith because of a discovery that it some-how answers all our questions. Even less decisive in such an option is a realization that all dogmatic pronouncements by Church authorities are true. Faith is not an intellectual tranquilizer. Faith is essentially "heuristic." It never gives up its investigation into the inexhaustible Truth. Or to use the Apostle Paul's words: "What we see now is like a dim image in a mirror; then we shall see face to face. What I know now is only partial; then it will be complete" (1 Cor 13:12).

For this reason any act of faith will have an element of anxiety, of "sudden impulse" (Luther) and even of agnosticism. The poet W.H. Auden wrote of Christ in the following terms:

> He is the Truth.
> Seek Him in the Kingdom of Anxiety,
> You will come to a great city
> that has expected your return for years.[5]

Science speaks of established laws and principles when, on the basis of repeated controlled experiments, one has established that the same circumstances always produce the same effect. In a case of firm faith in a person, we are dealing with a completely different kettle of fish. We simply cannot get the "full picture." One can never know the loved one like the back of one's hand.

> What we know of other people
> Is only our memory of the moments
> During which we knew them. And they have changed since then.
> To pretend that they and we are the same
> Is a useful and convenient social convention
> Which must sometimes be broken. We must also remember
> That at every meeting we are meeting a stranger.[6]

5. Quoted by Thomas Merton in *Conjectures of a Guilty Bystander*, New York, 1965, 251.
6. T. S. Eliot, *Cocktail Party*, in *Collected Plays*, London, 1962, 156–157.

God is and will always be different to the image we have formed of him and carry round with us. This image is always the result of our experience of God to date (or our *lack* of experience for that matter, in which case our image of God remains very theoretical and abstract) as well as what we have heard (or not heard) about him. The real danger of a radically conservative faith lies precisely in the fact that a claim is made that one knows once and for all who God is and is not. Flying in the face of the biblical command not to make an image or likeness of God, one binds oneself to the creature of one's own mental invention which one then proceeds to defend with the armory of orthodoxy. Those whose faith is genuine never give up searching. They know that "the other's true face, i.e. the way in which the other presents himself, transcends all ideas which they had of him. At every new encounter the other destroys the picture of himself he had left behind after the previous encounter."[7] Levinas makes it perfectly clear that this is the case between people at the psychological level and between people and God at the religious level. I only discover God's face bit by bit and then on the basis of my religious experience, however poor that may be. My search for God is no lonely pilgrimage; it is not a journey I undertake alone. I do not start out with an intellectual "tabula rasa." The experience which others have had of God as mirrored in literature, such as for example that which I find in the gospel and in the whole tradition of the Church (i.e., in the testimony of saints, mystics or ordinary members of the faithful), helps me on my way. The places where God is to be found are suggested to me and described. What I experience brings me to or keeps me within a particular church community. That church community then carries me along towards a deeper encounter with God. Christ has promised us that the Church—despite all her weaknesses and infidelity—is God's spiritual and sacramental *pied à terre* here on earth.

The encounter itself which takes place in prayer remains a matter of personal faith. This is even truer in our day because, while the believer is surrounded by others who are searching, one is living with an even larger number of people who claim that even if God might possibly exist, it is still quite impossible to discover him. Those who dig for gold tend to drop tools when "experts" among them "prove"

7. E. Lévinas, *Totalité et Infini*, 21.

that there is no more gold in the ground by their silent departure from the mine.

True faith is not only searching or "heuristic," but in our day, to use P. Berger's word, it is also "heretical" in the original etymological sense of the word. Philo of Alexandria viewed a "hairesis" as a current of thought, spirituality or religious sensitivity of a particular theological school. It is thus clear that the image which Mother Teresa, Billy Graham or Alexander Solzhenitsyn have of God will reflect their individual spirituality and thus be different. The way they read the gospel story, the features of Christian teaching that strike them and what they themselves preach or proclaim will vary considerably. This was also true to a great extent in the past. The way that Francis of Assisi, Nicholas of Cusa or Ignatius of Loyola viewed God and envisaged the perfect religious life or the main thrust of their religious message admitted of major differences. Each of them chose to emphasize certain features of the Christian message simply because no one single person can exhaust all aspects of the infinite richness of God, however holy their life. Even the happiest couple on earth who has the most successful of marriages does not enjoy all those things which have contributed to happy marriages down through the ages. Each individual couple takes a different approach to life. And yet in our own day something has changed. In former times the various Christian spiritualities had a fixed reference point, namely the Scholastic theological substructure which they all had in common. Where it was a matter of theory the various charismatic luminaries reasoned in virtually the same way. Intellectually they were all formed by Aquinas' *Summa Theologica*. They lived in an age of doctrinal certainty. When it came to spirituality, theology's castoff, the magisterium left the faithful a free choice. Spirituality was generally viewed as an innocuous toy for the exempt religious orders to play around with. Today completely the reverse seems to apply. Whether they be Protestant or Catholic, of the Left or the Right, people are generally willing to accept the evangelical witness and respect the sensibilities of a figure such as Mother Teresa or Helder Camara, regardless of how wide the gap may be between the different theological substructures (and even in cases where a theological background is almost totally absent). The importance of a single theoretical infrastructure has been greatly relativized. The common enemy is no longer the heretic but rather the atheist.

"The modern situation is a world of religious uncertainty, occasionally staved off by more or less precarious constructions of religious affirmation by some religious personality or charismatic prophet."[8] Such a thing as a fixed, dogmatic frame of reference accepted by everyone and which one can use as a yardstick of orthodoxy quite simply no longer exists. To put it plainly, heretofore the essential contents of the faith were plain to everyone, while an individual's particular spirituality was a matter of choice. At the present time the central core of religious faith has been eaten away by pluralism, the general climate of intellectual insecurity and atheism. The widespread sensitivity towards social justice and solidarity with oppressed classes or peoples is ignored by committed Christians at their peril. Where doctrine is concerned we have become "heretical," i.e., one can pick and choose out of the traditional teaching of the Church to which one happens to belong, those elements which appeal most directly to the mood of the age or the spirit of the times and consequently still seem "to hold water."

A number of prominent French Catholics, including Jean Guitton, Jean Marie Domenach and Maurice Clavel, have published books entitled *Ce que je crois* (What I Believe); it is natural that the contemporary reader should expect there to be fundamental differences between the contents of these respective works. Actually, it is the differences which make the series so interesting and worthwhile. What each of these individuals believes within Christian revelation (or what they reject as the case may be) will always be a particular concept, choice or "hairesis." "Do you not believe *everything* that the Church requires you to believe?" the Grand Inquisitor asks. Someone like Jean Guitton will not deny anything of substance (and for that reason people like to label him a "conservative"). The fact that he seems to ignore or relativize certain elements of the Christian message which are very fashionable in contemporary ethical discussion, makes many progressive Christians very cross. What makes the personal testimonies of Domenach and Clavel so interesting is their highly individual choice as to what they consider truly significant or as to what they have rediscovered in the Christian message.

In an earlier time a Christian would simply never have been asked, "Now what do you actually believe?" The fact that persons called themselves Christian made their answer self-evident. For those with a

8. P. Berger, *The Heretical Imperative*, 28.

theological formation their answer was the *Summa Theologica* (a very telling title: a summary of all the elements of the faith which had a theological articulation). For the layman his answer was the catechism. The fact that a catechism—despite repeated efforts, conservative as well as progressive to come up with the tried and tested approach in a new form—no longer works nor washes, is also a sign of the times and speaks volumes about the mentality of the contemporary Christian. Through the classical catechism the Church attempted to provide all the faithful with pithy formulas they could learn by heart and which summarized the central truths of the Christian faith in language the common people seemed to understand. The man or woman who knew their catechism had the safe feeling that they knew and could articulate what it was they actually believed. The contents of their faith were neither such a mystery or a problem that they were not able to talk reasonably coherently about it. It is undeniable that one did not fully grasp or understand everything, yet each word evoked images which with the passage of time (through Christian doctrine at school, sermons in the church or Catholic newspapers, periodicals and books) seemed more and more self-evident. When there were things which one could not understand one still assumed that there were expert theologians who did and who, if necessary, could demonstrate them and prove them to be true in a convincing way.

Today the words of the catechism are less and less familiar to the average believer (in so far as one knows them at all). The language and terminology of theology seem very puzzling, particularly to the younger generation. When youngsters ask for an explanation the experts come up a wide variety of interpretations (again in so far as the young people want religious doctrines "explained" or "interpreted"). Moreover, to those very people who have made religion their profession such doctrines are highly problematic, that they can no longer be expressed in the same terms, that particular statements must certainly not be interpreted liberally, that in the past various subjects were passed over all too easily in silence and must now get priority (e.g., social justice, racial equality, respect for the environment, etc.) and above all "that we must have the guts to live with our doubts." In other words, the cognitive security with which the catechism used to supply the faithful has now given way to a humble searching in an atmosphere of mental doubt or what R. Girard likes to call "cognitive nihilism." This very insecurity has become as it were an intellectual status-symbol of authenticity. It demonstrates a person's openness, critical spirit, lucidity and intellectual honesty.

Painfully aware that a little book with two-hundred-and-fifty questions and answers was totally inadequate to explain the great religious and philosophical a prioris of our time, a certain number of respectable theologians were asked to come up with a succinct summary of the Christian faith. The essential question still remains, though: what does one actually (still) exactly believe? A number of German theologians, with their characteristic talent for systematic thought and presentation, such as Karl Rahner, Walter Kasper and Joseph Ratzinger, have answered this question with some success. And yet it would seem that most Christians are more attracted by the spiritual witness of such figures as Marcel Légaud, Roger Schutz or Carlo Caretto, who make no attempt whatever to present an exhaustive summary of what being a Christian entails, but who in a "heretical" or "eclectic" way attempt to focus on a number of important fundamental Christian principles.

As Karl Rahner himself has repeatedly argued, one cannot expect any priest or theologian to know all aspects of Christian doctrine. Just like other branches of science, theology has become too complex for it not to be compartmentalized into various domains of specialization. There is no theologian on earth who can answer *all* the questions a believer might ask, to say nothing of the average convinced Christian. It is quite impossible to be at the same time an exegete, dogmatician, moralist, Church historian, philosopher and expert in Christian spirituality. Believing what the Church proposes to us is consequently for nobody just simply "credo quia intelligo." Faith and an ongoing search advance now more than ever hand in hand. This has, of course, always been the case. In our day the link between the two is much more conscious than was the case in the past. This searching faith, with its own peculiar sensitivity and personal slant, is what Peter Berger has called "the heretical imperative." One could of course simply call it a more personal faith. One of our contemporary mystics puts it rather well: "what I need is not so much an abstract general knowledge of God. Even less do I desire an intellectual-critical knowledge. I desire rather a personal and unique knowledge in flesh and blood, not transposable into any other form of knowledge, because it is an expression of myself, of my own history and my own nature. It is not necessary for me to serve "the truth," but rather my own truth, i.e. that truth within which God has revealed himself to me. In that sense it is a very 'subjective' truth because through the fact that I get to know God, I also come to know myself more clearly."[9]

Even if the idea is somewhat more abstract, it has the advantage of being less ambiguous: personal reflection on God has for most of the faithful become an "inductive" undertaking. A person's religious orientation is less the result of the school in which one received one's intellectual formation than of the way one has come to experience reality. We ought not to forget that what I see or experience depends very greatly on what I have been taught or instructed to see. For this reason it is vital for the person who seeks God to do so in a social-ecclesial context. Moreover, as has already been emphasized, the Church in the Christian perspective is much more than a heuristic medium or an intellectual signpost. It is above all else a sacramental meeting place with God.

The things which a person experiences, reads, studies or hears all combine to determine not only the tenor and profundity of one's faith, but also the nature of one's doubts and one's intellectual difficulties. It deserves to be emphasized that this has always been the case, except that in days of yore what a person heard or read was much less contradictory and what one experienced oneself was more likely to be endorsed and affirmed subsequently by others. Everyone lived and operated within the same context of faith. In a society where pluralism reigns believers miss that spiritual hearth where they used to feel so at home. Now they feel out in the cold. They feel alone and isolated with what they experience, miss, cherish, dread and regret. There is a striking paradox in the fact that on the one hand believers feel more than ever the need for the consensus of others "to affirm them in their faith," and yet on the other hand adopt a much more critical attitude towards official Church pronouncements or condemnations. On the one hand, because they have a social sense, they feel the need of consensus more than ever; on the other hand, they have developed an allergy to intervention from on high.

To sum up, it must be said that the corpus of Christian teaching is no mere rag bag of truths which a believer can take or leave as he or she wishes. If one decides to leave it, then we can consider such a one at best an agnostic. If one decides to pick and choose and just take on board some of it, then we can call that one a heretic. That

9. J. Bastiaire, *Croire au Printemps,* in *La nouvelle Revue Francaise,* 274, 1975, 352.

something is self-evident does not mean that it can be immediately understood and assented to by everybody, at every moment and in all possible circumstances. Doubts, gaps and problems are not only possible but unavoidable. Christian doctrine is far less a chessboard we can take in at a glance than a luxuriant botanical garden into which the believer is led step by step by God's providential pedagogy. (It is also a garden from which the believer is free to flee at any moment if ever the sheer luxuriance of the divine landscape were to arouse within him a feeling of spiritual agoraphobia).

The body of Christian doctrine is not a set of rational theses which we can decode once and for all, or reject as total nonsense. God is rather a person who reveals himself to us bit by bit. God does not bowl someone over "at one fell swoop" with an armory of eternal truths. One has only to think of the "messianic secret" in Mark's Gospel. Initially the Lord makes no allusion whatever to the fact that he might be the Messiah. When by degrees his apostles tumbled to the fact that he might be divine after they had seen his miracles and heard his evangelical message, he warned them quite emphatically: "See to it that you say nothing to anyone about these things." (Mark 1:44) The people were not yet ready for the radicality of his disconcerting message. The mystery of God's presence only sank into the apostles very gradually, its progress constantly interrupted by their doubts and lack of faith.

Our faith is something "organic." It is not a lifeless "thing" that you either "have or do not have." It is something which grows, having been implanted in us at the moment of our baptism or at some other stage in our life. Manès Sperber pointed out that "as soon as the truth is understood, it changes its profile. It is always a signpost which directs us to a deeper reality hiding behind it. I have hardly crossed the brow of a hill than I see another hill looming up behind it and they will probably go on in a never ending series."[10]

There is in fact no official standard by which one can fathom or control the depth and accuracy of a person's faith. One can test the accuracy of "things" such as weights and measures, but not the growth of a tree or the development of my emotional life. In some degree everyone's life of faith is unique. The faith of a twentieth-century missionary is different from that of a medieval monk. An old

10. Manès Sperber, *Die Wasserträger Gottes, All das Vergangene*, III, München, 1978, 123.

man's faith is different from that of a child. An English mystic describes God's tangible presence in different terms than a Greek patristic author.

The fact that our faith is essentially incomplete and is still feeling its way and that modern humanity is more acutely conscious of this fact than a medieval monk all suggests that Dietrich Bonhoeffer was quite right in his observation that the time of "cheap grace" was now over. A disciple of Christ today has "to pay a high price." It no longer goes without saying nor is it immediately obvious, either as a matter of personal conviction or social convention, that one should follow Christ and believe in him. "Cheap grace means grace as doctrine, as principle, as system. . . . Precious grace on the other hand is the hidden treasure in the field. . . . It is the gospel that has to be searched out again and again, the gift on account of which we must pray, the door on which one must knock. . . . With the expansion of Christianity and the growing conformity of the Church to society the knowledge of precious grace gradually disappeared. The world became Christian, grace had become common property. It became easy to obtain."[11] The great positive feature about our own time is that there is a "re-evaluation" of religious faith. From having been something everyone owned it has become the "hidden treasure in the field."

When Bonhoeffer concludes that grace is "so precious because it calls upon us to be disciples of Christ" then he is suggesting that the believer has only one fixed reference point and one anchor: Jesus Christ. Discipleship of the living Lord (and not the acceptance of fixed principles) will lead us in the direction of the full truth. The "buried treasure" is hidden, it is true, yet where the field is located has in the meantime become clear. That field is the Church. The treasure is sublime, yet the field is not necessarily a perfect plot of ground. There is little point in going digging for treasure in the desert because one has the feeling of freedom and one's movements are untrammeled, when the gospel never ceases reminding us that the search, if it is to be fruitful, has to concentrate on the field.

Bonhoeffer goes a step further and points out how to avoid real "hairesis" or heresy (in the strict sense of the word, i.e., only seeing a portion of reality). It must be admitted that not everyone is equally struck by every saying of Jesus or by each article of faith. There is no

11. D. Bonhoeffer, *Navolging*, Amsterdam, 1966, 13,15,16 and 17. (English transl: *The Cost of Discipleship, A Powerful Attack on Easy Christianity.*)

one who translates every word of Christ's into a totally consistent mode of Christian living. One can easily imagine how a twenty-year-old Christian "militant" might be more struck by Christ's concern for outcasts and lepers than by the Lord's lonely agony in the Garden of Olives. Developmental psychology teaches us that the interests and focus of attention of a growing adolescent pass through different stages. If one desires to be a genuine disciple of Christ's in Bonhoeffer's view, then it is imperative for one to take a radical option for at least one aspect of his message and attempt to live it out to the bitter end. To some extent it is possible to compare the evangelical counsels with a table cloth: if one presses hard on one particular spot, the rest of the cloth is pulled to the central position. Francis of Assisi opted for Christ's poverty one hundred percent, de Caussade threw himself without reserve on God's Providence as the centre of gravity of the Christian life while Ignatius of Loyola concentrated on discerning the Father's will.

Spiritualities can and will vary, yet there is only one Christian revelation. There are shifts of emphasis, yet contradictions at the heart of orthodox faith are quite impossible.

4. Faith Supposes Freedom

As Eric Fromm so rightly pointed out, it is important when treating of the concept of freedom to keep two factors clearly apart: "Free from what?" and "Free for what?" Libertines and fanatical advocates of freedom generally limit themselves to the first question. Young teenagers know from which constricting shackles they wish to release themselves. What they might do with their newly won freedom, or to what purpose they might put it, is generally surrounded by a bit of a mystery to them. Every choice we make has to be paid for by a bit of our freedom. Just the same way as a miser cultivates money for its own sake (and never spends it on some valuable object), so, too, libertines cultivate freedom for the sake of freedom. They revel in a comfortable feeling which the range of possibilities theoretically open to them induce. They do not wish to give up so much as an ounce of their freedom so as to make of something which up to then was mere potential, a reality freely chosen.

In the context of faith our first question would be along the following lines: From what would a person who genuinely wants to come to a religious faith need to set oneself free? There are three constricting obstacles which spring to mind: intrusive outside interference or indoctrination by others, an anxiety lest one might compromise oneself and the pressure exerted by a particular image of God which crushes one under a flood of proofs and leaves no space for questions, reserves or doubts.

Where the first factor is concerned, it is clear that no one can be forced to profess religious faith. Pressure is an obstacle rather than an enticement to belief. Many forms of contemporary atheism or agnosticism seem as if they are an angry protest against busybodies interfering in an individual's relationship with God, the very relationship which happens to be the most intimate in which a person engages during one's life. Indoctrination and mature faith cancel one another out. This is not to suggest, of course, that the tender shoot of a child's Christian faith would become a mature plant without catechism or religious instruction. Just like the language they speak, their religion (or their agnosticism) is something children learn. Where language is a political issue one can of course adopt a neutral stance. And yet there is no one who would push this "neutrality" so far that one would not wish to speak any language or at least desire to turn one's back on one's mother tongue. It is essential as a child to have developed a certain facility in one's native language if as an adolescent one is to write jottings in one's diary or the odd love letter in that language (even if initially one does resort to clichés and plagiarism).

"Freedom is possibility," as Kierkegaard put it. It is for that reason that initially freedom gives a feeling of insecurity and anxiety. Teachers and guardians thus all too often tend to "liberate" their subjects from that insecurity by channeling their freedom into "the straight and narrow" and thereby ruling out misguided possibilities (or potential mistakes). The two most prevalent avatars which this approach produces are conventional faith or total apostasy, by way of a radical protest. The anxiety which precedes a free decision one must take oneself creates the only authentic space which facilitates the growth towards spiritual maturity. This is something which so many in the field of education tend to overlook. On the other hand it would be naive to believe that the freedom of today's adolescent is principally curtailed by his parents or teachers. In most cases adolescents are so hyper-suspicious that they reject out of hand any advice or reprimand which smacks of traditional wisdom. They are sometimes disconcertingly naive in their complete lack of awareness of the pressure the spirit of the age, the opinions of their peers and above all the mass media exert on them. The great difficulty in developing a personal faith at the present day comes not so much from an authoritarian education as rather from the leveling effect of pluralism. The difficulty is rooted less in the crushing burden of inherited traditions than in ideological fashions. It is due less to parental interference than to what McLuhan has termed the "media massage."

In the second case a mature faith is also hampered by the anxiety of one's own ego. Persons can only give themselves to others in an act of faith once they have abandoned their psychological defence mechanism which they have built up around themselves like a rampart or wall. Agnosticism and scepticism are in many cases a sort of security system. The sceptic simply does not want to show his hand. He will never take the risk of being labeled "naive." Modern humanity reminds one of a child who discovers, in too rapid succession, that Santa Claus, Father Christmas and the biological stork are all only fairy tales intended for infants. The child is disconcerted and begins anxiously to ask whether perhaps such naive fictional inventions might not hide other areas of real life, too. They wonder whether religion, too, might not best be relegated to the ranks of myths and fairy tales. An ass is not going to bruise its hoof a second time against the same stone!

But there is more to it. Faith and love both tie a person. Every bond signifies a potential loss of freedom. In addition to the natural desire to cherish and be cherished, every individual has a second natural instinct to preserve one's own integrity. This latter instinct makes a person inclined to say "no" to any self-sacrifice or commitment which entails irreversible consequences. On the one hand, we have an instinctive desire for love and on the other the instinct of self-preservation or self-defense. We have a spontaneous urge to give ourselves generously to others which is mixed with a tendency carefully to avoid whatever can bind or tie us. This explains the widespread fear of the permanent marriage, solemn religious profession, ordination as a priest "forever" and even public membership in a church, regardless of which one it might be. When this attitude that one must always keep one's options open and "constantly toy with other possibilities" (Hammarskjöld) wins the upper hand, then genuine faith is immediately made impossible. This attitude is at the root of the hell of uncommitted loneliness, i.e., a love which is completely turned in (perverted) on oneself. To put it bluntly this is spiritual masturbation. Or as Sartre puts it, a "huis clos." This explains why

Sartre mistakenly believed that hell consisted in the other people with whom I live. "Hell" comes about rather as a consequence of an isolation and loneliness I myself have created through considering others *a priori* as interfering busybodies. "In that freedom he had thus achieved Harry suddenly realized that his freedom was a sort of death, that he was now alone, that the world left him alone in a most ghastly peace, that other people no longer concerned him, and that was simply suffocation in an ever more delirious air of isolation and loneliness. Independence was no longer his wish and his ideal, rather it had become his fate and his life sentence."[12]

God actually never intrudes. He does not do violence to humanity by overwhelming it with ringing proofs and irrefutable truths. God is no burglar who breaks into one's spirit; he awaits rather one's response. "See, I stand at the door and knock; if anyone hears my voice and opens the door, *then* will I come in to him" (Rev 3:20).

The reason why God never crushes a person with the weight of convincing arguments is because he does not want to *force* one to accept his proposal of love or gift of grace. God desires neither to seduce people, nor to dupe or mentally hypnotize them. Just as in any authentic relationship of love or friendship, it is up to God to wait for one's free response. As P. Evdokimov puts it, "Dieu peut tout faire, excepté nous contraindre à l'aimer."

Once people have acquired sufficient freedom for them to consider themselves as adults, what possibilities lie open before them then? Or to use Fromm's words, *for* what is that person actually free? The answer is disarmingly simple: free to choose themselves what they will love. The centre or kernel of all love is the choice or the preference. "The first and most precious thing that lives in man is his preference. God desires to get man's preference so that He is chosen in love above all other things that He Himself ever created."[13] This pithy pronouncement is Ruusbroec's masterly summary of Christian living. There are so many beautiful things to be enjoyed on God's earth. Our heart and mind can be fascinated by so many different worthy things. And yet what God desires most is to be preferred above all other realities. The first and greatest commandment, "Love God above all things" is and remains the most important commandment.

God is not a fretful lover who wants to monopolize us and have us

12. H. Hesse, *Der Steppenwolf*, Frankfurt, 1972, 52–53.
13. Ruusbroec, *Werken*, II, Tielt, 1946, 9.

disdain all else but him. After all, he created the world himself for humanity. That world, creation, is there precisely to make a choice possible because without predilection true love is impossible. A Christian is consequently he or she who—regardless of how many other attractive possibilities may present themselves—reechoes Joan of Arc's declaration: "Messire Dieu premier servi."